WHAT THEY'RE SAYING ABOUT THE NEW EDITION OF *"THEY SAY / I SAY"*

"The new chapter, 'In My Experience,' validates students' lived experiences and teaches them how to establish their ethos in their writing." —**Lorelei Blackburn,** *Michigan State University*

"This chapter is a worthy reminder of the value of story and a clear glimpse at the way professional writing is actually produced." —**Eric Wardell,** *Normandale Community College*

"Wow! I love the addition of this new chapter."

—**Cameron Wilson,** *William Jessup University*

"This chapter will be a great help in getting students to do what I'm already asking them to do, which is connect a controversy that we are reading and writing about with the world as they have seen, experienced, and read about it."

—**Douglas Swartz,** *Indiana University Northwest*

"I'm in love with this latest edition more than any other edition over the past handful of years I have assigned it."

—**Linda Rogers,** *California State University at Chico*

WHAT WOULD YOU SAY TO A COLLEAGUE ABOUT *"THEY SAY / I SAY"*?

"You need to teach with this text!"

—**Dagmar Van Engen,** *Arizona State University*

"I've never gotten student compliments on a textbook, and I get them every semester with *'They Say / I Say'.*"

—**Aaron Clark,** *Dallas College Brookhaven Campus*

"This book is integral to my writing course. I can't really imagine teaching college writing without it."

—**Nicole Wendt,** *University of Minnesota*

"The most effective book on teaching argumentative writing I have ever used."
—Selina Marcille, *Southern New Hampshire University*

"This book has been transformative for my composition classes."
—Doritta Fong, *Douglass College*

"The text isn't just about writing arguments—it's about reading and evaluating arguments, understanding who is saying what and why. *That's* the heart of research and inquiry."
—Kay Halasek, *The Ohio State University*

"Many students say that it is the first book they've found that actually helps them with writing in all disciplines."
—Laura Sonderman, *Marshall University*

"A beautifully lucid way to approach argument—different from any rhetoric I've ever seen."
—Anne-Marie Thomas, *Austin Community College, Riverside*

"The best tribute to 'They Say / I Say' I've heard is this, from a student: 'This is one book I'm not selling back to the bookstore.' Nods all around the room. The students love this book."
—Christine Ross, *Quinnipiac University*

"It's the anti-composition text: Fun, creative, humorous, brilliant, effective."
—Perry Cumbie, *Durham Technical Community College*

"This book explains in clear detail what skilled writers take for granted."   —John Hyman, *American University*

"Practical advice for writers in a welcoming tone, as if to say, 'We're all writers here. Let's talk about what actually works.' The approach is so different from every other book about writing."
—Tiffaney Tiffin, *Hope International University*

"The templates make academic writing accessible to a wide range of students."   —Farah Marklevits, *Augustana College*

SIXTH EDITION

"THEY SAY/I SAY"

SIXTH EDITION

"THEY SAY / I SAY"

The Moves That Matter in Academic Writing

GERALD GRAFF

CATHY BIRKENSTEIN

both of the University of Illinois at Chicago

W. W. NORTON & COMPANY
Celebrating a Century of Independent Publishing

W. W. Norton & Company has been independent since its founding in 1923, when William Warder Norton and Mary D. Herter Norton first published lectures delivered at the People's Institute, the adult education division of New York City's Cooper Union. The firm soon expanded its program beyond the Institute, publishing books by celebrated academics from America and abroad. By midcentury, the two major pillars of Norton's publishing program—trade books and college texts—were firmly established. In the 1950s, the Norton family transferred control of the company to its employees, and today—with a staff of five hundred and hundreds of trade, college, and professional titles published each year—W. W. Norton & Company stands as the largest and oldest publishing house owned wholly by its employees.

Composition: KnowledgeWorks Global Ltd
Manufacturing: LSC Crawfordsville

Permission to use copyrighted material is included in the credits section
of this book, which begins on page 371.

Library of Congress Control Number: 2023949206

ISBN: 9781324046219

W. W. Norton & Company, Inc., 500 Fifth Avenue, New York, NY 10110
wwnorton.com

W. W. Norton & Company Ltd., 15 Carlisle Street, London W1D 3BS

1 2 3 4 5 6 7 8 9 0

For
Aaron David

CONTENTS

New to this edition

Contents

*New to this edition

SEE ALSO

*New to this edition

PREFACE
TO THE SIXTH EDITION

—▭—

SINCE ITS INCEPTION, this book has been animated by several interlocking goals:

- To demystify academic argument by showing that it involves one central move: that of stating one's own view (what "I say") not in isolation, but in conversation or debate with the views of others (what "they say").
- To provide flexible, user-friendly templates—"Although it is often said that _____, I argue _____," for instance—that help students put this "they say / I say" move into practice, showing that such formulas need not result in writing that is "formulaic."
- To show how important the "they say / I say" move is to a healthy democracy, which requires that we step outside our increasingly polarized comfort zones and listen carefully to those who see things differently.
- To show that, despite the many differences between the academic disciplines, the "they say / I say" move is central to them all, as well as high order workplace and public sphere communication.
- To refute the common perception that academic writing must be dry, lifeless, and devoid of personality, by showing that it can often accommodate different dialects, colloquial expressions, and personal voices.

WHAT'S NEW IN THIS EDITION

"In My Experience": Using Personal Stories to Energize Your Argument—one of the two chapters new to this edition—advances this last goal by encouraging students to draw on their personal experiences. Written for students who feel, as an undergraduate once told us, that academic writing "just isn't me," the chapter shows how personal stories can be used in such writing to make virtually any of the moves we cover in this book, including summarizing and challenging what "they say," revising what you "used to think," planting a naysayer, and answering the "so what?" question. Personal stories, we show, can be a great way to connect the academic world to our lives outside the classroom. They can also help students demonstrate that the essay they have submitted was written by a real human being and not artificial intelligence.

"Help Me Understand . . .": When Your "They Say" Is a Bot. Speaking of generative AI, the second new chapter addresses how today's hyper-advanced chatbots can be used not as substitutes for students' own writing skills but as tools for advancing them. When used responsibly, we show, these new chatbots can be deployed in the service of "they say / I say" argument, and we provide templates for prompting these technologies to help us understand our own positions and those of others, to identify naysayers, to address the ever-important "so what?" and "who cares?" questions, and to make a host of other moves that matter in academic writing.

New and updated examples. In most of the core chapters of the book, we have replaced the examples used to illustrate the rhetorical moves with more recent writing from a wide range of academic and popular sources and a range of authors, from established writers such as Michelle Alexander, Anne-Marie Slaughter, Suketu Mehta, Maya Phillips, and Kenneth Goldsmith to emerging voices such as Damond Williams, Joe Garcia, and students like Yael Lenga and Felicity Noahubi.

New readings. We have also included three new full-length selections that model the rhetorical moves and are documented in MLA and APA style: "Go Ahead, Waste Time on the Internet" by Kenneth Goldsmith, "Disability in Higher Education: Building Access and Building Futures" by Yael Lenga, and "Left Behind" by Joe Garcia, a powerful argument advocating that people who are incarcerated should be granted access to the internet.

New appendix, "Citing What 'They Say'." This appendix offers a quick-start guide to documenting sources, including examples of how to cite generative AI, and points students to where they can find additional models and advice.

A reading experience that is more hands-on than ever with the new Norton Illumine Ebook. Students don't just read *"They Say / I Say"*—they interact with it. Building on the book's already popular templates, exercises, and tutorials, the new Norton Illumine Ebook gets students practicing the moves while they read, through interactive new features written by author Laura J. Panning Davies. Each chapter offers "Check Your Understanding" questions that are auto-graded with immediate feedback. And instructors can easily embed their own notes, videos, or links to share with their students, customizing each chapter as they see fit.

A collection of new videos. The Sixth Edition offers a new collection of animated videos on key concepts—from understanding academic argument to using signal phrases—that help students visualize and apply the book's advice. Each video is two to three minutes long. Some videos are embedded directly in the ebook, and all are available for streaming online.

Tutorials give students hands-on practice using the rhetorical moves taught in the book. Each tutorial helps students analyze an essay with an eye to the "moves that matter" and then use the book's templates to begin writing themselves. The Sixth Edition is updated with a new tutorial for Chapter 7, "In My Experience," as well as new essay examples.

InQuizitive for Writers assignments allow students to practice new writing, editing, and research skills in a low-stakes, feedback-driven environment. Interactive questions are adaptive, so students receive additional practice in the areas where they need more help, and explanatory feedback offers advice precisely when it's needed, along with direct links to *The Little Seagull Handbook* ebook, which is automatically included with all new copies of *"They Say / I Say."* New activities cover rhetorical situations, elements of argument, thesis statements, critical reading strategies, and more.

Norton Teaching Tools is a new, searchable website that can be filtered by chapter or by resource type, making it easy to find exactly what you need, download, customize, and import it into your LMS course. Written by new co-author Laura J. Panning Davies, with special contributions from instructors across the country, all of the revised contents from the instructor's guide for *"They Say / I Say"* can now be found here: summaries of the rhetoric chapters and each of the essays; in-class activities, discussion prompts, and assignment suggestions for each chapter; advice and assignment ideas for using theysayiblog.com; teaching notes, lists of related essays, and suggested responses to the "Joining the Conversation" questions; and sample syllabi. New to the Sixth Edition is a comprehensive guide to teaching first-year writing that covers everything from designing a course to assessing student writing to engaging difficult conversations in the classroom. You will also find tips and best practices for assigning Check Your Understanding questions in the Norton Illumine Ebook, InQuizitive for Writers, *The Little Seagull Handbook* ebook, the new collection of animated videos, and other digital resources.

"They Say / I Blog" provides current readings that use the rhetorical moves covered in the book, along with questions that prompt students to join the conversation online. Updated monthly by author Laura J. Panning Davies, the blog offers a rich archive of additional readings on important issues. Visit **theysayiblog.com**.

Resources for your learning management system (LMS) files provide integrated links to all of Norton's high-quality digital resources. All activities can be accessed from within your existing learning management system, and graded activities can be configured to report to the LMS course gradebook.

Even as we have updated *"They Say / I Say,"* our basic goals remain unchanged: to help students engage closely with others, particularly those who challenge what we say. Our additions, in other words, are meant to reinforce our longstanding goal of demystifying academic discourse by identifying its key moves in forms that students can put into practice. Given the deeply divided society we continue to live in, this practice of engaging in dialogue and entertaining counterarguments seems more urgent than ever.

PREFACE

Demystifying Academic Conversation

EXPERIENCED WRITING INSTRUCTORS have long recognized that writing well means entering into conversation with others. Academic writing in particular calls on writers not simply to express their own ideas but to do so as a response to what others have said. The first-year writing program at our own university, according to its mission statement, asks "students to participate in ongoing conversations about vitally important academic and public issues." A similar statement by another program holds that "intellectual writing is almost always composed in response to others' texts." These statements echo the ideas of many recent rhetorical theorists, who argue that writing well means engaging the voices of others and letting them in turn engage us.

Yet despite this growing consensus that writing is a social, conversational act, helping student writers actually participate in these conversations remains a formidable challenge. This book aims to meet that challenge. Its goal is to demystify academic writing by isolating its basic moves, explaining them clearly, and representing them in the form of templates. In this way, we hope to help students become active participants in the important conversations of the academic world and the wider public sphere.

HIGHLIGHTS

- *Shows that writing well means entering a conversation*, summarizing others ("they say") to set up one's own argument ("I say")
- *Demystifies academic writing*, showing students "the moves that matter" in language they can readily apply
- *Provides user-friendly templates* to help writers make those moves in their own writing
- *Includes a chapter on reading*, showing students how the authors they read are part of a conversation that they themselves can enter—and thus to see reading as a matter not of passively absorbing information but of understanding and actively entering dialogues and debates

HOW THIS BOOK CAME TO BE

The original idea for this book grew out of our shared interest in democratizing academic culture. First, it grew out of arguments that Gerald Graff has been making throughout his career that schools and colleges need to invite students into the conversations and debates that surround them. More specifically, it is a practical, hands-on companion to his book *Clueless in Academe: How Schooling Obscures the Life of the Mind*, in which he looks at academic conversations from the perspective of those who find them mysterious and proposes ways in which such mystification can be overcome. Second, this book grew out of writing templates that Cathy Birkenstein developed in the 1990s, for use in writing and literature courses she was teaching. Many students, she found, could readily grasp what it meant to support a thesis with evidence, to entertain a counterargument, to identify a textual contradiction, and ultimately to summarize and respond to challenging arguments, but they often had trouble putting these concepts into practice in their own writing. When Cathy sketched out templates on the board, however, giving her students some of the language and patterns that these sophisticated moves require, their writing—and even their quality of thought—significantly improved.

This book began, then, when we put our ideas together and realized that these templates might have the potential to open up and clarify academic conversation. We proceeded from the premise that all writers rely on certain stock formulas that they themselves didn't invent—and that many of these formulas are so commonly used that they can be represented in model templates that students can use to structure and even generate what they want to say.

As we developed a working draft of this book, we began using it in first-year writing courses that we teach at UIC. In classroom exercises and writing assignments, we found that students who otherwise struggled to organize their thoughts, or even to think of something to say, did much better when we provided them with templates like the following:

▶ **In discussions of _____ , a controversial issue is whether _____ . While some argue that _____ , others contend that _____ .**

▶ **This is not to say that _____ .**

One virtue of such templates, we found, is that they focus writers' attention not just on what is being said but also on the *forms* that structure what is being said. In other words, they make students more conscious of the rhetorical patterns that are key to academic success but often pass under the classroom radar.

THE CENTRALITY OF "THEY SAY / I SAY"

The central rhetorical move that we focus on in this book is the "they say / I say" template that gives our book its title. In our view, this template represents the deep, underlying structure, the internal DNA as it were, of all effective arguments. Effective persuasive writers do more than make well-supported claims ("I say"); they also map those claims relative to the claims of others ("they say").

Here, for example, the "they say / I say" pattern structures a passage from an essay by the media and technology critic Steven Johnson:

> For decades, we've worked under the assumption that mass culture follows a path declining steadily toward lowest-common-denominator standards, presumably because the "masses" want dumb, simple pleasures and big media companies try to give the masses what they want. But . . . the exact opposite is happening: the culture is getting more cognitively demanding, not less.
>
> STEVEN JOHNSON, "Watching TV Makes You Smarter"

In generating his own argument from something "they say," Johnson suggests *why* he needs to say what he is saying: to correct a popular misconception.

Even when writers do not explicitly identify the views they are responding to, as Johnson does, an implicit "they say" can often be discerned, as in the following passage by Zora Neale Hurston:

> I remember the day I became colored.
>
> ZORA NEALE HURSTON, "How It Feels to Be Colored Me"

In order to grasp Hurston's point here, we need to be able to reconstruct the implicit view she is responding to and questioning: that racial identity is an innate quality we are simply born with. On the contrary, Hurston suggests, our race is imposed on us by society—something we "become" by virtue of how we are treated.

As these examples suggest, the "they say / I say" model can improve not just student writing but student reading comprehension as well. Since reading and writing are deeply reciprocal activities, students who learn to make the rhetorical moves represented by the templates in this book figure to become more adept at identifying these same moves in the texts they read. And if we are right that effective arguments are always in dialogue with other arguments, then it follows that in order to understand the types of challenging texts assigned in college, students need to identify the views to which those texts are responding.

Working with the "they say / I say" model can also help with invention, finding something to say. In our experience, students best discover what they want to say not by thinking about a subject in an isolation booth but by reading texts, listening closely to what other writers say, and looking for an opening through which they can enter the conversation. In other words, listening closely to others and summarizing what they have to say can help writers generate their own ideas.

THE USEFULNESS OF TEMPLATES

Our templates also have a generative quality, prompting students to make moves in their writing that they might not otherwise make or even know they should make. The templates in this book can be particularly helpful for students who are unsure about what to say or who have trouble finding enough to say, often because they consider their own beliefs so self-evident that they need not be argued for. Students like this are often helped, we've found, when we give them a simple template like the following one for entertaining a counterargument (or planting a naysayer, as we call it in Chapter 6):

▶ **Of course some might object that** _____. **Although I concede that** _____, **I still maintain that** _____.

What this particular template helps students do is make the seemingly counterintuitive move of questioning their own beliefs, of looking at them from the perspective of those who disagree. In so doing, templates can bring out aspects of students' thoughts that, as they themselves sometimes remark, they didn't even realize were there.

Other templates in this book help students make a host of sophisticated moves that they might not otherwise make: summarizing what someone else says, framing a quotation in one's own words, indicating the view that the writer is responding to, marking the shift from a source's view to the writer's own view, offering evidence for that view, entertaining and answering counterarguments, and explaining what is at stake in the first place. In showing students how to make such moves, templates do more than organize students' ideas; they help bring those ideas into existence.

"OK—BUT TEMPLATES?"

We are aware, of course, that some instructors may have reservations about templates. Some, for instance, may object that such formulaic devices represent a return to prescriptive forms of instruction that encourage passive learning or lead students to put their writing on automatic pilot.

This is an understandable reaction, we think, to kinds of rote instruction that have indeed encouraged passivity and drained writing of its creativity and dynamic relation to the social world. The trouble is that many students will never learn on their own to make the key intellectual moves that our templates represent. While seasoned writers pick up these moves unconsciously through their reading, many students do not. Consequently, we believe, students need to see these moves represented in the explicit ways that the templates provide.

The aim of the templates, then, is not to stifle critical thinking but to be direct with students about the key rhetorical moves that it comprises. Since we encourage students to modify and adapt the templates to the particularities of the arguments they are making, using such prefabricated formulas as learning tools need not result in writing and thinking that are themselves formulaic. Admittedly, no teaching tool can guarantee that students will engage in hard, rigorous thought. Our templates do, however, provide concrete prompts that can stimulate and shape such thought: What do "they say" about my topic? How would a naysayer respond to my argument? What is my evidence? Do I need to qualify my point? Who cares?

In fact, templates have a long and rich history. Public orators from ancient Greece and Rome through the European Renaissance studied rhetorical *topoi* or "commonplaces," model passages and formulas that represented the different strategies available to public speakers. In many respects, our templates echo this classical rhetorical tradition of imitating established models.

The journal *Nature* requires aspiring contributors to follow a guideline that is like a template on the opening page of their manuscript: "Two or three sentences explaining what the main result [of their study] reveals in direct comparison with what was thought to be the case previously, or how the main result adds to previous knowledge." In the field of education, a form designed by the education theorist Howard Gardner asks postdoctoral fellowship applicants to complete the following template: "Most scholars in the field believe _____. As a result of my study, _____." That these two examples are geared toward post-doctoral fellows and veteran researchers shows that it is not only struggling undergraduates who can use help making these key rhetorical moves but experienced academics as well.

Templates have even been used in the teaching of personal narrative. The literary and educational theorist Jane Tompkins devised the following template to help student writers make the often difficult move from telling a story to explaining what it means: "X tells a story about _____ to make the point that _____. My own experience with _____ yields a point that is similar / different / both similar and different. What I take away from my own experience with _____ is _____. As a result, I conclude _____." We especially like this template because it suggests that "they say / I say" argument need not be mechanical, impersonal, or dry and that telling a story and making an argument are more compatible activities than many think.

WHY IT'S OK TO USE "I"

But wait—doesn't the "I" part of "they say / I say" flagrantly encourage the use of the first-person pronoun? Aren't we aware that some teachers prohibit students from using "I" or "we" on the grounds that these pronouns encourage ill-considered, subjective opinions rather than objective and reasoned arguments?

Yes, we are aware of this first-person prohibition, but we think it has serious flaws. First, expressing ill-considered, subjective opinions is not necessarily the worst sin beginning writers can commit; it might be a starting point from which they can move on to more reasoned, less self-indulgent perspectives. Second, prohibiting students from using "I" is simply not an effective way of curbing students' subjectivity, since one can offer poorly argued, ill-supported opinions just as easily without it. Third and most important, prohibiting the first person tends to hamper students' ability not only to take strong positions but also to differentiate their own positions from those of others, as we point out in Chapter 5. To be sure, writers can resort to various circumlocutions—"it will here be argued," "the evidence suggests," "the truth is"—and these may be useful for avoiding a monotonous series of "I believe" sentences. But except for avoiding such monotony, we see no good reason why "I" should be set aside in persuasive writing. Rather than prohibit "I," then, we think a better tactic is to give students practice at using it well and learning its use, both by supporting their claims with evidence and by attending closely to alternative perspectives—to what "they" are saying.

HOW THIS BOOK IS ORGANIZED

Because of its centrality, we have allowed the "they say / I say" format to dictate the structure of this book. So while Part 1 addresses the art of listening to others, Part 2 addresses how to offer one's own response. Part 1 opens with the chapter "Starting with What Others Are Saying," which explains why it is generally advisable to begin a text by citing others rather than plunging directly into one's own views. Subsequent chapters take up the arts of summarizing and quoting what these others have to say. Part 2 begins with a chapter on different ways of responding, followed by chapters on marking the shift between what "they say" and what "I say," on introducing and answering objections, on using personal stories, and on answering the all-important questions "so what?" and "who cares?" Part 3, "Tying It All Together," includes a chapter on connection and coherence; one on academic language, which encourages students to draw on their everyday voice as a tool for writing; and others on the art of metacommentary and using the templates to revise a text. Part 4 offers guidance for entering conversations in specific academic contexts, with chapters on entering class discussions, writing online, and reading and writing in the social sciences. It also includes a new chapter on how to use and cite chatbots in essays. Finally, we provide forty-three readings and an index of templates.

WHAT THIS BOOK DOESN'T DO

There are some things that this book does not try to do. We do not, for instance, cover logical principles of argument, such as syllogisms, warrants, logical fallacies, or the differences between inductive and deductive reasoning. Although such concepts can be useful, we believe most of us learn the ins and outs of argumentative writing not by studying logical principles in the abstract but by plunging into actual discussions and debates, trying out different patterns of response, and in this way getting a sense of what works to persuade different audiences and what doesn't. In our view, people learn more about arguing from hearing someone say, "You miss my point. What I'm saying is not _____ but _____," or "I agree with you that

_____ and would even add that _____ ," than they do from studying the differences between inductive and deductive reasoning. Such formulas give students an immediate sense of what it feels like to enter a public conversation in a way that studying abstract warrants and logical fallacies does not.

ENGAGING WITH THE IDEAS OF OTHERS

One central goal of this book is to demystify academic writing by returning it to its social and conversational roots. Although writing may require some degree of quiet and solitude, the "they say / I say" model shows students that they can best develop their arguments not just by looking inward but by doing what they often do in a good conversation with friends and family—listening carefully to what others are saying and engaging with other views.

This approach to writing therefore has an ethical dimension, since it asks writers not simply to keep proving and reasserting what they already believe but also to stretch what they believe by putting it up against beliefs that differ, sometimes radically, from their own. In an increasingly diverse, global society, this ability to engage with the ideas of others is especially crucial to democratic citizenship.

Gerald Graff
Cathy Birkenstein

SIXTH EDITION

"THEY SAY/I SAY"

INTRODUCTION

Entering the Conversation

THINK ABOUT AN ACTIVITY that you do particularly well: cooking, playing the piano, shooting a basketball, even something as basic as driving a car. If you reflect on this activity, you'll realize that once you mastered it you no longer had to give much conscious thought to the various moves that go into doing it. Performing this activity, in other words, depends on your having learned a series of complicated moves—moves that may seem mysterious or difficult to those who haven't yet learned them.

The same applies to writing. Often without consciously realizing it, accomplished writers routinely rely on a stock of established moves that are crucial for communicating sophisticated ideas. What makes writers masters of their trade is not only their ability to express interesting thoughts but also their mastery of an inventory of basic moves that they probably picked up by reading a wide range of other accomplished writers. Less experienced writers, by contrast, are often unfamiliar with these basic moves and unsure how to make them in their own writing. Hence this book, which is intended as a short, user-friendly guide to the basic moves of academic writing.

One of our key premises is that these basic moves are so common that they can be represented in *templates* that you can use right away to structure and even generate your own writing. Perhaps the most distinctive feature of this book is its presentation of many such templates, designed to help you successfully enter not only the world of academic thinking and writing but also the wider worlds of civic discourse and work.

Instead of focusing solely on abstract principles of writing, then, this book offers model templates that help you put those principles directly into practice. Working with these templates will give you an immediate sense of how to engage in the kinds of critical thinking you are required to do at the college level and in the vocational and public spheres beyond.

Some of these templates represent simple but crucial moves, like those used to summarize some widely held belief:

▸ **Many Americans assume that _____.**

Others are more complicated:

▸ **On the one hand, _____. On the other hand, _____.**

▸ **Author X contradicts herself. At the same time that she argues _____, she also implies _____.**

▸ **I agree that _____. However, _____.**

▸ **This is not to say that _____.**

It is true, of course, that critical thinking and writing go deeper than any set of linguistic formulas, requiring that you question assumptions, develop strong claims, offer supporting reasons and evidence, consider opposing arguments, and so on. But these deeper habits of thought cannot be put into practice unless you have a language for expressing them in clear, organized ways.

STATE YOUR OWN IDEAS AS A
RESPONSE TO OTHERS

The single most important template that we focus on in this book is the "they say _____ ; I say _____" formula that gives our book its title. If there is any one point that we hope you will take away from this book, it is the importance not only of expressing your ideas ("I say") but also of presenting those ideas as a *response to some other person or group* ("they say"). For us, the underlying structure of effective academic writing—and of responsible public discourse—resides not just in stating our own ideas but in listening closely to others around us, summarizing their views in a way that they will recognize, and responding with our own ideas in kind. Broadly speaking, academic writing is argumentative writing, and we believe that to argue well you need to do more than assert your own position. You need to enter a conversation, using what others say (or might say) as a launching pad or sounding board for your own views. For this reason, one of the main pieces of advice in this book is to write the voices of others into your text.

In our view, then, the best academic writing has one underlying feature: it is deeply engaged in some way with other people's views. Too often, however, academic writing is taught as a process of saying "true" or "smart" things in a vacuum, as if it were possible to argue effectively without being in conversation *with* someone else. If you have been taught to write a traditional five-paragraph essay, for example, you have learned how to develop a thesis and support it with evidence. This is good advice as far as it goes, but it leaves out the important fact that in the real world we don't make arguments without being provoked. Instead, we make arguments because someone has said or done something (or perhaps *not* said or done something) and we need to respond: "I can't see why you like football so much"; "I agree: it was a great film"; "That argument is contradictory." If it weren't for other people and our need to challenge, agree with, or otherwise respond to them, there would be no reason to argue at all.

"WHY ARE YOU TELLING ME THIS?"

To make an impact as a writer, then, you need to do more than make statements that are logical, well supported, and consistent. You must also find a way of entering into conversation with the views of others, with something "they say." The easiest and most common way writers do this is by *summarizing* what others say and then using it to set up what they want to say.

"But why," as a student of ours once asked, "do I always need to summarize the views of others to set up my own view? Why can't I just state my own view and be done with it?" Why indeed? After all, "they," whoever they may be, will have already had their say, so why do you have to *repeat* it? Furthermore, if they had their say in print, can't readers just go and read what was said themselves?

The answer is that if you don't identify the "they say" you're responding to, your own argument probably won't have a point. Readers will wonder what prompted you to say what you're saying and therefore motivated you to write. As the figure on the following page suggests, without a "they say," *what* you are saying may be clear to your audience, but *why* you are saying it won't be.

Even if we don't know what film he's referring to, it's easy to grasp what the speaker means here when he says that its characters are very complex. But it's hard to see why the speaker

4

feels the need to say what he is saying. "Why," as one member of his imagined audience wonders, "is he telling us this?" So the characters are complex—so what?

Now look at what happens to the same proposition when it is presented as a response to something "they say":

We hope you agree that the same claim—"the characters in the film are very complex"—becomes much stronger when presented as a response to a contrary view: that the film's characters "are sexist stereotypes." Unlike the speaker in the first cartoon, the speaker in the second has a clear goal or mission: to correct what he sees as a mistaken characterization.

THE AS-OPPOSED-TO-WHAT FACTOR

To put our point another way, framing your "I say" as a response to something "they say" gives your writing an element of contrast without which it won't make sense. It may be helpful to think of this crucial element as an "as-opposed-to-what factor" and, as you write, to continually ask yourself, "Who says otherwise?" and "Does anyone dispute it?" Behind the audience's "Yeah, so?" and "Why is he telling us this?" in the first cartoon above lie precisely these types of "As opposed to what?" questions. The speaker in the second cartoon, we think, is more satisfying because he answers these questions, helping us see his point that the film presents complex characters *rather than* simple sexist stereotypes.

HOW IT'S DONE

Many accomplished writers make explicit "they say" moves to set up and motivate their own arguments. One famous example is Martin Luther King Jr.'s "Letter from Birmingham Jail," which consists almost entirely of King's eloquent responses to a public statement by eight clergymen deploring the civil rights protests he was leading. The letter—which was written in 1963, while

King was in prison for leading a demonstration against racial injustice in Birmingham—is structured almost entirely around a framework of summary and response, in which King summarizes and then answers their criticisms. In one typical passage, King writes as follows:

> You deplore the demonstrations taking place in Birmingham. But your statement, I am sorry to say, fails to express a similar concern for the conditions that brought about the demonstrations.
>
> MARTIN LUTHER KING JR., "Letter from Birmingham Jail"

King goes on to agree with his critics that "it is unfortunate that demonstrations are taking place in Birmingham," yet he hastens to add that "it is even more unfortunate that the city's white power structure left the Negro community with no alternative." King's letter is so thoroughly conversational, in fact, that it could be rewritten in the form of a dialogue or play.

    King's critics:
    King's response:
    Critics:
    Response:

Clearly, King would not have written his famous letter were it not for his critics, whose views he treats not as objections to his already-formed arguments but as the motivating source of those arguments, their central reason for being. He quotes not only what his critics have said ("Some have asked: 'Why didn't you give the new city administration time to act?'"), but also things they *might* have said ("One may well ask: 'How can you advocate breaking some laws and obeying others?'")—all to set the stage for what he himself wants to say.

The "they" you respond to in crafting an argument need not be a famous author or someone known to your audience. It can be a friend or family member, a classmate who has made a provocative claim, or something a group or individual might say. It can even be a side of yourself: something you partly believe but also doubt, or something you once believed but no longer do, as Michelle Alexander suggests in the introduction to her 2010 book, *The New Jim Crow: Mass Incarceration in the Age of Colorblindness* (included in this book):

> I reached the conclusions presented in this book reluctantly. Ten years ago, I would have argued strenuously against the central claim made here—namely, that something akin to a racial caste system currently exists in the United States. Indeed, if Barack Obama had been elected president back then, I would have argued that his election marked the nation's triumph over racial caste—the final nail in the coffin of Jim Crow. (349)
>
> MICHELLE ALEXANDER, *The New Jim Crow: Mass Incarceration in the Age of Colorblindness*

In this passage, Alexander identifies a view that she used to hold and that many to this day continue to hold: namely, that the United States is a caste-free, colorblind society that, as Barack Obama's election illustrates, has finally left Jim Crow–style racism behind. In so doing, Alexander avoids two common temptations: to either bury challenges to her argument, or to acknowledge them but in mocking, dismissive ways. Instead, Alexander writes this counterview into her text—and in a way that does it justice. She then uses the remainder of her book to answer it, arguing that today's penal system inflicts so much undeserved damage on the Black community that it can only be understood as an extension of Jim Crow–era repression.

See Chapter 4 for more on agreeing, but with a difference.

While King and Alexander both identify the views they are responding to, some authors do not, instead allowing readers to infer what view they're responding to on their own. See, for instance, if you can identify the implied or unnamed "they say" that the following claim is responding to:

> I like to think I have a certain advantage as a teacher of literature because when I was growing up I disliked and feared books.
>   GERALD GRAFF, "Disliking Books at an Early Age"

In case you haven't figured it out already, the phantom "they say" here is the common belief that in order to be a good teacher of literature, one must have grown up liking and enjoying books.

COURT CONTROVERSY, BUT...

As you can see from these examples, many writers use the "they say / I say" format to challenge standard ways of thinking and thus to stir up controversy. This point may come as a shock to you if you have always had the impression that in order to succeed academically you need to play it safe and avoid controversy in your writing, making statements that nobody can possibly disagree with. Though this view of writing may appear logical, it is actually a recipe for flat, lifeless writing and for writing that fails to answer what we call the "so what?" and "who cares?" questions. "William Shakespeare wrote many famous plays and sonnets" may be a perfectly true statement, but precisely because nobody is likely to disagree with it, it goes without saying and thus would seem pointless if said.

But just because controversy is important doesn't mean you have to become an attack dog who automatically disagrees with everything others say. We think this is an important point to underscore because some who are not familiar with this book have gotten the impression from the title that our goal is to train writers simply to disparage whatever "they say."

LISTEN BEFORE YOU LEAP

There certainly are occasions when strong critique is needed. It's hard to live in a deeply polarized society like our current one and not feel the need at times to criticize what others think. But even the most justified critiques fall flat, we submit, unless we really listen to and understand the views we are criticizing:

▶ **While I understand the impulse to _____, my own view is _____.**

Even the most sympathetic audiences, after all, tend to feel manipulated by arguments that scapegoat and caricature the other side.

Furthermore, genuinely listening to views we disagree with can have the salutary effect of helping us see that beliefs we'd initially disdained may not be as thoroughly reprehensible as we'd imagined. Thus the type of "they say / I say" argument that we promote in this book can take the form of agreeing up to a point or of both agreeing and disagreeing simultaneously, as in:

▶ **While I agree with X that _____, I cannot accept her overall conclusion that _____.**

▶ **While X argues _____, and I argue _____, in a way we're both right.**

Agreement cannot be ruled out, however:

▸ I agree with _____ that _____.

THE TEMPLATE OF TEMPLATES

There are many ways, then, to enter a conversation and respond to what "they say." But our discussion of ways to do so would be incomplete were we not to mention the most comprehensive way that writers enter conversations, which incorporates all the major moves discussed in this book:

▸ In recent discussions of _____, a controversial issue has been whether _____. On the one hand, some argue that _____. From this perspective, _____. On the other hand, however, others argue that _____. In the words of X, one of this view's main proponents, "_____." According to this view, _____. In sum, then, the issue is whether _____ or _____.

My own view is that _____. Though I concede that _____, I still maintain that _____. For example, _____. Although some might object that _____, I would reply that _____. The issue is important because _____.

This "template of templates," as we like to call it, represents the internal DNA of countless articles and even entire books. Writers commonly use a version of it not only to stake out their "they say" and "I say" at the start of their manuscript, but—just as important—to form the overarching blueprint that structures what they write over the entire length of their text.

Taking it line by line, this master template first helps you open your text by identifying an issue in some ongoing conversation or debate ("In recent discussions of _____, a controversial issue has been _____") and then map some of the voices in this controversy (by using the "on the one hand / on the other hand" structure). The template then helps you introduce a quotation ("In the words of X") and explain the quotation in your own words ("According to this view"). Then, in a new paragraph, it helps you state your own argument ("My own view is that"), qualify your argument ("Though I concede that"), and support your argument with evidence ("For example"). In addition, the template helps you make one of the most crucial moves in argumentative writing, what we call "planting a naysayer in your text," in which you summarize and then answer a likely objection to your own central claim ("Although it might be objected that _____, I reply _____"). Finally, this template helps you shift between general, overarching claims ("In sum, then") and smaller-scale, supporting claims ("For example").

Again, none of us is born knowing these moves, especially when it comes to academic writing—hence the need for this book.

BUT ISN'T THIS PLAGIARISM?

"But isn't this plagiarism?" at least one student each year will usually ask. "Well, is it?" we respond, turning the question around into one the entire class can profit from. "We are, after all, asking you to use language in your writing that isn't your own—language that you 'borrow' or, to put it less delicately, steal from other writers."

Often, a lively discussion ensues that raises important questions about authorial ownership and helps everyone better understand the frequently confusing line between plagiarism and the legitimate use of what others say and how they say it. Students are quick to see that no one person owns a conventional formula like "on the one hand / on the other hand." Phrases like "a controversial issue" are so commonly used and recycled that they are generic— community property that can be freely used without fear of committing plagiarism. It *is* plagiarism, however, if the words used to fill in the blanks of such formulas are borrowed from others without proper acknowledgment. In sum, then, while it is not plagiarism to recycle conventionally used formulas, it is a serious academic offense to take the substantive content from others' texts without citing the authors and giving them proper credit.

"OK—BUT TEMPLATES?"

Nevertheless, if you are like some of our students, your initial response to templates may be skepticism. At first, many of our students complain that using templates will take away their originality and creativity and make them all sound the same. "They'll turn us into writing robots," one of our students insisted. "I'm in college now," another student asserted. "This is third-grade-level stuff."

In our view, however, the templates in this book, far from being "third-grade-level stuff," represent the stock-in-trade of sophisticated thinking and writing, and they often require a great deal of practice and instruction to use successfully. As for the belief that preestablished forms undermine creativity, we think it rests on a very limited vision of what creativity is all about. In our view, the templates in this book will actually help your writing become *more* original and creative, not less. After all, even the most creative forms of expression depend on established patterns and structures. Most songwriters, for instance, rely on a time-honored verse-chorus-verse pattern, and few people would call Shakespeare uncreative because he didn't invent the sonnet or the dramatic forms that he used to such dazzling effect. Even the most avant-garde, cutting-edge artists like improvisational jazz musicians need to master the basic forms that their work improvises on, departs from, and goes beyond, or else their work will come across as uneducated child's play. Ultimately, then, creativity and originality lie not in the avoidance of established forms but in the imaginative use of them.

Furthermore, these templates do not dictate the *content* of what you say, which can be as original as you can make it, but only suggest a way of formatting *how* you say it. In addition, once you begin to feel comfortable with the templates in this book, you will be able to improvise creatively on them to fit new situations and purposes and find others in your reading. In other words, the templates offered here are learning tools to get you started, not structures set in stone. Once you get used to using them, you can even dispense with them altogether, for the rhetorical moves they model will be at your fingertips in an unconscious, instinctive way.

But if you still need proof that writing templates need not make you sound stiff and artificial, consider the following opening to an essay by Kelly Coryell that we've included in the book:

> I've never understood the popular saying "Sticks and stones may break my bones, but words will never hurt me." I grew up as a tomboy; I've had more than my fair share of scrapes, bruises, and stitches. But I've found that words inflict the most painful injuries.
>
> KELLY CORYELL, "All Words Matter: The Manipulation behind 'All Lives Matter'"

Although Coryell relies on a version of the "they say / I say" formula—they say that words are less harmful than physical wounds, but I say the opposite is the case—her writing is anything but dry, robotic, or uncreative. A few things that add warmth to the passage are Coryell's use of everyday colloquial language (a technique we discuss in Chapter 10) and her inclusion of her own personal experience (a technique we discuss in Chapter 7).

PUTTING IN YOUR OAR

Though the immediate goal of this book is to help you become a better writer, at a deeper level it invites you to become a certain type of person: a critical, intellectual thinker who, instead of sitting passively on the sidelines, can participate in the debates and conversations of your world in an active and empowered way. Ultimately, this book invites you to become a critical thinker who can enter the types of conversations described eloquently by the philosopher Kenneth Burke in the following widely cited passage. Likening the world of intellectual exchange to a never-ending conversation at a party, Burke writes:

> You come late. When you arrive, others have long preceded you, and they are engaged in a heated discussion, a discussion too heated for them to pause and tell you exactly what it is about. . . . You listen for a while, until you decide that you have caught the tenor of the argument; then you put in your oar. Someone answers; you answer him; another comes to your defense; another aligns himself against you. . . . The hour grows late, you must depart. And you do depart, with the discussion still vigorously in progress.
>
> KENNETH BURKE, *The Philosophy of Literary Form*

What we like about this passage is its suggestion that stating an argument (putting in your oar) can only be done in conversation with others; that entering the dynamic world of ideas must be done not as isolated individuals but as social beings deeply connected to others.

This ability to enter complex, many-sided conversations has taken on a special urgency in today's polarized red state / blue state America, where the future for all of us may depend on our ability to put ourselves in the shoes of those who think very differently from us. The central piece of advice in this book—that we listen carefully to others, including those who disagree with us, and then engage with them thoughtfully and respectfully—can help us see beyond our own pet beliefs, which may not be shared by everyone. The mere act of crafting a sentence that begins "Of course, someone might object that _____" may not seem like a way to change the world; but it does have the potential to jog us out of our comfort zones, to get us thinking critically about our own beliefs, and even to change minds, our own included.

Exercises

1. Write two paragraphs in which you first summarize our rationale for the templates in this book and then articulate your own position in response. If you want, you can use the template below to organize your paragraphs, expanding and modifying it as necessary to fit what you want to say:

   In the Introduction to *"They Say / I Say": The Moves That Matter in Academic Writing,* Gerald Graff and Cathy Birkenstein provide templates designed to _____. Specifically, Graff and Birkenstein argue that the types of writing templates they offer _____. As the authors themselves put it, "_____." Although some people believe _____, Graff and Birkenstein insist that _____. In sum, then, their view is that _____.

   I [agree / disagree / have mixed feelings]. In my view, the types of templates that the authors recommend _____. For instance, _____. In addition, _____. Some might object, of course, on the grounds that _____. Yet I would argue that _____. Overall, then, I believe _____—an important point to make given _____.

2. Read the following paragraph from an essay by Emily Poe, written when she was a student at Furman University. Disregarding for the moment what Poe says, focus your attention on the phrases she uses to structure what she says (italicized here). Then write a new paragraph using Poe's as a model but replacing her topic, vegetarianism, with one of your own.

   The term "vegetarian" tends to be synonymous with "tree-hugger" in many people's minds. *They see* vegetarianism as a cult that brainwashes its followers into eliminating an essential part of their daily diets for an abstract goal of "animal welfare." *However*, few vegetarians choose their lifestyle just to follow the crowd. *On the contrary*, many of these supposedly brainwashed people are actually independent thinkers, concerned citizens, and compassionate human beings. *For the truth is* that there are many very good reasons for giving up meat. Perhaps the best reasons are to improve the environment, to encourage humane treatment of livestock, or to enhance one's own health. *In this essay, then*, closely examining a vegetarian diet as compared to a meat-eater's diet will show that vegetarianism is clearly the better option for sustaining the Earth and all its inhabitants.

ONE

"THEY SAY"

Starting with What Others Are Saying

—▫—

NOT LONG AGO we attended a talk at an academic conference where the speaker's central claim seemed to be that a certain sociologist—call him Dr. X—had done very good work in a number of areas of the discipline. The speaker proceeded to illustrate his thesis by referring extensively and in great detail to various books and articles by Dr. X and by quoting long passages from them. The speaker was obviously both learned and impassioned, but as we listened to his talk, we found ourselves somewhat puzzled: the argument—that Dr. X's work was very important—was clear enough, but why did the speaker need to make it in the first place? Did anyone dispute it? Were there commentators in the field who had argued against X's work or challenged its value? Was the speaker's interpretation of what X had done somehow novel or revolutionary? Since the speaker gave no hint of an answer to any of these questions, we could only wonder why he was going on and on about X. It was only after the speaker finished and took questions from the audience that we got a clue: in response to one questioner, he referred to several critics who had

The hypothetical audience in the figure on p. 5 reacts similarly.

vigorously questioned Dr. X's ideas and convinced many sociologists that Dr. X's work was unsound.

This story illustrates an important lesson: that to give writing
the most important thing of all—namely, a point—writers need
to indicate clearly not only what their thesis is but also what larger
conversation that thesis is responding to. Because our speaker
failed to mention what others had said about Dr. X's work, he
left his audience unsure about why he felt the need to say what
he was saying. Perhaps the point was clear to other sociologists
in the audience who were more familiar with the debates over
Dr. X's work than we were. But even they, we bet, would have
understood the speaker's point better if he'd sketched in some
of the larger conversation his own claims were a part of and
reminded the audience about what "they say."

This story also illustrates an important lesson about the *order*
in which things are said: to keep an audience engaged, writers
need to explain what they are responding to—either before
offering that response or, at least, very early in the discussion.
Delaying this explanation for more than one or two paragraphs
in a very short essay or blog entry, three or four pages in a
longer work, or more than ten or so pages in a book reverses
the natural order in which readers process material—and in
which writers think and develop ideas. After all, it seems very
unlikely that our conference speaker first developed his defense
of Dr. X and only later came across Dr. X's critics. As someone
knowledgeable in his field, the speaker surely encountered the
criticisms first and only then was compelled to respond and, as
he saw it, set the record straight.

Therefore, when it comes to constructing an argument
(whether orally or in writing), we offer you the following
advice: remember that you are entering a conversation and
therefore need to start with "what others are saying," as the

title of this chapter recommends, and then introduce your own ideas as a response. Specifically, we suggest that you summarize what "they say" as soon as you can in your text and remind readers of it at strategic points as your text unfolds. Though it's true that not all texts follow this practice, we think it's important for all writers to master it before they depart from it.

This is not to say that you must start with a detailed list of everyone who has written on your subject before you offer your own ideas. Had our conference speaker gone to the opposite extreme and spent most of his talk summarizing Dr. X's critics with no hint of what he himself had to say, the audience probably would have had the same frustrated "why is he going on like this?" reaction. What we suggest, then, is that as soon as possible you state your own position and the one it's responding to *together*, and that you think of the two as a unit. It is generally best to summarize the ideas you're responding to briefly, at the start of your text, and to delay detailed elaboration until later. The point is to give your readers a quick preview of what is motivating your argument, not to drown them in details right away.

Starting with a summary of others' views may seem to contradict the common advice that writers should lead with their own thesis or claim. Although we agree that you shouldn't keep readers in suspense too long about your central argument, we also believe that you need to present that argument as part of some larger conversation, indicating something about the arguments of others that you are supporting, opposing, amending, complicating, or qualifying. One added benefit of summarizing others' views as soon as you can: you let those others do some of the work of framing and clarifying the issue you're writing about.

Consider, for example, how George Orwell starts his famous essay "Politics and the English Language" with what others are saying:

Most people who bother with the matter at all would admit that the English language is in a bad way, but it is generally assumed that we cannot by conscious action do anything about it. Our civilization is decadent and our language—so the argument runs—must inevitably share in the general collapse. . . .

[But] the process is reversible. Modern English . . . is full of bad habits . . . which can be avoided if one is willing to take the necessary trouble.

GEORGE ORWELL, "Politics and the English Language"

Orwell is basically saying, "Most people assume that we cannot do anything about the bad state of the English language. But I say we can."

Of course, there are many other powerful ways to begin. Instead of opening with someone else's views, you could start with an illustrative quotation, a revealing fact or statistic, or—as we do in this chapter—a relevant anecdote. If you choose one of these formats, however, be sure that it in some way illustrates the view you're addressing or leads you to that view directly, with a minimum of steps.

In opening this chapter, for example, we devote the first paragraph to an anecdote about the conference speaker and then move quickly at the start of the second paragraph to the misconception about writing exemplified by the speaker. In the following opening, from an opinion piece in the *New York Times Book Review*, Christina Nehring also moves quickly from an anecdote illustrating something she dislikes to her own claim—that book lovers think too highly of themselves:

"I'm a reader!" announced the yellow button. "How about you?" I looked at its bearer, a strapping young guy stalking my town's Festival of Books. "I'll bet you're a reader," he volunteered, as though we were two geniuses well met. "No," I replied. "Absolutely not," I wanted to yell, and fling my Barnes & Noble bag at his feet. Instead, I mumbled something apologetic and melted into the crowd.

There's a new piety in the air: the self-congratulation of book lovers.

CHRISTINA NEHRING, "Books Make You a Boring Person"

Nehring's anecdote is really a kind of "they say": book lovers keep telling themselves how great they are.

TEMPLATES FOR INTRODUCING
WHAT "THEY SAY"

There are lots of conventional ways to introduce what others are saying. Here are some standard templates that we would have recommended to our conference speaker:

▶ **A number of sociologists have recently suggested <u>that X's work has several fundamental problems</u>.**

▶ **It has become common today to dismiss _____.**

▶ **In their recent work, Y and Z have offered harsh critiques of _____ for _____.**

TEMPLATES FOR INTRODUCING
"STANDARD VIEWS"

The following templates can help you make what we call the "standard view" move, in which you introduce a view that has become so widely accepted that by now it is essentially the conventional way of thinking about a topic:

- Americans have always believed that <u>individual effort can triumph over circumstances</u>.

- Conventional wisdom has it that _____.

- Common sense seems to dictate that _____.

- The standard way of thinking about topic X has it that _____.

- It is often said that _____.

- My whole life I have heard it said that _____.

- You would think that _____.

- Many people assume that _____.

These templates are popular because they provide a quick and efficient way to perform one of the most common moves that writers make: challenging widely accepted beliefs, placing them on the examining table, and analyzing their strengths and weaknesses.

TEMPLATES FOR MAKING WHAT "THEY SAY" SOMETHING *YOU* SAY

Another way to introduce the views you're responding to is to present them as your own. That is, the "they say" that you respond to need not be a view held by others; it can be one that you yourself once held or one that you are ambivalent about:

- I've always believed that <u>museums are boring</u>.

- When I was a child, I used to think that _____.

- ▸ Although I should know better by now, I cannot help thinking that _____.

- ▸ At the same time that I believe _____, I also believe _____.

TEMPLATES FOR INTRODUCING
SOMETHING IMPLIED OR ASSUMED

Another sophisticated move a writer can make is to summarize a point that is not directly stated in what "they say" but is implied or assumed:

- ▸ Although none of them have ever said so directly, my teachers have often given me the impression that <u>education will open doors</u>.

- ▸ One implication of X's treatment of _____ is that _____.

- ▸ Although X does not say so directly, she apparently assumes that _____.

- ▸ While they rarely admit as much, _____ often take for granted that _____.

These are templates that can help you think analytically—to look beyond what others say explicitly and to consider their unstated assumptions, as well as the implications of their views.

TEMPLATES FOR INTRODUCING
AN ONGOING DEBATE

Sometimes you'll want to open by summarizing a debate that presents two or more views. This kind of opening demonstrates your awareness that there are conflicting ways to look at your subject, the clear mark of someone who knows the subject and therefore is likely to be a reliable, trustworthy guide. Furthermore, opening with a summary of a debate can help you explore the issue you are writing about before declaring your own view. In this way, you can use the writing process itself to help you discover where you stand instead of having to commit to a position before you are ready to do so.

Here is a basic template for opening with a debate:

▶ **In discussions of X, one controversial issue has been _____.
On the one hand, _____ argues _____. On the other
hand, _____ contends _____. Others even maintain
_____. My own view is _____.**

The cognitive scientist Mark Aronoff uses this kind of template in an essay on the workings of the human brain:

> Theories of how the mind/brain works have been dominated for centuries by two opposing views. One, rationalism, sees the human mind as coming into this world more or less fully formed— preprogrammed, in modern terms. The other, empiricism, sees the mind of the newborn as largely unstructured, a blank slate.
>
> MARK ARONOFF, "Washington Slept Here"

A student writer, Michaela Cullington, uses a version of this template near the beginning of an essay to frame a debate over online writing abbreviations like "LOL" ("laughing out loud") and to indicate her own position in this debate:

> Some people believe that using these abbreviations is hindering the writing abilities of students, and others argue that texting is

actually having a positive effect on writing. In fact, it seems likely that texting has no significant effect on student writing.

  MICHAELA CULLINGTON, "Does Texting Affect Writing?"

Another way to open with a debate involves starting with a proposition many people agree with in order to highlight the point(s) on which they ultimately disagree:

▸ **When it comes to the topic of _____, most of us will readily agree that _____. Where this agreement usually ends, however, is on the question of _____. Whereas some are convinced that _____, others maintain that _____.**

The political writer Thomas Frank uses a variation on this move:

That we are a nation divided is an almost universal lament of this bitter election year. However, the exact property that divides us—elemental though it is said to be—remains a matter of some controversy.

  THOMAS FRANK, "American Psyche"

KEEP WHAT "THEY SAY" IN VIEW

We can't urge you too strongly to keep in mind what "they say" as you move through the rest of your text. After summarizing the ideas you are responding to at the outset, it's very important to continue to keep those ideas in view. Readers won't be able to follow your unfolding response, much less any complications you may offer, unless you keep reminding them what claims you are responding to.

In other words, even when presenting your own claims, you should keep returning to the motivating "they say." The longer and more complicated your text, the greater the chance that readers will forget what ideas originally motivated it—no matter how clearly you lay them out at the beginning. At strategic moments throughout your text, we recommend that you include what we call "return sentences." Here is an example:

▶ **In conclusion, then, as I suggested earlier, defenders of _____ can't have it both ways. Their assertion that _____ is contradicted by their claim that _____ .**

We ourselves use such return sentences at every opportunity in this book to remind you of the view of writing that our book questions—that good writing means making true or smart or logical statements about a given subject with little or no reference to what others say about it.

By reminding readers of the ideas you're responding to, return sentences ensure that your text maintains a sense of mission and urgency from start to finish. In short, they frame your argument as a genuine response to others' views rather than just a set of observations about a given subject. The difference is huge. To be responsive to others and the conversation you're entering, you need to start with what others are saying and continue keeping it in the readers' view.

Exercises

1. Following is a list of topics people have debated. Working by yourself or with a partner, compose a "they say" argument

for each of these topics, using any of the templates from this chapter.

Example:

Self-driving vehicles. "Many people think that self-driving cars will make roads safer by reducing accidents caused by unavoidable human errors."

a. Free college tuition at public universities
b. Social media use among teenagers
c. The value of studying the humanities in college
d. Public-funded clean needle exchanges
e. Assigning homework in elementary school

When you finish, read aloud and compare your "they say" arguments with a partner or a small group. Which template moves were more challenging than others to use? Why do you think so?

2. Read the following passage from Kenneth Goldsmith's 2016 *Los Angeles Times* op-ed, "Go Ahead: Waste Time on the Internet."

The notion that the Internet is bad for you seems premised on the idea that the Internet is one thing—a monolith. In reality it's a befuddling mix of the stupid and the sublime, a shattered, contradictory, and fragmented medium. Internet detractors seem to miss this simple fact, which is why so many of their criticisms disintegrate under observation.

The way Internet pundits tell it, you'd think we stare for three hours at clickbait—those articles with hypersensational headlines—the way we once sat down and watched three hours of cartoons on Saturday morning TV. But most of us don't do any one thing on the Internet. Instead, we do many things, some of it frivolous, some of it heavy. Our time spent in front of the computer is a mixed time, a time that reflects our desires—as opposed to the time spent sitting in front of the television where we were fed shows we didn't necessarily enjoy. TV gave us few choices. Many of us truly did feel like we wasted our time—as our parents so often chided us—"rotting away" in front of the TV.

I keep reading—on screens—that in the age of screens we've lost our ability to concentrate, that we've become distracted. But when I look around me and see people riveted to their devices, I notice a great wealth of concentration, focus, and engagement.

a. Where in this passage do you see Goldsmith introducing what others are saying about the internet and the amount of time we spend on screens? What do you notice about the different ways Goldsmith introduces "they say" arguments?

b. Summarize Goldsmith's argument by using the following template for introducing an ongoing debate (p. 26):

In discussions of **how the internet affects people**, one controversial issue has been _____. On one hand, _____ argues _____. On the other hand, _____ contends _____. Others even maintain _____. My own view is _____.

3. Read over something you've written for one of your classes—a paragraph, a short response, or an essay—and then respond to the following questions. You can do this exercise with a partner or by yourself.

a. Where do you introduce what others are saying? Underline or highlight where you include a "they say." If you can't find a "they say" in your writing, add one using one of the templates from this chapter.

b. How soon in your argument do you introduce these other views? Make sure that you include a "they say" early in your writing (in the first paragraph or two for a short response or essay). If the views you're responding to are buried later in your piece, revise your writing so that they appear earlier.

TWO

"HER POINT IS"

The Art of Summarizing

———🜚———

IF IT IS TRUE, as we claim in this book, that to argue persuasively you need to be in dialogue with others, then summarizing others' arguments is central to your arsenal of basic moves. Because writers who make strong claims need to map their claims relative to those of other people, it is important to know how to summarize effectively what those other people say. (We're using the word "summarizing" here to refer to any information from others that you present in your own words, including that which you paraphrase.)

Many writers shy away from summarizing—perhaps because they don't want to take the trouble to go back to the text in question and wrestle with what it says, or because they fear that devoting too much time to other people's ideas will take away from their own. When assigned to write a response to an article, such writers might offer their own views on the article's *topic* while hardly mentioning what the article itself argues or says. At the opposite extreme are those who do nothing *but* summarize. Lacking confidence, perhaps, in their own ideas, these writers so overload their texts with summaries of others' ideas that their own voice gets lost. And since these summaries are not animated by the writers' own interests, they often read like mere lists of things that X thinks or Y says—with no clear focus.

As a general rule, a good summary requires balancing what the original author is saying with the writer's own focus. Generally speaking, a summary must at once be true to what the original author says while also emphasizing those aspects of what the author says that interest you, the writer. Striking this delicate balance can be tricky, since it means facing two ways at once: both outward (toward the author being summarized) and inward (toward yourself). Ultimately, it means being respectful of others but simultaneously structuring how you summarize them in light of your own text's central argument.

ON THE ONE HAND, PUT YOURSELF IN *THEIR* SHOES

To write a really good summary, you must be able to suspend your own beliefs for a time and put yourself in the shoes of someone else. This means playing what the writing theorist Peter Elbow calls the "believing game," in which you try to inhabit the worldview of those whose conversation you are joining—and whom you are perhaps even disagreeing with—and try to see their argument from their perspective. This ability to temporarily suspend one's own convictions is a hallmark of good actors, who must convincingly "become" characters whom in real life they may detest. As a writer, when you play the believing game well, readers should not be able to tell whether you agree or disagree with the ideas you are summarizing.

If, as a writer, you cannot or will not suspend your own beliefs in this way, you are likely to produce summaries that are so clearly biased that they undermine your credibility with readers. Consider the following summary of an article by Kenneth Goldsmith that we've included in the book:

> Kenneth Goldsmith's article "Go Ahead: Waste Time on the Internet" is a total defense of the internet against its critics. I disagree because I see so much on the internet that's just terrible.

If you review what Goldsmith actually says (pp. 361–65), you should immediately see that this summary amounts to a distortion. While Goldsmith does defend the internet, he does not do so in a "total" or categorical way. Instead, he argues, the internet is "a befuddling mix of the stupid and the sublime" (361).

Another problem here is the hasty way the writer abandons the summary after only one sentence and rushes on to their own response. So eager is this writer to disagree, apparently, that they not only caricature what Goldsmith says but also give it a hasty, perfunctory reading. Granted, there are many writing situations in which, because of matters of proportion, a one- or two-sentence summary is precisely what you want. Indeed, as writing professor Karen Lunsford (whose own research focuses on argument theory) points out, it is standard in the natural and social sciences to summarize the work of others quickly, in one pithy sentence or phrase, as in the following example:

> Several studies (Crackle, 2021; Pop, 2019; Snap, 2023) suggest that these policies are harmless; moreover, other studies (Dick, 2019; Harry, 2022; Tom, 2020) argue that they even have benefits.

But if your assignment is to respond in writing to a single author, like Goldsmith, you will need to tell your readers enough about the argument so they can assess its merits on their own, independent of you.

When summarizing something you've read, be sure to provide a rigorous and thoughtful summary of the author's words, or you may fall prey to what we call "the closest cliché syndrome," in which what gets summarized is not the view the author in question has actually expressed but a familiar cliché that the writer mistakes for the author's view (sometimes because the writer believes it and mistakenly assumes the author must too). So, for example, Martin Luther King Jr.'s passionate defense of civil disobedience in "Letter from Birmingham Jail" might be summarized not as the defense of political protest that it actually is but as a plea for everyone to "just get along."

Whenever you enter into a conversation with others in your writing, then, it is extremely important that you go back to what those others have said, that you study it very closely, and that you not confuse it with something you already believe. Writers who fail to do this end up essentially conversing with imaginary others who are really only the products of their own biases and preconceptions.

ON THE OTHER HAND, KNOW WHERE *YOU* ARE GOING

Even as writing an effective summary requires you to temporarily adopt the worldview of another person, it does not mean ignoring your own view altogether. Paradoxically, at the same time that summarizing another text requires you to represent fairly what it says, it also requires that your own response exert a quiet influence. A good summary, in other words, has a focus or spin that allows the summary to fit with your own agenda while still being true to the text you are summarizing.

Thus if you are writing in response to the essay by Gold-smith, you should be able to see that an essay addressing the internet's impact on our social skills will call for a different summary than one addressing the internet's impact on our ability to concentrate. If you want to address both these topics, you'll need to subordinate them both to one of Goldsmith's general claims, then summarize this larger claim in a way that sets up your own two-pronged argument.

For example, suppose you want to argue that, far from being a blend of both good and bad qualities, as Goldsmith asserts, online technologies are mostly bad, that they actually do dis-courage sustained and serious thinking. To set up this argu-ment, you will want to compose a summary that foregrounds what Goldsmith says about the internet's effect on thought, while keeping any other aspects of Goldsmith's argument in the background:

> In his essay "Go Ahead, Waste Time on the Internet," Kenneth Goldsmith argues that, instead of being the big "waste of time" that many see it as, the internet, as Goldsmith himself puts it, "is a befuddling mix of the stupid and the sublime" (341). Specifically, Goldsmith argues that the internet does not always undermine our social skills, as many contend, or always dumb us down, as others assume. With respect to this last concern, Goldsmith describes an incident in which his wife was reading an online version of Freder-ick Douglass's autobiography with such great rapture that she didn't even notice Goldsmith's presence in the room. The implication here is that, instead of simply "making us shallow" and "destroying our ability to concentrate," the internet often enables us to focus intensely on high-quality, edifying material. Although it is often said that the internet encourages "skimming, not reading," Gold-smith claims that it can actually encourage intellectual thought.

I disagree. The internet may improve a few people's cognitive functioning, but nobody I know has ever read Frederick Douglass's writings or anything like them on the internet—unless they were forced to do so in school. In suggesting the internet can make us smarter, Goldsmith seems to be thinking of cerebral types like (apparently) his wife, who comprise a small percentage of the population . . .

The summary in this first paragraph works, we think, because, unlike the flawed summary we saw earlier, it generously quotes Goldsmith, hugging up closely to Goldsmith's own words (see Chapter 3, pp. 47–58, on the art of quoting). Furthermore, at the same time this successful summary stays true to Goldsmith's argument, it also simultaneously moves the focus in the writer's own direction. While the writer acknowledges Goldsmith's concern with both our social and cognitive functioning, their emphasis falls on the latter. In this way, they do justice to Goldsmith's argument while paving the way for their own ensuing critique.

This advice—to summarize authors in light of your own agenda—may seem painfully obvious. But writers often summarize a given author on one issue even though their text actually focuses on another. To avoid this problem, you need to make sure that your "they say" and "I say" are well matched. In fact, aligning what they say with what you say is a good thing to work on when revising what you've written.

Often writers who summarize without regard to their own agenda fall prey to what might be called "list summaries," summaries that simply inventory the original author's various points but fail to focus those points around any larger overall claim. If you've ever heard a talk in which the points were connected only by words like "and then," "also," and "in addition,"

THE EFFECT OF A TYPICAL LIST SUMMARY

you know how such lists can put listeners to sleep—as shown in the figure above. A typical list summary sounds like this:

> The author says many different things about his subject. *First* he says . . . *Then* he makes the point that . . . *In addition* he says . . . *And then* he writes . . . *Also* he shows that . . . *And then* he says . . .

It may be boring list summaries like this that give summaries in general a bad name and even prompt some instructors to discourage their students from summarizing at all.

Not all lists are bad, however. A list can be an excellent way to organize material—but only if, instead of being a miscellaneous grab bag, it is organized around a larger argument that informs each item listed. Many well-written summaries, for instance, list various points made by an author, sometimes itemizing those points ("First, she argues . . . ," "Second, she argues . . . ," "Third . . ."), and sometimes even itemizing those points in bullet form.

Many well-written arguments are organized in a list format as well. In "The New Liberal Arts," Sanford J. Ungar lists what he sees as seven common misperceptions that discourage college students from majoring in the liberal arts, the first of which begin:

> Misperception No. 1: A liberal-arts degree is a luxury that most families can no longer afford. . . .
> Misperception No. 2: College graduates are finding it harder to get good jobs with liberal-arts degrees. . . .
> Misperception No. 3: The liberal arts are particularly irrelevant for low-income and first-generation college students. They, more than their more-affluent peers, must focus on something more practical and marketable.
>
> SANFORD J. UNGAR, "The New Liberal Arts"

What makes Ungar's list so effective, and makes it stand out in contrast to the type of disorganized lists our cartoon parodies, is that it has a clear, overarching goal: to defend the liberal arts. Had Ungar's article lacked such a unifying agenda and instead been a miscellaneous grab bag, it almost assuredly would have lost its readers, who wouldn't have known what to focus on or what the final "message" or "takeaway" should be.

In conclusion, writing a good summary means not just representing an author's view accurately but doing so in a way that fits what you want to say, the larger point you want to make. On the one hand, it means playing Peter Elbow's believing game and doing justice to the source; if the summary ignores or misrepresents the source, its bias and unfairness will show. On the other hand, even as it does justice to the source, a summary has to have a slant or spin that prepares the way for your own claims. Once a summary enters your text, you should think of it as joint property—reflecting not just the source you are summarizing but your own perspective or take on it as well.

SUMMARIZING SATIRICALLY

Thus far in this chapter we have argued that, as a general rule, good summaries require a balance between what someone else has said and your own interests as a writer. Now, however, we want to address one exception to this rule: the satiric summary, in which writers deliberately give their own spin to someone else's argument in order to reveal a glaring shortcoming in it. Despite our previous comments that well-crafted summaries generally strike a balance between heeding what someone else has said and your own independent interests, the satiric mode can at times be a very effective form of critique because it lets the summarized argument condemn itself without overt editorializing by you, the writer.

One such satiric summary can be found in Sanford J. Ungar's essay "The New Liberal Arts," which we just mentioned. In his discussion of the "misperception," as he sees it, that a liberal arts education is "particularly irrelevant for low-income and first-generation college students," who "must focus on something more practical and marketable," Ungar restates this view as "another way of saying, really, that the rich folks will do the important thinking, and the lower classes will simply carry out their ideas." Few who would dissuade disadvantaged students from the liberal arts would actually state their position in this insulting way. But in taking their position to its logical conclusion, Ungar's satire suggests that this is precisely what their position amounts to.

USE SIGNAL VERBS THAT FIT THE ACTION

In introducing summaries, try to avoid bland formulas like "she says" or "they believe." Though language like this is sometimes serviceable enough, it often fails to reflect accurately what's been said. Using these weaker verbs may lead you to summarize the topic instead of the argument. In some cases, "he says" may even drain the passion out of the ideas you're summarizing.

We suspect that the habit of ignoring the action when summarizing stems from the mistaken belief we mentioned earlier, that writing is about playing it safe and not making waves, a matter of piling up truths and bits of knowledge rather than a dynamic process of doing things to and with other people. People who wouldn't hesitate to *say* "X totally misrepresented," "attacked," or "loved" something when chatting with friends will in their writing often opt for far tamer and even less accurate phrases like "X said."

But the authors you summarize at the college level seldom simply "say" or "discuss" things; they "urge," "emphasize," and "complain about" them. For example, in the introduction to her 2010 book, *The New Jim Crow: Mass Incarceration in the Age of Colorblindness* (pp. 347–60), Michelle Alexander doesn't just *say* that today's prison system oppresses African Americans; she condemns the system for doing so, *indicting* and *deploring* it. The Declaration of Independence doesn't just *talk about* the treatment of the colonies by the British; it *protests against* it.

To do justice to the authors you cite, we recommend that when summarizing—or when introducing a quotation—you use vivid and precise signal verbs as often as possible. Though "he says" or "she believes" will sometimes be the most appropriate language for the occasion, your text will often be more accurate and lively if you tailor your verbs to suit the precise actions you're describing.

TEMPLATES FOR WRITING SUMMARIES

To introduce a summary, use one of the signal verbs above in a template like these:

▸ **In her essay X, she advocates <u>a radical revision of the juvenile justice system</u>.**

▸ **They celebrate the fact that _____.**

▸ **_____, he admits.**

When you tackle the summary itself, think about what else is important beyond the central claim of the argument. For example, what are the conversations the author is responding to? What kinds of evidence does the author's argument rely on? What are the implications of what the author says, both for your own argument and for the larger conversation?

Here is a template that you can use to develop your summary:

▸ **X and Y, in their article _____, argue that _____. Their research, which demonstrates that _____, challenges the idea that _____. They use _____ to show _____. X and Y's argument speaks to _____ about the larger issue of _____.**

VERBS FOR INTRODUCING
SUMMARIES AND QUOTATIONS

VERBS FOR MAKING A CLAIM

argue	insist
assert	observe
believe	remind us
claim	report
emphasize	suggest

VERBS FOR EXPRESSING AGREEMENT

acknowledge	do not deny
admire	endorse
admit	extol
agree	praise
celebrate	reaffirm
concede	support
corroborate	verify

VERBS FOR QUESTIONING OR DISAGREEING

complain	qualify
complicate	question
contend	refute
contradict	reject
deny	renounce
deplore the tendency to	repudiate

VERBS FOR MAKING RECOMMENDATIONS

advocate	implore
call for	plead
demand	recommend
encourage	urge
exhort	warn

Exercises

1. To get a feel for Peter Elbow's believing game, think about a debate you've heard recently—perhaps in class, at your workplace, or at home. Write a summary of one of the arguments you heard. Then write a summary of another position in the same debate. Give both your summaries to a classmate or two. See if they can tell which position you endorse. If you've succeeded, they won't be able to tell.

2. Read the following passage from "Our Manifesto to Fix America's Gun Laws," an argument written by the editorial board of the *Eagle Eye*, the student newspaper at Marjory Stoneman Douglas High School in Parkland, Florida, in response to the mass shooting that occurred there on February 14, 2018.

   We have a unique platform not only as student journalists but also as survivors of a mass shooting. We are firsthand witnesses to the kind of devastation that gross incompetence and political inaction can produce. We cannot stand idly by as the country continues to be infected by a plague of gun violence that seeps into community after community and does irreparable damage to the hearts and minds of the American people. . . .

The changes we propose:

Ban semi-automatic weapons that fire high-velocity rounds
Civilians shouldn't have access to the same weapons that soldiers do. That's a gross misuse of the second amendment . . .

Ban accessories that simulate automatic weapons
High-capacity magazines played a huge role in the shooting at our school. In only 10 minutes, 17 people were killed, and 17 others were injured. This is unacceptable . . .

Establish a database of gun sales and universal background checks
We believe that there should be a database recording which guns are sold in the United States, to whom, and of what caliber and capacity they are . . .

Raise the firearm purchase age to 21
In a few months from now, many of us will be turning 18. We will not be able to drink; we will not be able to rent a car. Most of us will still be living with our parents. We will not be able to purchase a handgun. And yet we will be able to purchase an AR-15 . . .

a. Do you think the list format is appropriate for this argument? Why or why not?
b. Write a one-sentence summary of this argument, using one of the verbs from the list on pages 43–44.
c. Compare your summary with a classmate's. What are the similarities and differences between them?

3. A student was asked to summarize an essay by writer Ben Adler, "Banning Plastic Bags Is Great for the World, Right? Not So Fast." Here is the draft: "Ben Adler says that

climate change is too big of a problem for any one person to solve."

a. How does this summary fall prey to the "closest cliché syndrome" (p. 35)?
b. What's a better verb to use than "say"? Why do you think so?

THREE

"AS HE HIMSELF PUTS IT"
The Art of Quoting

—▢—

A KEY PREMISE OF THIS BOOK is that to launch an effective argument you need to write the arguments of others into your text. One of the best ways to do so is not only by summarizing what "they say," as suggested in Chapter 2, but also by quoting their exact words. Quoting someone else's words gives a tremendous amount of credibility to your summary and helps ensure that it is fair and accurate. In a sense, then, quotations function as a kind of proof of evidence, saying to readers: "Look, I'm not just making this up. She makes this claim, and here it is in her exact words."

Yet many writers make a host of mistakes when it comes to quoting, not the least of which is the failure to quote enough in the first place, if at all. Some writers quote too little—perhaps because they don't want to bother going back to the original text and looking up the author's exact words or because they think they can reconstruct the author's ideas from memory. At the opposite extreme are writers who so overquote that they end up with texts that are short on commentary of their own—maybe because they lack confidence in their ability to comment on the quotations, or because they don't fully understand what they've quoted and therefore have trouble explaining what the quotations mean.

But the main problem with quoting arises when writers assume that quotations speak for themselves. Because the meaning of a quotation is obvious to *them*, many writers assume that this meaning will also be obvious to their readers, when often it is not. Writers who make this mistake think that their job is done when they've chosen a quotation and inserted it into their text. They draft an essay, slap in a few quotations, and whammo, they're done. Such writers fail to see that quoting means more than simply enclosing what "they say" in quotation marks. In a way, quotations are orphans: words that have been taken from their original contexts and that need to be integrated into their new textual surroundings. This chapter offers two key ways to produce this sort of integration: (1) by choosing quotations wisely, with an eye to how well they support a particular part of your text, and (2) by surrounding every major quotation with a frame explaining whose words they are, what the quotation means, and how the quotation relates to your own text. The point we want to emphasize is that quoting what "they say" must always be connected with what *you* say.

QUOTE RELEVANT PASSAGES

Before you can select appropriate quotations, you need to have a sense of what you want to do with them—that is, how they will support your text at the particular point where you insert them. Be careful not to select quotations just for the sake of demonstrating that you've read the author's work; you need to make sure they support your own argument.

However, finding relevant quotations is not always easy. In fact, sometimes quotations that were initially relevant to your argument, or to a key point in it, become less so as your text changes during the process of writing and revising. Given the evolving and messy nature of writing, you may sometimes think that you've found the perfect quotation to support your argument, only to discover later on, as your text develops, that your focus has changed and the quotation no longer works. It can be somewhat misleading, then, to speak of finding your thesis and finding relevant quotations as two separate steps, one coming after the other. When you're deeply engaged in the writing and revising process, there is usually a great deal of back-and-forth between your argument and any quotations you select.

MAKE A QUOTATION SANDWICH

Finding relevant quotations is only part of your job; you also need to present them in a way that makes their relevance and meaning clear to your readers. Since quotations do not speak for themselves, you need to build a frame around them in which you do that speaking for them.

Quotations that are inserted into a text without such a frame are sometimes called "dangling" quotations for the way they're left dangling without any explanation. One teacher we've worked with, Steve Benton, calls these "hit-and-run" quotations, likening them to car accidents in which the driver speeds away and avoids taking responsibility for the dent in your fender or the smashed taillights, as in the figure that follows.

DON'T BE A HIT-AND-RUN QUOTER.

GG

What follows is a typical hit-and-run quotation that might be written in response to the 2021 essay "Left Behind" by Joe Garcia, an incarcerated journalist who writes for the *San Quentin News*:

> Joe Garcia writes about technology and prison. "Without more open and frequent internet access, there's no way we'll ever truly keep pace with the changing world outside our prison walls."
>
> This is an excellent point. I have always felt that . . .

See Appendix, "Citing What 'They Say,'" for examples of how to document a quotation in an essay.

Since this student fails to introduce the quotation adequately or explain why they find it worth quoting, readers will have a hard time reconstructing what Garcia argued. First, the student simply gives us the quotation from Garcia without telling us who Garcia is (a family friend? a scholar? a journalist?) or even indicating that the quoted words are his. In addition, the student does not explain what they take Garcia to be saying or how his claims connect with their own. Instead, it's as if the student could stay focused on the quotation only long enough to transcribe it and hurry on to what they have "always felt."

To adequately frame a quotation, you need to insert it into what we like to call a "quotation sandwich," with the statement introducing it serving as the top slice of bread and the explanation following it serving as the bottom slice. The introductory or lead-in claims should explain who is speaking and set up what the quotation says; the follow-up statements should explain why you consider the quotation to be important and what you take it to say. Finally, don't forget that in researched academic writing, quoting what someone else says means citing what they say, to give credit where credit is due, but also to help others follow the conversation. The templates below are shown without documentation, but you can find more information and examples in the Appendix, "Citing What 'They Say,'" on pp. 387–92.

TEMPLATES FOR INTRODUCING QUOTATIONS

▸ X states, "<u>Not all steroids should be banned from sports</u>."

▸ As the prominent philosopher X puts it, "_____."

▸ According to X, "_____."

▸ X himself writes, "_____."

▸ In her book, _____, X maintains that "_____."

▸ Writing in the journal _____, X complains that "_____."

▸ In X's view, "_____."

▸ X agrees when she writes, "_____."

▸ X disagrees when he writes, "_____."

▸ X complicates matters further when she writes, "_____."

TEMPLATES FOR EXPLAINING QUOTATIONS

The one piece of advice about quoting that our students say they find most helpful is to get in the habit of following every major quotation by explaining what it means, using a template like one of the ones below.

▸ Basically, X is warning <u>that the proposed solution will only make the problem worse.</u>

▸ In other words, X believes _____.

▸ In making this comment, X urges us to _____.

▸ X is corroborating the age-old adage that _____.

▸ X's point is that _____.

▸ The essence of X's argument is that _____.

When offering such explanations, it is important to use language that accurately reflects the spirit of the quoted passage. It is often serviceable enough in introducing a quotation to write "X states" or "X asserts," but in most cases you can add precision to your writing by introducing the quotation in more vivid terms. Since, in the article referred to above, Garcia is clearly alarmed by prisoners' lack of access to computer technologies, it would be more accurate to use evaluative language that reflects that alarm: "Garcia is dismayed that," "Garcia is disturbed by," "Garcia worries that," or "Garcia deplores."

See pp. 43–44 for a list of verbs for introducing summaries.

Using some of these moves, the passage above might be revised as follows:

52

Joe Garcia, a staff writer for the *San Quentin News* at the San Quentin State Prison where he is incarcerated, complains in his 2021 article "Left Behind" that prisoners like him are denied access to the very technologies that they will eventually need to re-enter society. As Garcia himself puts it, "without more open and frequent internet access, there's no way we'll ever truly keep pace with the changing world outside our prison walls." In this way, Garcia makes us wonder how prisoners are supposed to prepare for the job market that awaits them when they cannot develop the very technology skills that the market now runs on. Ultimately, he challenges what he sees as the overly draconian treatment of prisoners, suggesting that it undermines our national belief in rehabilitation.

This is an excellent point. As reports show, . . .

This revision succeeds, we think, because it frames or "sand-wiches" Garcia's words, integrating them into the surrounding discussion and thus guiding readers about how they should be read. Instead of leaving us to guess whom the quoted words belong to, as the previous draft had done, this revised version clearly indicates that the words belong to Garcia ("As Garcia himself puts it"), identifies who Garcia is ("a staff writer for the *San Quentin News* at the San Quentin State Prison"), and tells us when he wrote ("2021"). In addition, instead of being presented as an illustration of the overly broad domains of "technology and prison," the quotation is now presented as an illustration of a very specific point that is repeated in different ways: that the prison system sets up prisoners for failure. (See our discussion of how to repeat yourself without being repetitive, pp. 134–35). In this way, the writer explains the quotation while restating it in their own words, using it purposefully instead of simply to pad an essay or a Works Cited list.

BLEND THE AUTHOR'S WORDS
WITH YOUR OWN

This new framing material also works because it accurately represents Garcia's words while emphasizing what the writer deems important. Instead of simply repeating Garcia's claim word-for-word, the writer now keeps echoing its language in the sentences around it. Garcia's "internet access," for instance, gets reinforced in the surrounding references to "access to . . . technologies" and the ability to "develop technology skills." Similarly, Garcia's "keep pace with" is echoed in the related phrase "prepare for," while Garcia's reference to "the changing world outside our prison walls" is translated as "society," "the job market," and "the market." In this way, the new framing material creates a kind of hybrid mix of Garcia's words and those of the writer.

CAN YOU OVERANALYZE A QUOTATION?

But is it possible to overexplain a quotation? And how do you know when you've explained a quotation thoroughly enough? After all, not all quotations require the same amount of explanatory framing, and there are no hard-and-fast rules for knowing how much explanation any quotation needs. As a general rule, the most explanatory framing is needed for quotations that may be hard for readers to process: quotations that are long and complex, that are filled with details or jargon, or that contain hidden complexities.

And yet, though the particular situation usually dictates when and how much to explain a quotation, we will still offer one piece of advice: when in doubt, go for it. It is better to risk being overly explicit about what you take a quotation to mean than to leave the quotation dangling and your readers in doubt. Indeed, we encourage you to provide such explanatory framing even when writing to an audience that you know to be familiar with the author being quoted and able to interpret your quotations on their own. Even in such cases, readers need to see how *you* interpret the quotation, since words—especially those of controversial figures—can be interpreted in various ways and used to support different, sometimes opposing, agendas. Your readers need to see what you make of the material you've quoted, if only to be sure that your reading of the material and theirs are on the same page.

HOW *NOT* TO INTRODUCE QUOTATIONS

We want to conclude this chapter by surveying some ways *not* to introduce quotations. Although some writers do so, you should not introduce quotations by saying something like "Orwell asserts an idea that" or "A quote by Shakespeare says." Introductory phrases like these are both redundant and misleading. In the first example, you could write either "Orwell asserts that" or "Orwell's assertion is that" rather than redundantly combining the two. The second example misleads readers, since it is the writer who is doing the quoting, not Shakespeare (as "a quote by Shakespeare" implies).

The templates in this book will help you avoid such mistakes. Once you have mastered templates like "as X puts it" or "in X's own words," you probably won't even have to think about them—and will be free to focus on the challenging ideas that templates help you frame.

Exercises

1. Examine the ways in which journalism professor Suketu Mehta embeds quotations from former mayor of New York City, Michael Bloomberg, in a passage below from his 2019 book, *This Land is Our Land*, which argues that immigrants do not steal jobs or undermine the US economy. Mehta writes:

Bloomberg said there were half a millon undocumented immigrants in New York City. "And let's be honest: they arrive for a good reason—they want a better life for themselves and their families, and our businesses need them and hire them! . . . [O]ur City's economy . . . would collapse if they were deported. The same holds true for the nation."

The self-made billionaire laid out the business case for immigration: many other countries are growing their economies faster than the United States is, reversing the century-long advantage America has enjoyed. Baby boomers are retiring, America's birthrate is slowing, and there aren't enough young workers to pay for the old folks' pensions. "The economics are very simple: We need more workers than we have."

He called for increasing immigration, because it's good for the economy, and for legalizing those who're already here. "There is only one practical solution, and it is a solution that respects the history of our nation: Offer those already here the opportunity to earn permanent status and keep their families together." It is a moral argument. "For decades, the Federal government has tacitly welcomed them into the workforce, collected their income and social security taxes, which about two-thirds of undocumented workers pay, and benefited immeasurably from their contributions to our country." (659)

a. How well does Mehta set up his quotations?

b. How successfully does Mehta integrate Bloomberg's words with his own? Can you identify which of Mehta's words echo Bloomberg's words?

c. Notice that Mehta ends three of his paragraphs with quotations—a practice we suggest you avoid. Are these quotations "dropped" or "dangled"? Why or why not? How, if at all, would you revise what Mehta wrote?

2. Below is a passage from Christine Michel Carter's 2019 *Harper's Bazaar* essay, "How Feminism Is Stifling Our Sons." In this essay, Carter points out how gender stereotypes are harmful to both girls and boys, and she argues that popular media needs to present more positive models of masculinity. Read this passage and choose a phrase or sentence to quote as a "they say" for an argument of your own. Use the templates from this chapter to sandwich this quote: introduce the quote, explain what it means, and connect it to your own ideas. Your entire response (the introduction, quote, explanation, and connection to your ideas) should be three or four sentences long.

We've committed so strongly to teaching girls they're equal to boys that we've forgotten to extend the message to the boys themselves in a healthy, inclusive way. Along with our focus on feminism, we need to embrace a new men's movement too—one that pays attention to the young boys who are discovering their manhood against a backdrop of hashtags and equality campaigns that tend to either overlook or vilify where masculinity fits in.

3. Read over something you've written for one of your classes. Have you quoted any sources? If so, highlight or underline all the quotations. How have you integrated each quotation into your own text? How have you introduced it? explained what it means? indicated how it relates to *your* text? If you haven't done all these things, revise your text to do so using the list of verbs for introducing summaries and quotations (pp. 43–44) and the templates for introducing quotations (p. 51) and explaining quotations (p. 52). If you haven't written anything with quotations, revise an academic text you've written so that it uses quotations.

FOUR

"YES / NO / OK, BUT"

Three Ways to Respond

THE FIRST THREE CHAPTERS of this book discuss the "they say" stage of writing, in which you devote your attention to the views of some other person or group. In this chapter, we move to the "I say" stage, in which you offer your own argument as a response to what "they" have said.

Moving to the "I say" stage can be daunting in academia, where it often may seem that you need to be an expert in a field to have an argument at all. Many students have told us that they have trouble entering some of the high-powered conversations that take place in college or graduate school because they do not know enough about the topic at hand or because, they say, they simply are not "smart enough." Yet often these same students, when given a chance to study in depth the contribution that some scholar has made in a given field, will turn around and say things like "I can see where they are coming from, how they make their case by building on what other scholars have said. Perhaps if I had studied the situation longer, *I* could have come up with a similar argument." What these students come to realize is that good arguments are based not on knowledge that only a special class of experts has access to but on everyday habits of mind that can be isolated, identified, and used by almost anyone. Though there's certainly no substitute for expertise and for knowing as much as possible about one's topic, the arguments that finally win the day are built, as the title of this chapter suggests, on some very basic rhetorical patterns that most of us use on a daily basis.

There are a great many ways to respond to others' ideas, but this chapter concentrates on the three most common and recognizable ways: agreeing, disagreeing, or some combination of both. Although each way of responding is open to endless variation, we focus on these three because readers come to any text needing to learn fairly quickly where the writer stands, and they do this by placing the writer on a mental map consisting of a few familiar options: the writer agrees with those being responded to, disagrees with them, or presents some combination of both agreeing and disagreeing.

When writers take too long to declare their position relative to views they've summarized or quoted, readers get frustrated, wondering, "Is this guy agreeing or disagreeing? Is he *for* what this other person has said, *against* it, or what?" For this reason, this chapter's advice applies to reading as well as to writing. Especially with difficult texts, you need not only to find the position the writer is responding to—the "they say"—but also to determine whether the writer is agreeing with it, challenging it, or some mixture of the two.

ONLY *THREE* WAYS TO RESPOND?

Perhaps you'll worry that fitting your own response into one of these three categories will force you to oversimplify your argument or lessen its complexity, subtlety, or originality. This is certainly a serious concern for academics who are rightly skeptical of writing that is simplistic and reductive. We would argue, however, that the more complex and subtle your argument is, and the more it departs from the conventional ways people think, the more your readers will need to be able to place it on their mental map in order to process the complex details you present. That is, the complexity, subtlety, and originality of your response are more likely to stand out and be noticed if readers have a baseline sense of where you stand relative to any ideas you've cited. As you move through this chapter, we hope you'll agree that the forms of agreeing, disagreeing, and both agreeing and disagreeing that we discuss, far from being simplistic or one-dimensional, are able to accommodate a high degree of creative, complex thought.

It is always a good tactic to begin your response not by launching directly into a mass of details but by stating clearly whether you agree, disagree, or both, using a direct, no-nonsense formula such as: "I agree," "I disagree," or "I am of two minds. I agree that _____ , but I cannot agree that _____." Once you have offered one of these straightforward statements (or one of the many variations discussed below), readers will have a strong grasp of your position and then be able to appreciate the complications you go on to offer as your response unfolds.

See Chapter 1 for suggestions on previewing where you stand.

Still, you may object that these three basic ways of responding don't cover all the options—that they ignore interpretive or analytical responses, for example. In other words, you might think that when you interpret a literary work, you don't necessarily agree or disagree with anything but simply explain the work's meaning, style, or structure. Many essays about literature and the arts, it might be said, take this form—they interpret a work's meaning, thus rendering matters of agreeing or disagreeing irrelevant.

We would argue, however, that the most interesting interpretations tend to be those that agree, disagree, or both—that
instead of being offered solo, the best interpretations take strong
stands relative to other interpretations. In fact, there would be
no reason to offer an interpretation of a work of literature or
art unless you were responding to the interpretations or possible
interpretations of others. Even when you point out features or
qualities of an artistic work that others have not noticed, you
are implicitly disagreeing with what those interpreters have said
by pointing out that they missed or overlooked something that,
in your view, is important. In any effective interpretation, then,
you need not only to state what you yourself take the work
of art to mean but also to do so relative to the interpretations of other readers—be they professional scholars, teachers,
classmates, or even hypothetical readers (as in, "Although some
readers might think that this poem is about _____, it is
in fact about _____ ").

DISAGREE—AND EXPLAIN WHY

Disagreeing may seem like one of the simpler moves a writer
can make, and it is often the first thing people associate with
the celebrated skill of critical thinking. Disagreeing can also
be the easiest way to generate an essay: find something you
can disagree with in what has been said or might be said about
your topic, summarize it, and argue with it. But disagreement
in fact poses hidden challenges. Perhaps the biggest of these
challenges is the temptation to scapegoat those we disagree
with. Academic writing, as we keep insisting in this book, is
an act of entering into conversation with others; but conversations often go south when, instead of listening to others, we

caricature them, attributing beliefs to them that they simply don't hold and might even find repugnant. Though the goal in scapegoating is to garner sympathy for our own position, the unintended result is that we end up looking unreliable, if not dishonest. A far better approach, we submit, is to play the "believing game" (see pp. 33–34), which requires us to seriously imagine what it would be like to hold another's perspective before we allow ourselves to disagree with it.

Another challenge posed by disagreeing with others has to do with what might be called "is too" / "is not" thinking. When disagreeing, you need to do more than simply assert that you disagree with a particular view; you also have to offer persuasive reasons *why* you disagree. After all, disagreeing means more than adding "not" to what someone else has said, more than just saying, "Although they say women's rights are improving, I say women's rights are *not* improving." Such a response merely contradicts the view it responds to and fails to add anything interesting or new. To turn it into an argument, you need to give reasons to support what you say: because another's argument fails to take relevant factors into account; because it is based on faulty or incomplete evidence; because it rests on questionable assumptions; or because it uses flawed logic, is contradictory, or overlooks what you take to be the real issue. To move the conversation forward (and, indeed, to justify your very act of writing), you need to demonstrate that you have something to contribute.

This does not mean that, in disagreeing with another view, you cannot be strong and direct in your opposition. Consider, for instance, the 2015 essay on artificial intelligence by the education scholar Michael Littman. In no uncertain terms, Littman insists that "the nightmare scenario . . . in which humans are enslaved or destroyed by superintelligent machines of our own creation *is purely science fiction*." Along similar lines, consider how the freelance journalist Anna Clark, in her 2015 article "Why We Need to Keep the 'Community' in Community Colleges," offers an equally hard-hitting critique of the "escalating movement of community colleges dropping the word 'community' from their names." Without mincing words—and in a one-sentence paragraph that's sure to get noticed—she states: "This is a bad move." One thing that saves these critiques from being caricatures is how generously the authors entertain the views they're challenging. Clark, for instance, devotes seven sentences to the counterview she's challenging before declaring it "a bad move," and over three more paragraphs to the counterview after making this bold declaration.

TEMPLATES FOR DISAGREEING, WITH REASONS

▸ **X is mistaken because she overlooks <u>recent fossil discoveries in the South</u>.**

▸ **X's claim that _____ rests on the questionable assumption that _____.**

▸ **I disagree with X's view that _____ because, as recent research has shown, _____.**

▸ **X contradicts herself/can't have it both ways. On the one hand, she argues _____. On the other hand, she also says _____.**

▸ **By focusing on _____, X overlooks the deeper problem of _____.**

You can also disagree by making what we call the "twist it" move, in which you agree with the evidence that someone else has presented but show through a twist of logic that this evidence actually supports your own, contrary position. For example:

> X argues for stricter gun control legislation, saying that the crime rate is on the rise and that we need to restrict the circulation of guns. I agree that the crime rate is on the rise, but that's precisely why I oppose stricter gun control legislation. With proper training, people should be able to own a gun to protect themselves against criminals.

In this example of the "twist it" move, the writer agrees with X's claim that the crime rate is on the rise but then argues that this increasing crime rate is in fact a valid reason for *opposing* gun control legislation.

At times you might be reluctant to express disagreement, for any number of reasons—not wanting to be unpleasant, to hurt someone's feelings, or to make yourself vulnerable to being disagreed with in return. One of these reasons may in fact explain why the conference speaker we described at the start of Chapter 1 avoided mentioning the disagreement he had with other scholars until he was provoked to do so in the discussion that followed his talk.

As much as we understand such fears of conflict and have experienced them ourselves, we nevertheless believe it is better to state our disagreements in frank yet considerate ways than to deny them. After all, suppressing disagreements doesn't make them go away; it only pushes them underground, where they can fester in private unchecked. Nevertheless, disagreements do not need to take the form of personal put-downs. Furthermore, there is usually no reason to take issue with *every* aspect of someone else's views. You can single out for criticism only those aspects of what someone else has said that are troubling and then agree with the rest—although such an approach, as we will see later in this chapter, leads to the somewhat more complicated terrain of both agreeing and disagreeing at the same time.

AGREE—BUT WITH A DIFFERENCE

Like disagreeing, agreeing is less simple than it may appear. Just as you need to avoid simply contradicting views you disagree with, you also need to do more than simply echo views you agree with. Even as you're agreeing, it's important to bring something new and fresh to the table, adding something that makes you a valuable participant in the conversation.

There are many moves that enable you to contribute something of your own to a conversation even as you agree with what someone else has said. You may point out some unnoticed evidence or line of reasoning that supports X's claims that X herself hadn't mentioned. You may cite some corroborating personal experience or a situation not mentioned by X that her views help readers understand. If X's views are particularly challenging or esoteric, what you bring to the table could be an accessible translation—an explanation for readers not already in the know. In other words, your text can usefully contribute to the conversation simply by pointing out unnoticed implications or explaining something that needs to be better understood.

Whatever mode of agreement you choose, the important thing is to open up some difference or contrast between your position and the one you're agreeing with rather than simply parroting what it says.

TEMPLATES FOR AGREEING

▸ I agree that <u>diversity in the student body is educationally valuable</u> because my experience <u>at Central University</u> confirms it.

▸ X is surely right about _____ because, as they may not be
   aware, recent studies have shown that _____.

▸ X's theory of _____ is extremely useful because it sheds
   light on the difficult problem of _____.

▸ Those unfamiliar with this school of thought may be interested
   to know that it basically boils down to _____.

Some writers avoid the practice of agreeing almost as much
as others avoid disagreeing. In a culture like America's, which
prizes originality, independence, and competitive individualism,
writers sometimes don't like to admit that anyone else has made
the same point, seemingly beating them to the punch. In our
view, however, as long as you can support a position taken by
someone else without merely restating what was said, there is no
reason to worry about being "unoriginal." Indeed, there is good
reason to rejoice when you agree with others since those others
can lend credibility to your argument. While you don't want to
present yourself as a mere copycat of someone else's views, you
also need to avoid sounding like a lone voice in the wilderness.

   But do be aware that whenever you agree with one person's
view, you are likely disagreeing with someone else's. It is hard
to align yourself with one position without at least implicitly
positioning yourself against others. The psychologist Carol
Gilligan does just that in an essay in which she agrees with
scientists who argue that the human brain is "hard-wired" for
cooperation but in so doing aligns herself against anyone who
believes that the brain is wired for selfishness and competition:

> These findings join a growing convergence of evidence across the
> human sciences leading to a revolutionary shift in consciousness. . . .
> If cooperation, typically associated with altruism and self-sacrifice,

sets off the same signals of delight as pleasures commonly associated with hedonism and self-indulgence; if the opposition between selfish and selfless, self vs. relationship biologically makes no sense, then a new paradigm is necessary to reframe the very terms of the conversation.

CAROL GILLIGAN, "Sisterhood Is Pleasurable:
A Quiet Revolution in Psychology"

In agreeing with some scientists that "the opposition between selfish and selfless . . . makes no sense," Gilligan implicitly disagrees with anyone who thinks the opposition *does* make sense. Basically, what Gilligan says could be boiled down to a template:

▸ **I agree that _____, a point that needs emphasizing since so many people still believe _____.**

▸ **If group X is right that _____, as I think they are, then we need to reassess the popular assumption that _____.**

What such templates allow you to do, then, is to agree with one view while challenging another—a move that leads into the domain of agreeing and disagreeing simultaneously.

AGREE AND DISAGREE SIMULTANEOUSLY

This last option is often our favorite way of responding. One thing we particularly like about agreeing and disagreeing simultaneously is that it helps us get beyond the kind of "is too" / "is not" exchanges that often characterize the disputes of young children and the more polarized shouting matches of talk radio and TV.

Sanford J. Ungar makes precisely this move in his essay "The New Liberal Arts" when, in critiquing seven common "misperceptions" of liberal arts education, he concedes that several contain a grain of truth. For example, after summarizing "Misperception No. 2," that "college graduates are finding it harder to get good jobs with liberal-arts degrees," that few employers want to hire those with an "irrelevant major like philosophy or French," Ungar writes: "Yes, recent graduates have had difficulty in the job market. . . ." But then, after making this concession, Ungar insists that this difficulty affects graduates in all fields, not just those from the liberal arts. In this way, we think, Ungar paradoxically strengthens his case. By admitting that the opposing argument has a point, Ungar bolsters his credibility, presenting himself as a writer willing to acknowledge facts as they present themselves rather than one determined to cheerlead only for his own side.

TEMPLATES FOR AGREEING AND DISAGREEING SIMULTANEOUSLY

"Yes and no." "Yes, but . . ." "On the one hand, . . . On the other hand, . . ." These are just some of the phrases you can use to make one of the most impressive academic moves: both agreeing and disagreeing simultaneously. The parallel structure— "yes and no," "on the one hand, I agree; on the other hand, I disagree"—allows you to make a complicated response while containing it in a clear, reader-friendly framework, thus helping readers to place your claim on that mental map of positions we spoke of earlier.

Look, for instance, at how Charles Murray uses this parallel structure in his 2008 essay "Are Too Many People Going to College?" In this essay, Murray responds to what he sees as the prevailing wisdom about a college, liberal arts degree, which holds that

> We should not restrict the availability of a liberal education to a rarified intellectual elite. More people should be going to college, not fewer.

He answers:

> Yes and no. More people should be getting the basics of a liberal education. But for most students, the places to provide these basics are elementary and middle school.

In other words, Murray answers "Yes" to more students getting a liberal arts education, but "No" to their getting this education in college.

TEMPLATES FOR AGREEING AND DISAGREE-ING SIMULTANEOUSLY

▸ Yes, it's true that _____. But _____.

▸ I'm of two minds about X's claim that _____. On the one hand, X seems right that _____. On the other hand, X seems wrong to suggest _____.

Formats like these help you enter particularly challenging debates in which, after weighing all sides, you conclude that the smartest position is a divided verdict.

    One nice aspect of such moves like these is that the balance can be tipped subtly toward agreement or disagreement, depending on where you lay your stress. To emphasize the agreement end of the spectrum, you can use a template like:

▶ **Although I [must] question some of X's assumptions, I fully endorse the most important part of their argument: their conclusion that _____ .**

Conversely, to emphasize the disagreement end of the spectrum, you might write:

▶ **Although I have no problem with X's claim that _____ , I strongly disagree with their main conclusion that _____ .**

In short, then, whether you are agreeing, disagreeing, or a combination of both, you need to be as clear as possible with readers about what type of response you are making—even if, and perhaps especially if, your response is marked by ambivalence or mixed feelings.

IS BEING UNDECIDED OK?

Nevertheless, writers often have as many concerns about expressing ambivalence as they do about expressing disagreement or agreement. Some worry that by expressing ambivalence they will come across as evasive, wishy-washy, or unsure of themselves. Others worry that their ambivalence will end up confusing readers who require decisive, clear-cut conclusions.

The truth is that in some cases these worries are legitimate. At times ambivalence can frustrate readers, leaving them with the feeling that you failed in your obligation to offer the guidance they expect from writers. At other times, however, acknowledging that a clear-cut resolution of an issue is impossible can demonstrate your sophistication as a writer. In an academic culture that values complex thought, forthrightly declaring that you have mixed feelings can be impressive, especially after having ruled out the one-dimensional positions on your issue taken by others in the conversation. Ultimately, then, how ambivalent you end up being comes down to a judgment call based on different readers' responses to your drafts, on your knowledge of your audience, and on the challenges of your particular argument and situation.

Exercises

1. Below is a passage from Chris Nowinski's 2019 *Vox* essay, "Youth Tackle Football Will Be Considered Unthinkable 50 Years from Now." In this essay, Nowinski (director of the Concussion Legacy Foundation and former college football player) argues that tackle football should be banned for kids under fourteen years old.

   a. Read the passage. Then respond to Nowinski's argument using one of the templates from this chapter: one that responds by agreeing and one that responds by disagreeing.
   b. Work with a partner to compare your responses. Which response do you think is the strongest, and why?

   The science is clearer than ever: Exposure data shows children as young as 9 are getting hit in the head more than 500 times in one season of youth tackle football. That should not feel normal to us. Think of the last time, outside of sports, you allowed your child to get hit hard in the head 25 times in a day. Better yet, when was the last time you were hit hard in the head?

   Scientists are now beginning to understand the long-term consequences of all those hits. Chronic traumatic encephalopathy, or

CTE, is a degenerative brain disease that was once thought to be confined only to "punch-drunk" boxers. Yet in the past decade, Boston University and Veterans Affairs researchers have diagnosed CTE in American football, soccer, ice hockey, and rugby players, along with other collision sport athletes. . . .

Our society is committed to protecting children—that's why we ban smoking, remove children from homes with lead paint, and force parents to put their children in car seats. We should also protect children from unnecessary brain damage in youth sports.

2. Working together with a partner, write a response where you agree and disagree simultaneously—the "OK, but" move. You can write your response using the Nowinski passage above as your "they say," or you can respond to a reading posted on **theysayiblog.com**. Use the templates from this chapter to compose your response. Decide if you want to emphasize disagreement or agreement, and revise your response accordingly.

3. Read an essay that is posted on **theysayiblog.com**.

   a. Is the writer agreeing, disagreeing, or both? Where do you see the writer doing this? Point to a particular sentence or passage.

   b. How connected is the writer's argument ("I say") to the larger conversation ("they say")?

   c. If the writer is disagreeing, how considerate is the writer to the views being rebutted? Why do you think being considerate while disagreeing is important in academic writing?

FIVE

"AND YET"

Distinguishing What You Say from What They Say

—◻—

IF GOOD ACADEMIC WRITING involves putting yourself into dialogue with others, it is extremely important that readers be able to tell at every point when you are expressing your own view and when you are stating someone else's. This chapter takes up the problem of moving from what *they* say to what *you* say without confusing readers about who is saying what.

DETERMINE WHO IS SAYING WHAT
IN THE TEXTS YOU READ

Before examining how to signal who is saying what in your own writing, let's look at how to recognize such signals when they appear in the texts you read—an especially important skill when it comes to the challenging works assigned in school. Frequently, when students have trouble understanding difficult texts, it is not just because the texts contain unfamiliar ideas or words but also because the texts rely on subtle clues to let readers know when a particular view should be attributed to the writer or to someone else. Especially with texts that present a true dialogue of perspectives, readers need to be alert to the often subtle markers that indicate whose voice the writer is speaking in.

Consider how the social critic and educator Gregory Mantsios uses these "voice markers," as they might be called, to distinguish the different perspectives in his essay on America's class inequalities:

> "We are all middle-class," or so it would seem. Our national consciousness, as shaped in large part by the media and our political leadership, provides us with a picture of ourselves as a nation of prosperity and opportunity with an ever expanding middle-class life-style. As a result, our class differences are muted and our collective character is homogenized.
>
> Yet class divisions are real and arguably the most significant factor in determining both our very being in the world and the nature of the society we live in.
>
> GREGORY MANTSIOS, "Rewards and Opportunities:
> The Politics and Economics of Class in the U.S."

Although Mantsios makes it look easy, he is actually making several sophisticated rhetorical moves here that help him distinguish the common view he opposes from his own position.

In the opening sentence, for instance, the phrase "or so it would seem" shows that Mantsios does not necessarily agree with the view he is describing, since writers normally don't present views they themselves hold as ones that only "seem" to be true. Mantsios also places this opening view in quotation marks to signal that it is not his own. He then further distances himself from the belief being summarized in the opening paragraph by attributing it to "our national consciousness, as shaped in large part by the media and our political leadership," and then further attributing to this "consciousness" a negative, undesirable "result": one in which "our class differences" get "muted" and "our collective character" gets "homogenized," stripped of its diversity and distinctness. Hence, even before Mantsios has declared his own position in the second paragraph, readers can get a pretty solid sense of where he probably stands.

Furthermore, the second paragraph opens with the word "Yet," indicating that Mantsios is now shifting to his own view (as opposed to the common view he has thus far been describing). Even the parallelism he sets up between the first and second paragraphs—between the first paragraph's claim that class differences do not exist and the second paragraph's claim that they do—helps throw into sharp relief the differences between the two voices. Finally, Mantsios's use of a direct, authoritative, declarative tone in the second paragraph also suggests a switch in voice. Although he does not use the words "I say" or "I argue," he clearly identifies the view he holds by presenting it not as one that merely *seems* to be true or that *others tell us* is true but as a view that *is* true or, as Mantsios puts it, "real."

Paying attention to these voice markers is an important aspect of reading comprehension. Readers who fail to notice these markers often take an author's summaries of what someone else believes to be an expression of what the author himself or herself believes. Thus, when we teach Mantsios's essay, some students invariably come away thinking that the statement "we are all middle-class" is Mantsios's own position rather than the perspective he is opposing, failing to see that in writing these words Mantsios acts as a kind of ventriloquist, mimicking what others say rather than directly expressing what he himself is thinking.

To see how important such voice markers are, consider what the Mantsios passage looks like if we remove them:

> We are all middle-class. . . . We are a nation of prosperity and opportunity with an ever expanding middle-class life-style. . . .
>
> Class divisions are real and arguably the most significant factor in determining both our very being in the world and the nature of the society we live in.

In contrast to the careful delineation between voices in Mantsios's original text, this unmarked version leaves it hard to tell where his voice begins and the voices of others end. With the markers removed, readers cannot tell that "We are all middle-class" represents a view the author opposes and that "Class divisions are real" represents what the author himself believes. Indeed, without the markers, especially the "yet," readers might well miss the fact that the second paragraph's claim that "Class divisions are real" contradicts the first paragraph's claim that "We are all middle-class."

TEMPLATES FOR SIGNALING WHO IS SAYING WHAT IN YOUR OWN WRITING

To avoid confusion in your own writing, make sure that at every point your readers can clearly tell who is saying what. To do so, you can use as voice-identifying devices many of the templates presented in previous chapters.

▸ Although X makes the best possible case for <u>universal, government-funded health care</u>, I <u>am not persuaded</u>.

▸ My view, however, contrary to what X has argued, is that _____.

▸ Adding to X's argument, I would point out that _____.

▸ According to both X and Y, _____.

▸ Politicians, X argues, should _____.

▸ Most athletes will tell you that _____.

BUT I'VE BEEN TOLD NOT TO USE "I"

Notice that the first three templates above use the first person, as do many of the templates in this book, thereby contradicting the common advice about avoiding the first person in academic writing. Although you may have been told that the "I" word encourages subjective, self-indulgent opinions rather than well-grounded arguments, we believe that texts using "I" can be just as well supported—or just as self-indulgent—as those that don't. For us, well-supported arguments are grounded in persuasive reasons and evidence, not in the use or nonuse of any particular pronouns.

Furthermore, if you consistently avoid the first person in your writing, you will probably have trouble making the key move addressed in this chapter: differentiating your views from those of others or even offering your own views in the first place. But don't just take our word for it. See for yourself how freely the first person is used by the writers quoted in this book and by the writers assigned in your courses.

Nevertheless, certain occasions may warrant avoiding the first person and writing, for example, that "they are correct" instead of "I think that they are correct." Since it can be monotonous to read an unvarying series of "I" statements ("I believe . . . I think . . . I argue . . . "), it is a good idea to mix first-person assertions with ones like the following:

▸ **X is right that <u>certain common patterns can be found in the communities</u>.**

▸ **The evidence shows that _____ .**

▸ **X's assertion that _____ does not fit the facts.**

▸ **Anyone familiar with _____ should agree that _____ .**

One might even follow Mantsios's lead, as in the following template:

▸ **Yet _____ are real, and are arguably the most significant factor in _____ .**

On the whole, however, academic writing today, even in the sciences and social sciences, makes use of the first person fairly liberally.

ANOTHER TRICK FOR IDENTIFYING WHO IS SPEAKING

To alert readers about whose perspective you are describing at any given moment, you don't always have to use overt voice markers like "X argues" followed by a summary of the argument. Instead, you can alert readers about whose voice you're speaking in by *embedding* a reference to X's argument in your own sentences. Hence, instead of writing

> Liberals believe that cultural differences need to be respected. I have a problem with this view, however.

you might write

> I have a problem with *what liberals call cultural differences.*

> There is a major problem with the liberal doctrine of *so-called cultural differences.*

You can also embed references to something you yourself have previously said. So instead of writing two cumbersome sentences like

> Earlier in this chapter we coined the term "voice markers." We would argue that such markers are extremely important for reading comprehension.

you might write

> We would argue that "voice markers," as we identified them earlier, are extremely important for reading comprehension.

Embedded references like these allow you to economize your train of thought and refer to other perspectives without any major interruption.

TEMPLATES FOR EMBEDDING VOICE MARKERS

▸ **X overlooks what I consider an important point about <u>cultural differences</u>.**

▸ **My own view is that what X insists is a _____ is in fact a _____ .**

▸ **I wholeheartedly endorse what X calls _____ .**

▸ **These conclusions, which X discusses in _____ , add weight to the argument that _____ .**

When writers fail to use voice-marking devices like the ones discussed in this chapter, their summaries of others' views tend to become confused with their own ideas—and vice versa. When readers cannot tell if you are summarizing your own views or endorsing a certain phrase or label, they have to stop and think: "Wait. I thought the author disagreed with this claim. Has she actually been asserting this view all along?" or "Hmmm, I thought she would have objected to this kind of phrase. Is she actually endorsing it?" Getting in the habit of using voice markers will keep you from confusing your readers and help alert you to similar markers in the challenging texts you read.

Exercises

1. Look at the short passages below. Right now, it's unclear who is saying what. Use the templates from this chapter to revise these passages so they include voice markers that allow a reader to distinguish between the two voices.

Example:
Students who major in preprofessional programs like accounting or medical technology are trained for in-demand careers. Students who study the humanities learn valuable skills that prepare them for many jobs, including some that may not even exist today.

Revision:
<u>Well-meaning advisers</u> argue that students who major in preprofessional programs like accounting or medical technologies are trained for in-demand careers. <u>However, they overlook what I consider an important point</u>, that studying the humanities gives students valuable skills that prepare them for many jobs, including some that may not even exist today.

a. Fracking, or drilling deeply into the ground to reach natural gas, can contaminate drinking water in communities near the drilling operations. Natural gas is a cleaner form of energy than coal, and fracking is a cost-effective way to access the reserves of natural gas in the United States.

b. Charter schools give families in struggling school districts options to choose which schools their kids will attend. Charter schools, controlled by private individuals or corporations, divert essential funds away from the public education systems that serve all children.

2. To see how one writer signals when she is asserting her own views and when she is summarizing those of someone else, read the following passage from Anne-Marie Slaughter's essay "Why Women Still Can't Have It All." As you do so, identify those spots where Slaughter refers to the views of others and the signal phrases she uses to distinguish her views from theirs.

Seeking out a more balanced life is not a women's issue; balance would be better for us all. Bronnie Ware, an Australian blogger who worked for years in palliative care and is the author of the 2011 book *The Top Five Regrets of the Dying,* writes that the regret she heard most often was "I wish I'd had the courage to live a life true to myself, not the life others expected of me." The second-most common regret was "I wish I didn't work so hard." She writes: "This came from every male patient that I nursed. They missed their children's youth and their partner's companionship."

Juliette Kayyem, who several years ago left the Department of Homeland Security soon after her husband, David Barron, left a high position in the Justice Department, says their joint decision to leave Washington and return to Boston sprang from their desire to work on the "happiness project," meaning quality time with their three children. (She borrowed the term from her friend Gretchen Rubin, who wrote a best-selling book and now runs a blog with that name.)

It's time to embrace a national happiness project. As a daughter of Charlottesville, Virginia, the home of Thomas Jefferson and the university he founded, I grew up with the Declaration of Independence in my blood. Last I checked, he did not declare American independence in the name of life, liberty, and professional success. Let us rediscover the pursuit of happiness, and let us start at home.

3. Read over a draft of your own writing—a paragraph or an essay—and then respond to the following questions. How do you distinguish your own voice from the argument(s) you are summarizing, quoting, and responding to? How could you use a template from this chapter to clarify the distinction between *your* argument and *their* argument(s)? Where could you use first-person voice markers or embedded references in your writing?

SIX

"SKEPTICS MAY OBJECT"

Planting a Naysayer in Your Text

———

THE WRITER Jane Tompkins describes a pattern that repeats itself whenever she writes a book or an article. For the first couple of weeks when she sits down to write, things go relatively well. But then in the middle of the night, several weeks into the writing process, she'll wake up in a cold sweat, suddenly realizing that she has overlooked some major criticism that readers will surely make against her ideas. Her first thought, invariably, is that she will have to give up on the project or that she will have to throw out what she's written thus far and start over. Then she realizes that "this moment of doubt and panic is where my text really begins." She then revises what she's written in a way that incorporates the criticisms she's anticipated, and her text becomes stronger and more interesting as a result.

This little story contains an important lesson for all writers, experienced and inexperienced alike. It suggests that even though most of us are upset at the idea of someone criticizing our work, such criticisms can actually work to our advantage. Although it's naturally tempting to ignore criticism of our ideas, doing so may in fact be a big mistake, since our writing improves when we not only listen to these objections but also give them an explicit hearing in our writing. Indeed, no single device more quickly improves a piece of writing than planting a naysayer in the text—saying, for example, that "although some readers may object" to something in your argument, you "would reply that _____."

ANTICIPATE OBJECTIONS

But wait, you say. Isn't the advice to incorporate critical views a recipe for destroying your credibility and undermining your argument? Here you are, trying to say something that will hold up, and we want you to tell readers all the negative things someone might say against you?

Exactly. We *are* urging you to tell readers what others might say against you, but our point is that doing so will actually *enhance* your credibility, not undermine it. As we argue throughout this book, writing well does not mean piling up uncontroversial truths in a vacuum; it means engaging others in a dialogue or debate—not only by opening your text with a summary of what others *have* said, as we suggest in Chapter 1, but also by imagining what others *might* say against your argument as it unfolds. Once you see writing as an act of entering a conversation, you should also see how opposing arguments can work for you rather than against you.

Paradoxically, the more you give voice to your critics' objections, the more you tend to disarm those critics, especially if you go on to answer their objections in convincing ways. When you entertain a counterargument, you make a kind of preemptive strike, identifying problems with your argument before others can point them out for you. Furthermore, by entertaining counterarguments, you show respect for your readers, treating them not as gullible dupes who will believe anything you say but as independent, critical thinkers who are aware that your view is not the only one in town. In addition, by imagining what others might say against your claims, you come across as a generous, broad-minded person who is confident enough to be open to debate—like the writer in the figure on the following page.

Conversely, if you don't entertain counterarguments, you may very likely come across as closed-minded, as if you think your beliefs are beyond dispute. You might also leave important questions hanging and concerns about your arguments unaddressed. Finally, if you fail to plant a naysayer in your text, you may find that you have very little to say. Our own students often say that entertaining counterarguments makes it easier to generate enough text to meet their assignment's page-length requirements.

Planting a naysayer in your text is a relatively simple move, as you can see by looking at the following passage from the essay "Why Women Still Can't Have it All" by Anne-Marie Slaughter, a professor who formerly served in the U.S. State Department. Slaughter's central argument is that, "given the way America's economy and society are currently structured," women cannot "have it all"—that women won't be able to strike a reasonable work/life balance until the workplace is radically restructured. Knowing that not everyone will agree with her, Slaughter explains:

> As I write this, I can hear the reaction of some readers to many of the proposals in this essay: It's all fine and well for a tenured professor to write about flexible working hours, investment intervals, and family-comes-first management. But what about the real world? Most American women cannot demand these things, particularly in a bad economy, and their employers have little incentive to grant them voluntarily.

"YOU WILL PROBABLY OBJECT THAT I HAVE MISREPRESENTED X'S WORK HERE, AND I CONCEDE THAT X NEVER SAYS _____ IN SO MANY WORDS. NEVERTHELESS ... "

One reason this naysayer works, we think, is that Slaughter stays with it for several sentences, as you can see above, and even adds one more sentence beyond the material we've quoted. Although it is often tempting to give views we disagree with short shrift, if not to mock them or ignore them altogether, Slaughter gives this objection a generous hearing before she proceeds to answer it, no sarcasm or ridicule included.

TEMPLATES FOR ENTERTAINING OBJECTIONS

To entertain an objection in your own writing, you might want to borrow some of Slaughter's language above:

▸ **As I write this, I can hear the reaction of some skeptics to many of the proposals in this essay: It's all fine and well for _____. But what about _____?**

You might also write:

▸ **Yet some may challenge my view on the grounds that _____.**

▸ **Yet some readers may challenge my view by insisting that _____.**

▸ **Of course, many will probably disagree on the grounds that _____.**

Note that the objections in the above templates are attributed not to any specific person or group but to "skeptics," "readers," "some," or "many." This kind of nameless, faceless naysayer is perfectly appropriate in many cases. But the ideas that motivate arguments and objections often can—and, where possible, should—be ascribed to a specific ideology or school of thought (for example, liberals, Christian fundamentalists, neopragmatists) rather than to anonymous anybodies. In other words, naysayers can be labeled, and you can add precision and impact to your writing by identifying what those labels are.

TEMPLATES FOR NAMING YOUR NAYSAYERS

▸ Here many *feminists* would probably object that <u>gender does influence language</u>.

▸ But *social Darwinists* would certainly take issue with the argument that _____.

▸ *Biologists*, of course, may want to question whether _____.

▸ Nevertheless, both *followers and critics of Malcolm X* will probably suggest otherwise and argue that _____.

To be sure, some people dislike such labels and may even resent having labels applied to themselves. Some feel that labels put individuals in boxes, stereotyping them and glossing over what makes each of us unique. And it's true that labels can be used inappropriately, in ways that ignore individuality and promote stereotypes. But since the life of ideas, including many of our most private thoughts, is conducted through groups and types rather than solitary individuals, intellectual exchange requires labels to give definition and serve as a convenient shorthand. If you categorically reject all labels, you give up an important resource and even mislead readers by presenting yourself and others as having no connection to anyone else. You also miss an opportunity to generalize the importance and relevance of your work to some larger conversation. When you attribute a position you are summarizing to liberalism, say, or historical materialism, your argument is no longer just about your own solitary views but also about the intersection of broad ideas and habits of mind that many readers may already have a stake in.

The way to minimize the problem of stereotyping, then, is not to categorically reject labels but to refine and qualify their use, as the following templates demonstrate:

▸ Although not all *gamers* think alike, some of them will probably dispute my claim that _____.

▸ *Local politicians* are so diverse in their views that it's hard to generalize about them, but some are likely to object on the grounds that _____.

Another way to avoid needless stereotyping is to qualify labels carefully, substituting "pro bono lawyers" for "lawyers" in general, for example, or "quantitative sociologists" for all "social scientists," and so on.

TEMPLATES FOR INTRODUCING OBJECTIONS INFORMALLY

Objections can also be introduced in more informal ways. For instance, you can frame objections in the form of questions:

▸ But is my proposal realistic? What are the chances of its actually being adopted?

▸ Yet is it necessarily true that _____? Is it always the case, as I have been suggesting, that _____?

▸ However, does the evidence I've cited prove conclusively
  that _____ ?

You can also let your naysayer speak directly:

▸ "Impossible," some will say. "You must be reading the research
  selectively."

REPRESENT OBJECTIONS FAIRLY

Once you've decided to introduce a differing or opposing view
into your writing, your work has only just begun, since you still
need to represent and explain that view with fairness and gen-
erosity. Although it is tempting to give opposing views short
shrift, to hurry past them, or even to mock them, doing so is
usually counterproductive. When writers make the best case they
can for their critics (playing Peter Elbow's "believing game"), they
actually bolster their credibility with readers rather   See Chapter 2
than undermine it. They make readers think, "This is   for more on the
                                                        believing game.
a writer I can trust."

We recommend, then, that whenever you entertain objections
in your writing, you stay with them for several sentences or even
paragraphs and take them as seriously as possible. We also recommend that you read your summary of opposing views with an
outsider's eye: put yourself in the shoes of someone who disagrees
with you and ask if such a reader would recognize themselves in
your summary. Would that reader think you have taken their views
seriously, as beliefs that reasonable people might hold? Or would
they detect a mocking tone or an oversimplification of their views?

There will always be certain objections, to be sure, that you
believe do not deserve to be represented, just as there will be

objections that seem so unworthy of respect that they inspire ridicule. Remember, however, that if you do choose to mock a view that you oppose, you are likely to alienate those readers who don't already agree with you—likely the very readers you want to reach. Also be aware that in mocking another's view you may contribute to a hostile argument culture in which someone may ridicule you in return.

ANSWER OBJECTIONS

Do be aware that when you represent objections successfully, you still need to be able to answer those objections persuasively. After all, when you write objections into a text, you take the risk that readers will find those objections more convincing than the argument you yourself are advancing. Some writers take the risk that readers will identify more with the view that's summarized than with the view they actually endorse.

This is precisely what Benjamin Franklin describes happening to himself in *The Autobiography of Benjamin Franklin* (1793), when he recalls being converted to Deism (a religion that exalts reason over spirituality) by reading *anti*-Deist books. When he encountered the views of Deists being negatively summarized by authors who opposed them, Franklin explains, he ended up finding the Deist position more persuasive. To avoid having this kind of unintentional reverse effect on readers, you need to do your best to make sure that any counterarguments you address are not more convincing than your own claims. It is good to address objections in your writing but only if you are able to overcome them.

One surefire way to *fail* to overcome an objection is to dismiss it out of hand—saying, for example, "That's just wrong." The difference between such a response (which offers no supporting reasons whatsoever) and the types of nuanced responses we're promoting in this book is the difference between bullying your readers and genuinely persuading them.

Often the best way to overcome an objection is not to try to refute it completely but to agree with part of it while challenging only the part you dispute. In other words, in answering counterarguments, it is often best to say "yes, but" or "yes and no," treating the counterview as an opportunity to revise and refine your own position. Rather than build your argument into an impenetrable fortress, it is often best to make concessions while still standing your ground, as Stephanie Owen and Isabel Sawhill do in their 2013 report for the Brookings Institute, "Should Everyone Go to College?" Owen and Sawhill are responding to the commonly held belief that

See Chapter 4 for more on agreeing, with a difference.

> a college degree is a prerequisite to entering the middle class . . .
> that, on average, college graduates make significantly more money
> over their lifetimes than those with only a high school education.

They assert:

> While the average return on obtaining a college degree is clearly
> positive, we emphasize that it is not universally so. For certain
> schools, majors, occupations, and individuals, college may not be
> a smart investment.

In this way, Owen and Sawhill show how you can improve and refine your argument by making a concession. Even as they concede that "the average return on . . . a college degree is clearly positive," Owen and Sawhill insist that this positive outcome is not realized for every student.

TEMPLATES FOR MAKING CONCESSIONS
WHILE STILL STANDING YOUR GROUND

▸ Although I grant that <u>the book is poorly organized</u>, I still maintain that <u>it raises an important issue</u>.

▸ Proponents of X are right to argue that _____. But they exaggerate when they claim that _____.

▸ While it is true that _____, it does not necessarily follow that _____.

▸ On the one hand, I agree with X that _____. But on the other hand, I still insist that _____.

Templates like these show that answering naysayers' objections does not have to be an all-or-nothing affair in which either you definitively refute your critics or they definitively refute you. Often the most productive engagements among differing views end with a combined vision that incorporates elements of each one.

But what if you've tried out all the possible answers you can think of to an objection you've anticipated and you *still* have a nagging feeling that the objection is more convincing than your argument itself? In that case, the best remedy is to go back and make some fundamental revisions to your argument, even reversing your position completely if need be. Although finding out late in the game that you aren't fully convinced by your own argument can be painful, it can actually make your final text more intellectually honest, challenging, and serious. After all, the goal of writing is not to keep proving that whatever you initially said is right, but to stretch the limits of your thinking. So if planting a strong naysayer in your text forces you to change your mind, that's not a bad thing. Some would argue that that is what the academic world is all about.

Exercises

1. Read the following passage from "A People's Democratic Platform" by the cultural critic Eric Schlosser. As you'll see, he hasn't planted any naysayers in this text. Do it for him. Insert a brief paragraph stating an objection to his argument and then responding to the objection as he might.

> The United States must declare an end to the war on drugs. This war has filled the nation's prisons with poor drug addicts and small-time drug dealers. It has created a multibillion-dollar black market, enriched organized crime groups and promoted the corruption of government officials throughout the world. And it has not stemmed the widespread use of illegal drugs. By any rational measure, this war has been a total failure.
>
> We must develop public policies on substance abuse that are guided not by moral righteousness or political expediency but by common sense. The United States should immediately decriminalize the cultivation and possession of small amounts of marijuana for personal use. Marijuana should no longer be classified as a Schedule I narcotic, and those who seek to use marijuana as medicine should no longer face criminal sanctions. We must shift our entire approach to drug abuse from the criminal justice system to the public health system. Congress should appoint an independent commission to study the harm-reduction policies that have been adopted in Switzerland, Spain, Portugal, and the Netherlands. The commission should

recommend policies for the United States based on one important criterion: what works.

In a nation where pharmaceutical companies advertise powerful antidepressants on billboards and where alcohol companies
run amusing beer ads during the Super Bowl, the idea of a "drug-
free society" is absurd. Like the rest of American society, our
drug policy would greatly benefit from less punishment and more
compassion.

2. Think of a debate you recently had with a friend or classmate. Compose a one-sentence summary of your argument.
Then, by yourself or with a partner, brainstorm a list of possible objections or alternative perspectives on the issue. Pick
one, and use it to write a naysayer objection that responds to
your argument. Use the templates in this chapter to introduce and respond to this naysayer fairly.

3. Read over something you've written that makes an argument. Work with a partner to review your draft to see if
you've anticipated and responded to any objections. Use
these questions to guide your review: Have you anticipated
all the likely objections to your argument? Whom, if anyone,
have you attributed the objections to? Have you represented
the objections fairly? Have you answered them well enough,
or do you think you now need to qualify your own argument?
Does the introduction of the naysayer strengthen your argument? Why or why not?

SEVEN

"IN MY EXPERIENCE"

Using Personal Stories to Energize Your Argument

———

OUR COLLEAGUE STEVE BENTON often finds that his students' writing significantly improves when it includes a personal story. In one such case, Benton tells us, he received an essay from a student named Felicity Noahubi, in which she defended going to college on the grounds that it helps people get better jobs. But when Benton asked Felicity why she thought it was important to make this argument—the "so what?" question, as we call it—she explained that she had an aunt who, in her job in a meat-processing factory, used to work a mechanical cutting saw that vibrated so intensely that she eventually required surgery on her hands. Why not revise your essay, Benton asked, and make this story central to your argument? Felicity did, and it made her essay much more powerful and compelling.

We open the chapter this way because it helps overturn the common perception that personal experiences and stories have no place in academic argumentative writing. All too often, it is thought, while such personal material is OK for the early grades, it's off limits in the advanced world of college, that personal experience and academic, college-level argument are opposites. To be sure, a more personal voice may not be welcome in the sciences and mathematics, but even in those fields the issue is far from simple. Ask even the most high-powered academics why they became physicists or economists and you'll likely hear a personal story. Once you start looking for it, you'll probably be surprised to find how often the writers you read in college draw on their personal experiences, and how you can energize your own writing by doing the same. Indeed, a personal story can be used to make virtually all the "moves that matter in academic writing" covered in this book, the "they say / I say" move chief among them:

> **Although it is often said that _____ , a recent experience I had suggests _____ .**

To be effective, however, personal stories need to be used with care. Such stories, once again, will not be appropriate for every academic assignment, especially in some sciences. And they cannot take the place of abstract scholarly claims, references to established research, or statistics, which enable us to move beyond our private experiences and generalize about large numbers of cases.

At the same time, personal stories can be an appealing way to enliven standard scholarly content and even to shape such content. Imagine, for instance, how an otherwise straightforward argument about an assigned text might be presented as a mini-story:

> **The other night, when I told my roommates about author X's argument, that _____ , they responded that X seemed to be overlooking _____ . I agree, and would even add that _____ .**

You might also imagine how a story could be used to address the kind of objection we discuss in Chapter 6:

▸ **When my stepmother read an early draft of this paper, she exclaimed, "_____?" And I had to admit that _____. Nevertheless, I still would argue _____.**

USE PERSONAL EXPERIENCE
TO ESTABLISH YOUR CREDIBILITY

Personal stories can also be a helpful way to establish your credibility as a writer. For instance, consider how the founder of the Chicago Basketball Academy (CBA), Damond Williams, uses personal experience to establish his credentials as someone who has "been there" and knows something about his subject from the inside. In a book Williams is writing that addresses the lack of career options available to young athletes from disadvantaged backgrounds, he writes:

> I know a lot about the challenges of life after basketball because I lived them. As an avid Black basketball player who grew up on the South Side of Chicago, I was always painfully unsure what would happen to me if I couldn't make a living as a professional athlete. I saw a lot of my peers who were just as passionate about basketball as I was eventually fall prey to idleness or even crime because they had nowhere to turn when they didn't make it to the pros. I didn't want to become another negative statistic in my low income community, and I felt like I was on an island all by myself. As it turned out, I did achieve a certain level of success in college and, afterward, in professional leagues overseas, but I always knew that my athletic career was only temporary,

and that something else would be needed when it was time to hang it up.

DAMOND WILLIAMS, *The Basketball Economy*

Williams founded the CBA, he explains, to be that "something else" and provide the kind of career alternatives that many disadvantaged athletes need. Without his personal story, readers might wonder what authority Williams has for writing about his subject, and why he in particular chose to make the CBA his life's mission.

USE STORIES TO DRAMATIZE YOUR "THEY SAY" AND "I SAY"

A personal story can also be a useful way to make the "they say / I say" move, as we can see in the opening to a 2022 article by Beth Macy, author of the book-turned-cable-series *Dopesick*. In "A Simple Way to End the Opioid Epidemic," Macy dramatizes one of the many fault lines in our increasingly polarized society, admitting that the Indiana sheriffs she gave a talk to in 2020 viewed her liberal position with open scorn. Macy explains that, as she stood at the podium, she made the case that, instead of arresting addicts and sending them to jail, we should enter them in treatment centers and offer them medication to curb their addiction. But her conservative audience would have none of it. One sheriff, for instance, caustically called out, "'They're clean when they leave my jail'"; and when her talk ended, she "was met with the sound of a solitary audience member slow-clapping."

You might think the last thing Macy would want to foreground would be this kind of ridicule she was greeted with. For an expert writer like Macy, however, it's a perfect "they say" to set up her own argument.

For another example of how stories can be used to make the "they say / I say" move, consider poet-critic Kenneth Goldsmith's 2016 essay, "Go Ahead: Waste Time on the Internet," in which Goldsmith complicates the view "that in the age of screens we've lost our ability to concentrate." To read Goldsmith's article, see pp. 361–65. Goldsmith writes:

> The other night I walked into the living room and my wife was glued to her iPad, reading *Narrative of the Life of Frederick Douglass*. Hours later, when I headed to bed, she hadn't moved an inch, still transfixed by the 171-year-old narrative on her 21st-century device. When I said good night, she didn't even look up.

Through this story, Goldsmith clearly challenges what "they say": that screens impair our ability to concentrate.

A few paragraphs later, Goldsmith tells another story to challenge a related "they say": the common view that computers make us "antisocial." He writes:

> After reading one of those hysterical "devices are ruining your child" articles, my sister-in-law decided to take action. She imposed a system whereby, after dinner, the children were to "turn in" their devices—computers, smartphones, and tablets. . . . Upon confiscating my nephew's cell phone one Friday night, she asked him on Saturday morning, "What plans do you have with your friends today?" "None," he responded. "You took away my phone."

In other words, these stories suggest, although we often vilify the internet, we need to appreciate its social and cultural virtues.

Using Goldsmith as a model, you might write:

▶ **Many often worry that** _____ **. But the other night I** _____ **.**

And following Macy's trick of transforming a potentially painful experience into a "they say / I say" story, you might use a template like:

▶ **I knew there was a problem the instant I** _____ **. When I suggested** _____ **, I was met with** _____ **. When I proposed** _____ **, X told me** _____ **. It may be true, I grant, that** _____ **. But I still hold to my belief that** _____ **.**

USE A STORY TO REVISE
WHAT YOU USED TO THINK

Stories can also help you answer not only what *others* say, but what you yourself used to say or think, as the legal theorist and political activist Michelle Alexander demonstrates in her 2010 book, *The New Jim Crow: Mass Incarceration in the Age of Colorblindness*. Recalling a day years earlier when she happened across a poster on a telephone pole that read, "THE DRUG WAR IS THE NEW JIM CROW," Alexander writes:

> I paused for a moment, and skimmed the text . . . about police brutality, the new three-strikes law in California, and the expansion of America's prison system. . . . I sighed, and muttered to myself something like, "Yeah, the criminal justice system is racist in many ways, but it really doesn't help to make such an absurd comparison. People will just think you're crazy."

Years later, however, Alexander realized that she'd been mistaken, that the comparison she'd formerly dismissed was actually right. After more than a decade of legal work against racial discrimination, she explains,

> I had come to suspect that I was wrong about the criminal justice system. It was not just another institution infected with racial bias but rather a different beast entirely. The activists who posted the sign on the telephone pole were not crazy. . . . Quite belatedly, I came to see that mass incarceration in the United States had, in fact, emerged as a stunningly comprehensive and well-disguised system of racialized social control that functions in a matter strikingly similar to Jim Crow.

In fact, Alexander came belatedly to see the poster as so convincing that she used its claim about the "New Jim Crow" as her book's very title. What we get here, then, is a classic "I used to think / but now I realize" argument presented in narrative form. Like Williams, Macy, and Goldsmith, Alexander could have relied solely on abstract generalizations to make her case, but it is made more engaging and powerful by her use of the kind of first-person language usually found in short stories and novels:

"I paused . . ."

"I sighed and muttered . . ."

"I came to see . . ."

Following Alexander, you might write:

▸ **There once was a time when I was passionately committed to the idea that** _____. **I remember encountering a** _____ **one day and thinking** _____. **Now, however, having** _____, **I have come to realize** _____.

USE A STORY TO BEGIN WITH A BANG

A personal story can also be an effective way to open a text, as the example above from Beth Macy suggests. Consider also how the journalist Anna Clark opens with a story about her parents in her 2015 article "Why We Need to Keep the 'Community' in Community Colleges":

My parents took turns going to college. While raising three kids, my father lost his left big toe in an accident at a tool-and-die shop and Mom babysat dozens of neighborhood rugrats. We didn't have enough. The kitchen cabinets were too bare. So, Dad signed up for classes at Lake Michigan College, the two-year school formerly known as Benton Harbor Community College.

With his hands cupping his chin at a lamplit table, he softly read aloud from his textbooks; for years, his murmuring carried down the hallway to my bedroom, like a lullaby. When I was 11, he earned his bachelor's degree through an extension program hosted by LMC and got a job at Whirlpool Corporation. Then it was Mom's turn. She did her homework alongside my siblings and [me] at the kitchen table. The same year I graduated high school, she earned her associate's degree, on her way to her own B.A. My mother and I posed in front of the fireplace, each in cap and gown, grinning for the camera, for each other, for wherever it was we were headed next.

It is not a coincidence that my parents are the only people I've witnessed who have worked their way out of poverty. With open admission and low-cost tuition, community colleges are the champions of people just like them: full-time workers and parents; older folks and younger ones; military veterans and people who speak English as a second language. That is, the true multiplicity of our communities.

But there is an escalating movement of community colleges dropping the word "community" from their names. . . .

This opening succeeds, we think, in grabbing the reader's attention. It also sets up the "they say" Clark is challenging: namely, the view that community colleges should drop the word "community" from their titles. Such a change, Clark insists, will only erase the institutions' most laudable and distinctive feature, their openness to everyone, including working adults like her parents.

VIEW YOUR STORY THROUGH
AN ARGUMENTATIVE LENS

Perhaps the most important thing to remember, then, when including personal experience in your writing is to use it in the service of a larger moral or argument.

▸ I tell this story because it shows _____.

Few things are more annoying than reading—or listening to!—a story that hooks you in with an engaging incident that, in the end, doesn't go anywhere and lacks a discernible point. To avoid this common problem, you need to think of your personal experiences through an academic lens and present them not just as events that are interesting in and of themselves, but as arguments in a larger debate or conversation. Though this intellectual way of thinking may feel strange at first and take some getting used to, it's precisely what allows Clark to present her parents' stories as critiques of a new trend in education, and what allows Goldsmith to present his sister-in-law's parenting experience as an argument in defense of surfing the internet.

This intellectual way of seeing is what allows the influential education writer Mike Rose to turn his mother's career as a waitress into an argument about working-class labor in his 2009 article "Blue Collar Brilliance." Challenging the common assumption that manual work requires brawn but not brains, Rose describes how his mother's waitressing job, far from being mindless, involved the kind of cognitive "brilliance" named in his title.

For instance, Rose explains, as a waitress, his mother had to master an esoteric, specialized vocabulary:

> *Fry four on two,* my mother would say as she clipped a check onto the metal wheel. Her tables were *deuces, four-tops,* or *six-tops* according to their size; seating areas also were nicknamed. The *racetrack,* for instance, was the fast-turnover front section. Lingo conferred authority and signaled know-how.

Waiting on as many as nine tables at a time, his mother also had to learn to juggle a host of competing demands and "devised memory strategies so that she could remember who ordered what."

> [She] took customers' orders, pencil poised over pad, while fielding questions about food. She walked full tilt through the room with plates stretching up her left arm and two cups of coffee somehow cradled in her right hand. She stood at a table or booth and removed a plate for this person, another for that person, then another, remembering who had the hamburger, who had the fried shrimp, almost always getting it right.

In general, Rose explains that, though his mother only had a seventh-grade education:

[She] learned *to work smart*, as she put it, *to make every move count*. She'd sequence and group tasks: What could she do first, then second, then third as she circled through her station? What tasks could be clustered? She did everything on the fly, and when problems arose—technical or human—she solved them within the flow of her work.

Rose's story, then, serves a clear argumentative purpose: to challenge our culture's tendency to see intelligence as an abstract quality "based solely on grades in school and numbers on IQ tests." On the contrary, Rose argues, there is an alternate type of intelligence that is just as important, one based on the sorts of "hands-on knowledge" and "thinking in motion" that blue collar work like his mother's embodies. In this way, Rose's story is not just a sequence of events, but an argument about the kind of work our culture does or does not value.

MAKE SURE YOUR STORY
AND ARGUMENT MATCH

Given how important it is to use any story you tell to make a larger argument, it is also important to ensure that your story and argument are in sync—that your story says what you *say* it says. Often, the two of us find, it's easy to come up with a personal story that looks from a distance as if it's going to support the argument we want to make, only to realize as we start writing that the story has gotten away from us and created the kind of "uh-oh moment" that we discuss in Chapter 12, on revision.

Such problems arise because, like other forms of evidence, personal narratives can have an unintended reverse effect that allows readers to wrest their meanings away from you. In fact, it might even be argued that such unintended effects are inevitable, that no matter how well chosen and crafted it may be, almost any personal story you tell can be used against you. After all, just because the personal experience you're relaying happens to be your own, it doesn't mean that you're the expert on it, that nobody else can say what it means. Readers can always make a version of the "twist it" move we discuss in Chapter 4 and interpret your experience very differently.

Imagine, for instance, how skeptical readers might use Kenneth Goldsmith's story about his wife's online reading against him. Couldn't they see her deep absorption in the ebook she was reading not as a point in favor of the internet, but as a strike against it? Specifically, couldn't they interpret his wife's near obliviousness to his presence as evidence that the internet, far from fostering social interaction as Goldsmith insists, actually undermines such interaction and even furthers anti-social behavior?

To disarm such unwelcome counter-readings, it's a good idea to follow any personal stories you tell with a template for anticipating naysayers like those we provide in Chapter 6, as in:

▶ **Lest anyone read this story as evidence that** _____, **I would point out that** _____.

DRAW ON YOUR *ACADEMIC* EXPERIENCE

Nevertheless, in the end you may still wonder if your personal experiences will carry much weight in the high-level academic arena. "Can I really make a trip to the mall or last week's family picnic relevant to academic subjects? Can an 'intellectual way of seeing' really make a story about my dog relevant to my course in macroeconomics?" Perhaps—or perhaps not. But there is at least one domain of your experience that's bound to be relevant to any course or assignment: what you learned in another academic setting—another college course, say, or even in elementary or high school.

Note, for instance, how the *New York Times* culture critic Maya Phillips opens a review of a play about women's suffrage. Drawing a contrast between the play and what she'd learned in her "grade school history books," Phillips writes:

> I don't remember my grade school history books dedicating more than a few sentences to the women's suffrage movement. The nearly 100-year history of women fighting for the right to vote is often trimmed down to two main talking points—Susan B. Anthony and the 19th Amendment—and the suffragists dismissed as self-serious rabble-rousers.
>
> To contradict those notions of these revolutionary women and their fight, the new musical "Suffs" . . . begins. . . .
>
> MAYA PHILLIPS, "Young, Scrappy, and Hungry for the Right to Vote"

Following Phillips, you might use a template like the following:

▸ **A central lesson of my English course last semester was that
_____. But author X, whom we are reading in this history
course, suggests _____. My own opinion is that _____
has the better argument, largely because _____.**

Templates like this can help you build bridges in your studies, making connections between texts, courses, and subjects that you might not otherwise notice and that educators should appreciate.

As we were writing this chapter, we couldn't stop thinking about a student we once had who said that, while he was willing to engage in it when necessary, "academic writing just isn't *me*." While we concede that some academic writing requires a degree of formality that can feel foreign, we also argue that it has room for deeply personal experiences that may initially look nonacademic. In this respect, our point in this chapter is similar to the one Gerald makes in his essay included in the back of this book, "Hidden Intellectualism": that there is no experience, no matter how seemingly humble—a spouse's leisure-time reading, your mother's waitressing job, a poster stapled to a telephone pole—that can't be made academically relevant if you view it "through academic eyes."

Exercises

1. Try using the following templates to practice connecting a personal experience to a broader debate or conversation. Feel free to modify the templates if necessary:

▸ **An experience I had sheds light on the controversial issue of** _____.

▸ **The point I draw from this incident is** _____.

2. Now imagine somebody objecting that the experience you related above should be interpreted differently from the way you interpreted it. Using the following template or a version

of it, add two or three sentences to what you wrote in which you summarize and answer this objection:

▸ **Of course, some may read my experience as illustrating not _____, but _____. They would argue, in other words, that _____. I would respond, however, by pointing out that _____.**

3. Following the example from Maya Phillips on page 109, tell a story about something that you learned in one course and explain how it supports or conflicts (or both) with something you learned in another course.

EIGHT

"SO WHAT? WHO CARES?"

Saying Why It Matters

—◻—

BASEBALL IS THE NATIONAL PASTIME. Langston Hughes was the greatest poet of the Harlem Renaissance. All writing is conversational. So what? Who cares? Why does any of this matter?

How many times have you had reason to ask these questions? Regardless of how interesting a topic may be to you as a writer, readers always need to know what is at stake in a text and why they should care. All too often, however, these questions are left unanswered—mainly because writers and speakers assume that audiences will know the answers already or will figure them out on their own. As a result, students come away from lectures feeling like outsiders to what they've heard, just as many of us feel left hanging after talks we've attended. The problem is not necessarily that the speakers lack a clear, well-focused thesis or that the thesis is inadequately supported with evidence. Instead, the problem is that the speakers don't address the crucial question of why their arguments matter.

That this question is so often left unaddressed is unfortunate since the speakers generally *could* offer interesting, engaging answers. When pressed, for instance, most academics will tell you that their lectures and articles matter because they address some belief that needs to be corrected or updated—and because their arguments have important, real-world consequences. Yet many academics fail to identify these reasons and consequences explicitly in what they say and write. Rather than assume that audiences will know why their claims matter, all writers need to answer the "so what?" and "who cares?" questions up front. Not everyone can claim to have a cure for cancer or a solution to end poverty. But writers who fail to show that others *should* care or already *do* care about their claims will ultimately lose their audiences' interest.

This chapter focuses on various moves that you can make to answer the "who cares?" and "so what?" questions in your own writing. In one sense, the two questions get at the same thing: the relevance or importance of what you are saying. Yet they get at this significance in different ways. Whereas "who cares?" literally asks you to identify a person or group who cares about your claims, "so what?" asks about the real-world applications and consequences of those claims—what difference it would make if they were accepted. We'll look first at ways of making clear who cares.

"WHO CARES?"

To see how one writer answers the "who cares?" question, consider the following passage from the science writer Denise Grady. Writing in the *New York Times*, she explains some of the latest research into fat cells:

> Scientists used to think body fat and the cells it was made of were pretty much inert, just an oily storage compartment. But within the past decade research has shown that fat cells act like chemical factories and that body fat is potent stuff: a highly active

tissue that secretes hormones and other substances with profound and sometimes harmful effects. . . .

In recent years, biologists have begun calling fat an "endocrine organ," comparing it to glands like the thyroid and pituitary, which also release hormones straight into the bloodstream.

DENISE GRADY, "The Secret Life of a Potent Cell"

Notice how Grady's writing reflects the central advice we give in this book, offering a clear claim and also framing that claim as a response to what someone else has said. In so doing, Grady immediately identifies at least one group with a stake in the new research that sees fat as "active," "potent stuff": namely, the scientific community, which formerly believed that body fat is inert. By referring to these scientists, Grady implicitly acknowledges that her text is part of a larger conversation and shows who besides herself has an interest in what she says.

Consider, however, how the passage would read had Grady left out what "scientists used to think" and simply explained the new findings in isolation:

Within the past few decades research has shown that fat cells act like chemical factories and that body fat is potent stuff: a highly active tissue that secretes hormones and other substances. In recent years, biologists have begun calling fat an "endocrine organ," comparing it to glands like the thyroid and pituitary, which also release hormones straight into the bloodstream.

Though this statement is clear and easy to follow, it lacks any indication that anyone needs to hear it. OK, one thinks while reading this passage, fat is an active, potent thing. Sounds plausible enough; no reason to think it's not true. But does anyone really care? Who, if anyone, is interested?

TEMPLATES FOR INDICATING WHO CARES

To address "who cares?" questions in your own writing, we suggest using templates like the following, which echo Grady in refuting earlier thinking:

▸ <u>Parents</u> used to think <u>yelling at their kids was necessary</u>. But recently <u>experts</u> suggest that <u>it can be counterproductive</u>.

▸ This interpretation challenges the work of those critics who have long assumed that _____ .

▸ These findings challenge the work of earlier researchers, who tended to assume that _____ .

▸ Recent studies like these shed new light on _____ , which previous studies had not addressed.

Grady might have been more explicit by writing the "who cares?" question directly into her text, as in the following template:

▸ But who really cares? Who besides me and a handful of recent researchers has a stake in these claims? At the very least, the researchers who formerly believed _____ should care.

To gain greater authority as a writer, it can help to name specific people or groups who have a stake in your claims and to go into some detail about their views:

▸ Researchers have long assumed that _____ . For instance, one eminent scholar of cell biology, _____ , assumed in _____ , her seminal work on cell structures and functions, that fat cells _____ . As _____ herself put it, "_____" (2012). Another leading scientist, _____ , argued that fat cells "_____" (2011). Ultimately, when it came to the nature of fat, the basic assumption was that _____.

But a new body of research shows that fat cells are far more complex and that _____.

In other cases, you might refer to certain people or groups who *should* care about your claims:

▸ If sports enthusiasts stopped to think about it, many of them might simply assume that the most successful athletes _____. However, new research shows _____.

▸ These findings challenge the common assumption that _____.

▸ At first glance, teenagers might say _____. But on closer inspection _____.

As these templates suggest, answering the "who cares?" question involves establishing the type of contrast between what others say and what you say that is central to this book. Ultimately, such templates help you create a dramatic tension or clash of views in your writing that readers will feel invested in and want to see resolved.

"SO WHAT?"

Although answering the "who cares?" question is crucial, in many cases it is not enough, especially if you are writing for general readers who don't necessarily have a strong investment in the particular clash of views you are setting up. In the case of Grady's argument about fat cells, such readers may still wonder why it matters that some researchers think fat cells are active, while others think they're inert. Or, to move to a different field of study, American literature, *so what* if some scholars disagree about Huck Finn's relationship with the Jim, an enslaved man who has run away, in Mark Twain's *Adventures of Huckleberry Finn*? Why should anyone besides a few specialists in the field care about such disputes? What, if anything, hinges on them?

The best way to answer such questions about the larger consequences of your claims is to appeal to something that your audience already figures to care about. Whereas the "who cares?" question asks you to identify an interested person or group, the "so what?" question asks you to link your argument to some larger matter that readers already deem important. Thus, in analyzing *Huckleberry Finn*, a writer could argue that seemingly narrow disputes about the hero's relationship with Jim actually shed light on whether Twain's canonical, widely read novel is a critique of racism in America or is itself marred by it.

Let's see how Grady invokes such broad, general concerns in her article on fat cells. Her first move is to link researchers' interest in fat cells to a general concern with obesity and health:

> Researchers trying to decipher the biology of fat cells hope to find new ways to help people get rid of excess fat or, at least, prevent obesity from destroying their health. In an increasingly obese world, their efforts have taken on added importance.

Further showing why readers should care, Grady's next move is to demonstrate the even broader relevance and urgency of her subject matter:

> Internationally, more than a billion people are overweight. Obesity and two illnesses linked to it, heart disease and high blood pressure, are on the World Health Organization's list of the top 10 global health risks. In the United States, 65 percent of adults weigh too much,

compared with about 56 percent a decade ago, and government researchers blame obesity for at least 300,000 deaths a year.

What Grady implicitly says here is "Look, dear reader, you may think that these questions about the nature of fat cells I've been pursuing have little to do with everyday life. In fact, however, these questions are extremely important—particularly in our 'increasingly obese world' in which we need to prevent obesity from destroying our health."

Notice that Grady's phrase "in an increasingly _____ world" can be adapted as a strategic move to address the "so what?" question in other fields as well. For example, a sociologist analyzing back-to-nature movements of the past thirty years might make the following statement:

> In a world increasingly dominated by cell phones and sophisticated computer technologies, these attempts to return to nature appear futile.

This type of move can be readily applied to other disciplines because no matter how much disciplines may differ from one another, the need to justify the importance of one's concerns is common to them all.

TEMPLATES FOR ESTABLISHING WHY YOUR CLAIMS MATTER

▸ *Huckleberry Finn* matters / is important because <u>it is one of the most widely taught novels in the American school system.</u>

▸ Although X may seem trivial, it is in fact crucial in terms of today's concern over _____ .

▸ Ultimately, what is at stake here is _____ .

▸ These findings have important implications for the broader domain of _____ .

▸ If we are right about _____ , then major consequences follow for _____ .

▸ These conclusions / This discovery will have significant applications in _____ as well as in _____ .

Finally, you can also treat the "so what?" question as a related aspect of the "who cares?" question:

▸ Although X may seem of concern to only a small group of _____ , it should in fact concern anyone who cares about _____ .

All these templates help you hook your readers. By suggesting the real-world applications of your claims, the templates not only demonstrate that others care about your claims but also tell your readers why *they* should care. Again, it bears repeating that simply stating and proving your thesis isn't enough. You also need to frame it in a way that helps readers care about it.

WHAT ABOUT READERS WHO ALREADY KNOW WHY IT MATTERS?

At this point, you might wonder if you need to answer the "who cares?" and "so what?" questions in *everything* you write. Is it really necessary to address these questions if you're proposing something so obviously consequential as, say, a treatment for autism or a program to eliminate illiteracy? Isn't it obvious that everyone cares about such problems? Does it really need to be spelled out? And what about when you're writing for audiences who you know are already interested in your claims and who understand perfectly well why they're important? In other words, do you always need to address the "so what?" and "who cares?" questions?

As a rule, yes—although it's true that you can't keep answering them forever and at a certain point must say enough is enough. Although a determined skeptic can infinitely ask why something matters—"Why should I care about earning a salary? And why should I care about supporting a family?"—you have to stop answering at some point in your text. Nevertheless, we urge you to go as far as possible in answering such questions. If you take it for granted that readers will somehow intuit the answers to "so what?" and "who cares?" on their own, you may make your work seem less interesting than it actually is, and you run the risk that readers will dismiss your text as irrelevant and unimportant. By contrast, when you are careful to explain who cares and why, it's a little like bringing a cheerleading squad into your text. And though some expert readers might already know why your claims matter, even they need to be reminded. Thus the safest move is to be as explicit as possible in answering the "so what?" question, even for those already in the know. When you step back from the text and explain why it matters, you are urging your audience to keep reading, pay attention, and care.

Exercises

1. Below are two claims. Who might have a stake in these arguments? Use the templates in this chapter to answer in

one or two sentences the "who cares?" question for both arguments.

   a. The benefits of online shopping don't justify the environmental consequences of shipping items purchased online.
   b. The federal government should fund universal health care.

2. Here are two more claims. What are the possible real-world consequences of these arguments? Use the templates in this chapter to answer, in one or two sentences, the "so what?" question for both arguments.

   a. Violent video games do not cause mass shootings.
   b. Because all combat roles are now open to women, both men and women should be required to register for the Selective Service.

3. Read the following passage from Elizabeth Silkes's 2020 essay "Cultural Heritage Reminds Us of Our Shared Humanity. That's Why Threats against Them Are So Dangerous" found on **theysayiblog.com**. Where do you see Silkes answering the "so what?" and "who cares?" questions? Who does she say should care about preserving cultural sites, and why should they?

> The destruction of cultural sites—from libraries to places of worship to museums—is ultimately about erasing a people's entire history. During the Bosnian war in the early 1990s, Serb and Croat forces destroyed or damaged hundreds of mosques in their efforts to rid the region of Muslims. In Zvornik, which had been a historic Muslim trading post on the Drina River, so many traces of the town's past had been eliminated that Brano Grujic, the Serb-installed mayor there, could falsely boast in 1993 that "there were never any mosques in Zvornik." As Helen Walasek,

the author of *Bosnia and the Destruction of Cultural Heritage*, writes, sites such as archives and museums were targeted in part because they reflected Bosnia's pluralistic past. Such attacks were aimed at "eradicating any trace of Bosnia-Herzegovina's historic diversity and traditions of coexistence." . . .

The current conversation around preservation of cultural heritage in the Middle East comes at a critical time for the region, when conflict and atrocity have put a number of marginalized cultures at risk. . . .

While cultural heritage is not the only way we form bonds with others, it is one of the most powerful and effective means of doing so across barriers. It is heartening to see the public outcry at this latest threat, but the risk to cultural sites during conflict remains extraordinarily high. This is especially so given the limited funding for multilateral organizations dedicated to their protection such as UNESCO, from which the United States formally withdrew a year ago. If our children and our children's children cannot access the most fundamental aspects of our own histories and those of others, they will never be able to identify the common threads that bind us all. And it is only through this binding that we can tap into—and act on—our shared humanity.

4. Read over the draft of an essay you are working on. Work with a partner to identify the answers to the "so what?" and "who cares?" questions for your argument. Then revise your draft to say why your argument matters by using the following template:

My point here, that _____, should interest those who _____. Beyond this limited audience, however, my point should speak to anyone who cares about the larger issue of _____.

NINE

"AS A RESULT"

Connecting the Parts

WE ONCE HAD A STUDENT named Alex, whose characteristic sentence pattern went something like this:

> Spot is a good dog. He has fleas.

"Connect your sentences," we urged in the margins of Alex's papers. "What does Spot's being good have to do with his fleas? These two statements seem unrelated. Can you connect them in some logical way?" When comments like these yielded no results, we tried inking in suggested connections for him:

> Spot is a good dog, *but* he has fleas.
> Spot is a good dog, *even though* he has fleas.

But our message failed to get across, and Alex's disconnected sentence pattern persisted to the end of the semester.

And yet Alex did focus well on his subjects. When he mentioned Spot the dog (or Plato or any other topic) in one sentence, we could count on Spot (or Plato) being the topic of the following sentence as well. This was not the case with some of Alex's classmates, who sometimes changed topic from sentence to sentence or even from clause to clause within a single sentence. But because Alex neglected to mark his connections, his writing was as frustrating to read as theirs. In all these cases, we had to struggle to figure out on our own how the sentences and paragraphs connected or failed to connect with one another.

What makes such writers so hard to read, in other words, is that they never gesture back to what they have just said or forward to what they plan to say. "Never look back" might be their motto, almost as if they see writing as a process of thinking of something to say about a topic and writing it down, then thinking of something else to say about the topic and writing that down, too, and on and on until Alex've filled the assigned number of pages and can hand the paper in. Each sentence basically starts a new thought rather than growing out of or extending the thought of the previous sentence.

When Alex talked about his writing habits, he acknowledged that he never went back and read what he had written. Indeed, he told us that, other than using his computer software to check for spelling errors and make sure that his tenses were all aligned, he never actually reread what he wrote before turning it in. As Alex seemed to picture it, writing was something one did while sitting at a computer, whereas reading was a separate activity generally reserved for an easy chair, book in hand. It had never occurred to Alex that to write a good sentence he had to think about how it connected to those that came before and after; that he had to think hard about how that sentence fit into the sentences that surrounded it. Each sentence for Alex existed in a sort of tunnel isolated from every other sentence on the page. He never bothered to fit all the parts of his essay together because he apparently thought of writing as a matter of piling up information or observations rather than building a sustained argument. What we suggest in this chapter, then, is that you converse not only with others in your writing but with yourself: that you establish clear relations between one statement and the next by connecting those statements.

This chapter addresses the issue of how to connect all the parts of your writing. The best compositions establish a sense of momentum and direction by making explicit connections among their different parts, so that what is said in one sentence (or paragraph) both sets up what is to come and is clearly informed by what has already been said. When you write a sentence, you create an expectation in the reader's mind that the next sentence will in some way echo and extend it, even if—*especially if*—that next sentence takes your argument in a new direction.

It may help to think of each sentence you write as having arms that reach backward and forward, as the figure below suggests. When your sentences reach outward like this, they establish connections that help your writing flow smoothly in a way readers appreciate. Conversely, when writing lacks such connections and moves in fits and starts, readers repeatedly have to go back over the sentences and guess at the connections on their own. To prevent such disconnection and make your writing flow, we advise

YOUR
LAST
SENTENCE

YOUR SENTENCE

GG

YOUR
NEXT
SENTENCE

following a "do-it-yourself" principle, which means that it is your job as a writer to do the hard work of making the connections rather than, as Alex did, leaving this work to your readers.

This chapter offers several strategies you can use to put this principle into action: (1) using transition terms (like "therefore" and "as a result"); (2) adding pointing words (like "this" or "such"); (3) developing a set of key terms and phrases for each text you write; and (4) repeating yourself, but with a difference—a move that involves repeating what you've said, but with enough variation to avoid being redundant. All these moves require that you always look back and, in crafting any one sentence, think hard about those that precede it.

Notice how we ourselves have used such connecting devices thus far in this chapter. The second paragraph of this chapter, for example, opens with the transitional "And yet," signaling a change in direction, while the opening sentence of the third includes the phrase "in other words," telling you to expect a restatement of a point we've just made. If you look through this book, you should be able to find many sentences that contain some word or phrase that explicitly hooks them back to something said earlier, to something about to be said, or both. And many sentences in *this* chapter repeat key terms related to the idea of connection: "connect," "disconnect," "link," "relate," "forward," and "backward."

USE TRANSITIONS

For readers to follow your train of thought, you need not only to connect your sentences and paragraphs to each other but also to mark the kind of connection you are making. One of the easiest ways to make this move is to use *transitions* (from the Latin root *trans*, "across"), which help you cross from one point to another in your text. Transitions are usually placed at or near the start of sentences so they can signal to readers where your text is going: in the same direction it has been moving or in a new direction. More specifically, transitions tell readers whether your text is echoing a previous sentence or paragraph ("in other words"), adding something to it ("in addition"), offering an example of it ("for example"), generalizing from it ("as a result"), or modifying it ("and yet").

The following is a list of commonly used transitions, categorized according to their different functions:

ADDITION

also	in fact
and	indeed
besides	moreover
furthermore	so too
in addition	

ELABORATION

actually	to put it another way
by extension	to put it bluntly
in other words	to put it succinctly
in short	ultimately
that is	

EXAMPLE

after all	for instance
as an illustration	specifically
consider	to take a case in point
for example	

CAUSE AND EFFECT

accordingly	so
as a result	then
consequently	therefore
hence	thus
since	

COMPARISON

along the same lines	likewise
in the same way	similarly

CONTRAST

although	nevertheless
but	nonetheless
by contrast	on the contrary
conversely	on the other hand
despite	regardless
even though	whereas
however	while
in contrast	yet

CONCESSION

admittedly	naturally
although it is true	of course
granted	to be sure

CONCLUSION

as a result	in sum
consequently	therefore
hence	thus
in conclusion	to sum up
in short	to summarize

Ideally, transitions should operate so unobtrusively in a piece of writing that they recede into the background and readers do not even notice that they are there. It's a bit like what happens when drivers use their turn signals before turning right or left: just as other drivers recognize such signals almost unconsciously, readers should process transition terms with a minimum of thought. But even though such terms should function unobtrusively in your writing, they can be among the most powerful tools in your vocabulary. Think how your heart sinks when someone, immediately after praising you, begins a sentence with "but" or "however." No matter what follows, you know it won't be good.

Notice that some transitions can help you not only move from one sentence to another but also combine two or more sentences into one. Combining sentences in this way helps prevent the choppy, staccato effect that arises when too many short sentences are strung together, one after the other. For instance, to combine Alex's two choppy sentences ("Spot is a good dog. He has fleas.") into one, better-flowing sentence, we suggested that he rewrite them as "Spot is a good dog, *even though* he has fleas."

Transitions like these not only guide readers through the twists and turns of your argument but also help ensure that you *have* an argument in the first place. In fact, we think of words like "but," "yet," "nevertheless," "besides," and others as argument words, since it's hard to use them without making some kind of argument. The word "therefore," for instance, commits you to making sure that the claims preceding it lead logically to the conclusion that it introduces. "For example" also assumes an argument, since it requires the material you are introducing to stand as an instance or proof of some preceding generalization. As a result, the more you use transitions, the more you'll be able not only to connect the parts of your text but also to construct a strong argument in the first place. And if you draw on them frequently enough, using them should eventually become second nature.

To be sure, it is possible to overuse transitions, so take time to read over your drafts carefully and eliminate any transitions that are unnecessary. But following the maxim that you need to learn the basic moves of argument before you can deliberately depart from them, we advise you not to forgo explicit transition terms until you've first mastered their use. In all our years of teaching, we've read countless essays that suffered from having few or no transitions, but we cannot recall one in which the transitions were overused. Seasoned writers sometimes omit explicit transitions but only because they rely heavily on the other types of connecting devices that we turn to in the rest of this chapter.

Before doing so, however, let us warn you about inserting transitions without really thinking through their meanings—using "therefore," say, when your text's logic actually requires "nevertheless" or "however." So beware. Choosing transition terms should involve a bit of mental sweat, since the whole point of using them is to make your writing *more* reader-friendly, not less. The only thing more frustrating than reading Alex-style passages like "Spot is a good dog. He has fleas" is reading mis-connected sentences like "Spot is a good dog. For example, he has fleas."

USE POINTING WORDS

Another way to connect the parts of your argument is by using pointing words—which, as their name implies, point or refer backward to some concept in the previous sentence. The most common of these pointing words include "this," "these," "that," "those," "their," and "such" (as in "these pointing words" near the start of this sentence) and simple pronouns like "his," "he," "her," "she," "it," and "their." Such terms help you create the flow we spoke of earlier that enables readers to move effortlessly through your text. In a sense, these terms are like an invisible hand reaching out of your sentence, grabbing what's needed in the previous sentences and pulling it along.

Like transitions, however, pointing words need to be used carefully. It's dangerously easy to insert pointing words into your text that don't refer to a clearly defined object, assuming that because the object you have in mind is clear to you it will also be clear to your readers. For example, consider the use of "this" in the following passage:

> Alexis de Tocqueville was highly critical of democratic socie-ties, which he saw as tending toward mob rule. At the same time, he accorded democratic societies grudging respect. *This* is seen in Tocqueville's statement that . . .

When "this" is used in such a way, it becomes an ambiguous or free-floating pointer since readers can't tell if it refers to Tocque-ville's critical attitude toward democratic societies, his grudging respect for them, or some combination of both. "This what?" readers mutter as they go back over such passages and try to figure them out. It's also tempting to try to cheat with pointing words, hoping that they will conceal or make up for conceptual confusions that may lurk in your argument. By referring to a fuzzy idea as "this" or "that," you might hope the fuzziness will somehow come across as clearer than it is.

You can fix problems caused by a free-floating pointer by making sure there is one and only one possible object in the vicinity that the pointer could be referring to. It also often helps

NINE   "AS A RESULT"

to name the object the pointer is referring to at the same time that you point to it, replacing the bald "this" in the example above with a more precise phrase like "this ambivalence toward democratic societies" or "this grudging respect."

REPEAT KEY TERMS AND PHRASES

A third strategy for connecting the parts of your argument is to develop a constellation of key terms and phrases, including their synonyms and antonyms, that you repeat throughout your text. When used effectively, your key terms should be items that readers could extract from your text in order to get a solid sense of your topic. Playing with key terms also can be a good way to come up with a title and appropriate section headings for your text.

Notice how often Martin Luther King Jr. uses the keywords "criticism," "statement," "answer," and "correspondence" in the opening paragraph of his famous "Letter from Birmingham Jail":

Dear Fellow Clergymen:

While confined here in the Birmingham city jail, I came across your recent *statement* calling my present activities "unwise and untimely." Seldom do I pause to *answer criticism* of my work and ideas. If I sought to *answer* all the *criticisms* that cross my desk, my secretaries would have little time for anything other than *such correspondence* in the course of the day, and I would have no time for constructive work. But since I feel that you are men of genuine good will and that your *criticisms* are sincerely set forth, I want to try to *answer* your *statement* in what I hope will be patient and reasonable terms.

MARTIN LUTHER KING JR., "Letter from Birmingham Jail"

Even though King uses the terms "criticism" and "answer" three times each and "statement" twice, the effect is not overly repetitive. In fact, these key terms help build a sense of momentum in the paragraph and bind it together.

For another example of the effective use of key terms, consider the following passage, in which the academic legal theorist, Michelle Alexander, develops a constellation of key terms around the idea of voting. In the opening paragraph of her best-selling book, *The New Jim Crow: Mass Incarceration in the Age of Colorblindness*, Alexander writes,

> Jarvious Cotton cannot vote. Like his father, grandfather, great-grandfather, and great-great-grandfather, he has been denied the right to participate in our electoral democracy. Cotton's family tree tells the story of several generations of black men who were born in the United States but who were denied the most basic freedom that democracy promises—the freedom to vote for those who will make the rules and laws that govern one's life. Cotton's great-great-grandfather could not vote as a slave. His great-grandfather was beaten to death by the Ku Klux Klan for attempting to vote. His grandfather was prevented from voting by Klan intimidation. His father was barred from voting by poll taxes and literacy tests. Today, Jarvious Cotton cannot vote because he, like many black men in the United States, has been labeled a felon and is currently on parole.
>
> MICHELLE ALEXANDER, *The New Jim Crow: Mass Incarceration in the Age of Colorblindness*

Note how many times Alexander refers to the concept of voting in this passage. She uses the term "vote" five times, the term "voting" twice, and echoes the concept in phrases like "the right to participate in our electoral democracy" and "the most basic freedom that democracy promises." Indeed, Alexander includes some version of the key terms in every sentence above, creating a tight and unified focus in the paragraph from start to finish.

REPEAT YOURSELF—BUT WITH A DIFFERENCE

The last technique we offer for connecting the parts of your text involves repeating yourself, but with a difference—which basically means saying the same thing you've just said but in a slightly different way that avoids sounding monotonous. To effectively connect the parts of your argument and keep it moving forward, be careful not to leap from one idea to a different idea or introduce new ideas cold. Instead, try to build bridges between your ideas by echoing what you've just said while simultaneously moving your text into new territory.

Several of the connecting devices discussed in this chapter are ways of repeating yourself in this special way. Key terms, pointing terms, and even many transitions can be used in a way that not only brings something forward from the previous sentence but in some way alters it, too.

In addition, when you use transition phrases like "in other words" and "to put it another way," you repeat yourself with a difference, since these phrases help you restate earlier claims but in a different register. When you open a sentence with "in other words," you are basically telling your readers that in case they didn't fully understand what you meant in the last sentence, you are now coming at it again from a slightly different angle, or that since you're presenting a very important idea, you're not going to skip over it quickly but will explore it further to make sure your readers grasp all its aspects.

We would even go so far as to suggest that after your first sentence, almost every sentence you write should refer back to previous statements in some way. Whether you are writing a "furthermore" comment that adds to what you have just said or a "for example" statement that illustrates it, each sentence should echo at least one element of the previous sentence in some discernible way. Even when your text changes direction and requires transitions like "in contrast," "however," or "but," you still need to mark that shift by linking the sentence to the one just before it, as in the following example:

> Cheyenne loved basketball. Nevertheless, she feared her height would put her at a disadvantage.

These sentences work because even though the second sentence changes course and qualifies the first, it still echoes key concepts from the first. Not only does "she" echo "Cheyenne," since both refer to the same person, but "feared" echoes "loved" by establishing the contrast mandated by the term "nevertheless." "Nevertheless," then, is not an excuse for changing subjects radically. It too requires repetition to help readers shift gears with you and follow your train of thought.

Repetition, in short, is the central means by which you can move from point A to point B in a text. To introduce one last analogy, think of the way experienced rock climbers move up a steep slope. Instead of jumping or lurching from one handhold to the next, good climbers get a secure handhold on the position they have established before reaching for the next ledge. The same thing applies to writing. To move smoothly from point to point in your argument, you need to firmly ground what you say in what you've already said. In this way, your writing remains focused while simultaneously moving forward.

"But hold on," you may be thinking. "Isn't repetition precisely what sophisticated writers should avoid, on the grounds that it will make their writing sound simplistic—as if they are belaboring the obvious?" Yes and no. On the one hand, writers certainly can run into trouble if they merely repeat themselves and nothing more. On the other hand, repetition is key to creating continuity in writing. It is impossible to stay on track in a piece of writing if you don't repeat your points throughout the length of the text. Furthermore, writers would never make an impact on readers if they didn't repeat their main points often enough to reinforce those points and make them stand out above subordinate points. The trick therefore is not to avoid repeating yourself but to repeat yourself in varied and interesting enough ways that you advance your argument without sounding tedious.

Exercises

1. The statements below aren't yet connected to each other. Use any of the transitions listed on pages 127 and 128 to connect them. You can combine the statements into one sentence, or you can keep them as two separate sentences, adding or deleting words. Once you're done, compare your responses with a partner's. How does your choice of transition words affect the meaning of the statements?

   a. Herd immunity is established when 93 percent of a population is vaccinated. Vaccinations can wear off in early adolescence.

   b. Writing can look like an individual pursuit. It requires other people. Other people help writers imagine how their audience will understand and respond to their claims.

c. Some ski resorts have begun to diversify their operations to increase year-round profitability. Some have added zip lines that draw in people in the summer months.

2. Read the following passage from MIT professor Sherry Turkle's essay "Stop Googling. Let's Talk." Annotate the connecting devices you see. Underline the transitions, circle the key terms, and put boxes around the pointing terms.

> Across generations, technology is implicated in this assault on empathy. We've gotten used to being connected all the time, but we have found ways around conversation—at least from conversation that is open-ended and spontaneous, in which we play with ideas and allow ourselves to be fully present and vulnerable. But it is in this type of conversation—where we learn to make eye contact, to become aware of another person's posture and tone, to comfort one another and respectfully challenge one another—that empathy and intimacy flourish. In these conversations, we learn who we are.
>
> Of course, we can find empathic conversations today, but the trend line is clear. It's not only that we turn away from talking face to face to chat online. It's that we don't allow these conversations to happen in the first place because we keep our phones in the landscape.
>
> In our hearts, we know this, and now research is catching up with our intuitions. We face a significant choice. It is not about giving up our phones but about using them with greater intention. Conversation is there for us to reclaim. For the failing connections of our digital world, it is the talking cure.

3. Read over something you've written with an eye for the devices you've used to connect the parts. Working either by yourself or with a partner, do the following:

   a. Underline all the transitions, pointing terms, key terms, and repetitions.
   b. Describe the patterns you see. Do you rely on certain devices more than others?
   c. Locate a passage that could use better connections. Revise it using the devices introduced in this chapter. Is it easier to read now?

TEN

"YOU MEAN I CAN JUST SAY IT THAT WAY?"

Academic Writing Doesn't Mean Setting Aside Your Own Voice

WE WISH WE HAD A DOLLAR for each time a student has asked us a version of the above question. It usually comes when the student is visiting us during our office hours, seeking advice about how to improve a draft of an essay. When we ask the student to tell us in simple words the point being made in the essay, the student will almost invariably produce a statement that is far clearer and more incisive than anything in the draft.

"Write that down," we will urge. "What you just said is sooo much better than anything you wrote in your draft. We suggest going home and revising your paper in a way that makes that claim the focal point of your essay."

"Really?" our student will ask, looking surprised. "You mean I can just say it that way?"

"Sure. Why not?"

"Well, saying it that way seems just so elementary—so obvious. I mean, I don't want to sound stupid."

The goal of this chapter is to counteract this common misconception: that relying in college on the straightforward, down-to-earth language you use every day will make you sound stupid; that to impress your teachers you need to set aside your everyday voice and write in a way that is hard to understand.

It's easy to see how this misconception took hold, since academic writing is notoriously obscure. Students can't be blamed for such obscurity when much of the writing they're assigned to read is so hard to understand—as we can see in the following sentence from a science paper that linguist Steven Pinker quotes in his essay "Why Academics Stink at Writing":

> Participants read assertions whose veracity was either affirmed or denied by the subsequent presentation of an assessment word.

After struggling to determine what the writer of this sentence was trying to say, Pinker finally decided it was probably something as simple as this:

> Participants read sentences, each followed by the word *true* or *false*.

Had the author revised the original statement by tapping into more relaxed, everyday language, as Pinker did in revising it, much of this struggle could have been avoided. In our view, then, mastering academic writing does not mean completely abandoning your normal voice for one that's stiff, convoluted, or pompous, as students often assume. Instead, it means creating a new voice that draws on the voice you already have.

This is not to suggest that any language you use among friends has a place in academic writing. Nor is it to suggest that you may fall back on your everyday voice as an excuse to remain in your comfort zone and avoid learning the rigorous forms and habits that characterize academic culture. After all, learning new words and rhetorical moves is a major part of getting an education. We do, however, wish to suggest that everyday language can often enliven such moves and even enhance your precision in using academic terminology. In our view, then, it is a mistake to assume that the academic and everyday are completely separate languages that can never be used together. Ultimately, we suggest, academic writing is often at its best when it combines what we call "everydayspeak" and "academicspeak."

BLEND ACADEMIC AND COLLOQUIAL STYLES

In fact, we would point out that many academics are highly successful writers who themselves blend everyday and academic styles. Note, for example, how Judith Fetterley, a prominent scholar in the field of literary studies, blends academic and everyday ways of talking in the following passage on the novelist Willa Cather:

> As Merrill Skaggs has put it, "[Cather] is neurotically controlling and self-conscious about her work, but she knows at all points what she is doing. Above all else, she is self-conscious."
> Without question, Cather was a control freak.
>
> JUDITH FETTERLEY, "Willa Cather and the Question of Sympathy: An Unofficial Story"

In this passage, Fetterley makes use of what is probably the most common technique for blending academic and everyday language: she puts them side by side, juxtaposing "neurotically controlling" and "self-conscious" from a quoted source with her own colloquial term, "control freak." In this way, Fetterley lightens a potentially dry subject and makes it more accessible and even entertaining.

A TRANSLATION RECIPE

But Fetterley does more than simply put academicspeak and everydayspeak side by side. She takes a step further by translating the one into the other. By translating Skaggs's polysyllabic description of Cather as "neurotically controlling and self-conscious" into the succinct, if blunt, "control freak," Fetterley shows how rarefied, academic ways of talking and more familiar language can not only coexist but can also actually enhance one another—her informal "control freak" serving to explain the formal language that precedes it.

To be sure, slangy, colloquial expressions like "control freak" may be far more common in the humanities than in the sciences, and even in the humanities such casual usages are a recent development. Fifty years ago academic writing in all disciplines was the linguistic equivalent of a black-tie affair. But as times have changed, so has the range of options open to academic writers—so much so that it is not surprising to find writers in all fields using colloquial expressions and referring to movies, music, and other forms of popular culture.

Indeed, Fetterley's passage offers a simple recipe for mixing styles that we encourage you to try out in your own writing: first state the point in academic language, and then translate the point into everyday language. Everyone knows that academic terms like "neurotically controlling" and "self-conscious"—and others you might encounter like "subject position" or "bifurcate"—can be hard to understand. But this translation recipe, we think, eases such difficulties by making the academic familiar. Here is one way you might translate academicspeak into everydayspeak:

▸ **Scholar X argues, "_____." In other words, _____.**

Instead of "In other words," you might try variations like the following:

▸ **Essentially, X argues _____.**

▸ **X's point, succinctly put, is that _____.**

▸ **Plainly put, _____.**

Following Fetterley's lead and making moves like these can help you not only demystify challenging academic material but also reinterpret it, showing you understand it (and helping readers understand it) by putting it into your own terms.

SELF-TRANSLATION

But this translation recipe need not be limited to clarifying the ideas of others. It can also be used to clarify your own complex ideas, as the following passage by the philosopher Rebecca Goldstein illustrates:

> We can hardly get through our lives—in fact, it's hard to get through a week—without considering what makes specific actions right and others wrong and debating with ourselves whether that is a difference that must compel the actions we choose. (Okay, it's wrong! I get it! But why should I care?)
>
> <div align="right">REBECCA GOLDSTEIN, <i>Plato at the Googleplex:
Why Philosophy Won't Go Away</i></div>

Though Goldstein's first sentence may require several rereadings, it is one that most of us, with varying degrees of effort, can come to understand: that we all wrestle regularly with the challenging philosophical questions of what the ethics of a given situation are and whether those ethics should alter our behavior. But instead of leaving us entirely on our own to figure out what she is saying, Goldstein helps us out in her closing parenthetical remarks, which translate the abstractions of her first sentence into the kind of concrete everydayspeak that runs through our heads.

Yet another example of self-translation—one that actually uses the word "translation"—can be found on the opening page of a book by scholar Helen Sword:

> There is a massive gap between what most readers consider to be good writing and what academics typically produce and publish. I'm not talking about the kinds of formal strictures necessarily imposed

by journal editors—article length, citation style, and the like—but about a deeper, duller kind of disciplinary monotony, a compulsive proclivity for discursive obscurantism and circumambulatory diction (translation: an addiction to big words and soggy syntax).

HELEN SWORD, *Stylish Academic Writing*

In this passage, Sword gives her own unique twist to the translation technique we've been discussing. After a stream of difficult polysyllabic words—"a compulsive proclivity for discursive obscurantism and circumambulatory diction"—she then concludes by translating these words into everydayspeak: "an addiction to big words and soggy syntax." The effect is to dramatize her larger point: the "massive gap between what most readers consider to be good writing and what academics typically produce and publish."

FAMOUS EXAMPLES

Even notoriously difficult thinkers could be said to use the translation practice we have been advocating in this chapter, as the following famous and widely quoted claims illustrate:

I think, therefore I am.
—RENÉ DESCARTES

The master's tools will never dismantle the master's house.
—AUDRE LORDE

The medium is the message.
—MARSHALL MCLUHAN

Form follows function.
—LOUIS SULLIVAN

These sentences can be read almost as sound bites—short, catchy statements that express a more complex idea. Though the term "sound bite" is usually used to refer to mindless media simplifications, the succinct statements above show what valuable work they can do. These distillations are admittedly reductive in that they do not capture all the nuances of the more complex ideas they represent. But consider their power to stick in the minds of readers. Without these memorable translations, we wonder if these authors' ideas would have achieved such widespread circulation.

Consider Descartes's "I think, therefore I am," for example, which comes embedded in the following passage, in which Descartes is struggling to find a philosophical foundation for absolute truth in the face of skeptical doctrines that doubt that anything can be known for certain. After putting himself in the shoes of a radical skeptic and imagining what it would be like to believe all apparent truths to be false, Descartes "immediately . . . observed," he writes:

> whilst I thus wished to think that all was false, it was absolutely necessary that I, who thus thought, should be somewhat; and as I observed that this truth, I think, therefore I am (*cogito ergo sum*), was so certain and of such evidence that no ground of doubt, however extravagant, could be alleged by the sceptics capable of shaking it, I concluded that I might, without scruple, accept it as the first principle of the philosophy of which I was in search.
>
> RENÉ DESCARTES, "Discourse on the Method, Part IV"

Had Descartes been less probing and scrupulous, we speculate, he would have stopped writing and ended the passage after the statement "it was absolutely necessary that I, who thus thought, should be somewhat." After all, the passage up to this point contains all the basic ingredients that the rest of it goes on to explain, the simpler, more accessible formulation

"I think, therefore I am" being merely a reformulation of this earlier material. But just imagine if Descartes had decided that his job as a writer was finished after his initial claim and had failed to add the more accessible phrase "I think, therefore I am." We suspect this idea of his would not have become one of the most famous touchstones of Western philosophy.

EVERYDAY LANGUAGE AS A THINKING TOOL

As the examples in this chapter suggest, then, translating academic language into everydayspeak can be an indispensable tool for clarifying and underscoring ideas for readers. But at an even more basic level, such translation can be an indispensable means for you as a writer to clarify your ideas to yourself. In other words, translating academicspeak into everydayspeak can function as a thinking tool that enables you to discover what you are trying to say to begin with.

For as writing theorists often note, writing is generally not a process in which we start with a fully formed idea in our heads that we then simply transcribe in an unchanged state onto the page. On the contrary, writing is more often a means of discovery in which we use the writing process to figure out what our idea is. This is why writers are often surprised to find that what they end up with on the page is quite different from what they thought it would be when they started. What we are trying to say here is that everydayspeak is often crucial for this discovery process, that translating your ideas into more common, simpler terms can help you figure out what your ideas really are, as opposed to what you initially imagined they were. Even Descartes, for example, may not have had the formulation "I think, therefore I am" in mind before he wrote the passage above; instead, he may have arrived at it as he worked through the writing process.

We ourselves have been reminded of this point when engaged in our own writing. One major benefit of writing collaboratively, as the two of us do, is that it repeatedly forces us to explain in simpler terms our less-than-clear ideas when one of us doesn't already know what the other means. In the process of writing and revising this book, for instance, we were always turning to each other after reading something the other had written and asking a version of the "Can you explain that more simply?" question that we described asking our students in our office in this chapter's opening anecdote: "What do you mean?" "I don't get it—can you explain?" "Huh!?" Sometimes, when the idea is finally stated in plain, everyday terms, we realize that it doesn't make sense or that it amounts to nothing more than a cliché—or that we have something worth pursuing. It's as if using everyday language to talk through a draft—as any writer can do by asking others to critique a draft—shines a bright light on our writing to expose its strengths and weaknesses.

STILL NOT CONVINCED?

To be sure, not everyone will be as enthusiastic as we are about the benefits of everydayspeak. Many will insist that, while some fields in the humanities may be open to everyday language, colloquial expressions, and slang, most fields in the sciences are not. And some people in both the humanities and the sciences will argue that some ideas simply can't be done justice to in everyday language. "Theory X," they will say, "is just too complex to be explained in simple terms," or "You have to be in the field to understand it." Perhaps so. But at least one distinguished scientist, the celebrated atomic physicist Enrico Fermi, thought otherwise. Fermi, it is said, believed that all faculty in his field should teach basic physics to undergraduates, because having to explain the science in relatively plain English helped clarify their thinking. This last point can be stated as a rule of thumb: if you can't explain it to your aunt Franny or your uncle Frank, chances are you don't understand it yourself.

Furthermore, when writers tell themselves that their ideas are just too complex to be explained to nonspecialists, they risk fooling themselves into thinking that they are making more sense than they actually are. Translating academicspeak into everydayspeak functions as a kind of baloney detector, a way of keeping us honest when we're in danger of getting carried away by our own verbosity.

CODE-MESHING

"But come on," some may say. "Get real! Academic writing must, in many cases, mean setting aside our own voices." Sure, it may be fine to translate challenging academic ideas into plain everyday language, as Goldstein, Sword, and Descartes do above, when it's a language that your audience will understand and find acceptable. But what if your everyday language—the one you use when you're most relaxed, with family and friends— is filled with slang? And what if your everyday language is an ethnic or regional dialect—or a different language altogether? Is there really a place for such language in academic, professional, or public writing?

Yes and no. On the one hand, there are many situations— like when you're applying for a job or submitting a proposal to be read by an official screening body—in which it's probably safest to write in standardized English. On the other hand, the line between language that might confuse audiences and language that engages or challenges them is not always obvious. Nor is the line between foreign words that readers don't already know and those that readers might happily learn. After all, standardized English is more open and inclusive than it may at first appear. And readers often appreciate writers who take risks and mix things up.

Many prominent writers mix standardized English with other dialects or languages, employing a practice that cultural and linguistic theorists Vershawn Ashanti Young and Suresh Canagarajah call "code-meshing." For instance, in the titles of two of her books, *Talkin and Testifyin: The Language of Black America* and *Black Talk: Words and Phrases from the Hood to the Amen Corner*, the language scholar Geneva Smitherman mixes African American vernacular phrases with more scholarly language in order to suggest, as she explicitly argues in these books, that Black vernacular English is as legitimate a variety of language as standardized English. Here are three typical passages:

> In Black America, the oral tradition has served as a fundamental vehicle for gittin ovah. That tradition preserves the Afro-American heritage and reflects the collective spirit of the race.

> Blacks are quick to ridicule "educated fools," people who done gone to school and read all dem books and still don't know nothin!

> It is a socially approved verbal strategy for black rappers to talk about how bad they is.
>
> GENEVA SMITHERMAN, *Talkin and Testifyin:*
> *The Language of Black America*

In these examples, Smitherman blends the types of terms we expect in scholarly writing like "oral tradition" and "fundamental vehicle" with Black vernacular phrases like "gittin ovah." She even blends the standard English spelling of words with African American English variants like "dem" and "ovah" in a way that evokes how some speakers of African American English sound. Some might object to these unconventional practices, but this is precisely Smitherman's point: that our habitual language practices need to be opened up, and that the number of participants in the academic conversation needs to be expanded.

Along similar lines, the writer and activist Gloria Anzaldúa mixes standard English with what she calls Chicano Spanish to make a political point about the suppression of the Spanish language in the United States. In one typical passage, she writes:

> From this racial, ideological, cultural, and biological cross-pollinization, an "alien" consciousness is presently in the making— a new *mestiza* consciousness, *una conciencia de mujer.*
>
> GLORIA ANZALDÚA,
> *Borderlands / La Frontera: The New Mestiza*

Anzaldúa gets her point across not only through *what* she says but also through the *way* she says it, showing that the new hybrid, or "*mestiza* consciousness," that she celebrates is, as she puts it, "presently in the making." Ultimately, such code-meshing suggests that languages, like the people who speak them, are not distinct, separate islands.

Because there are so many options in writing, then, there is no need to ever feel limited in your choice of words. You can always experiment with your language and improve it. Depending on your audience and purpose, and how much risk you're willing to take, you can dress up your language, dress it down, or some combination of both. You could even recast the title of this book, *"They Say / I Say,"* as a teenager might say it: "She Goes / I'm Like."

We hope you agree with us, then, that to succeed as a college writer, you need not always set aside your everyday voice, even when that voice may initially seem unwelcome in the academic world. It is by blending everyday language with standardized English that what counts as "standard" changes and the range of possibilities open to academic writers continues to grow.

Exercises

1. Take a paragraph from this book and dress it down, rewriting it in informal colloquial language. Then rewrite the same paragraph again by dressing it up, making it much more formal. Then rewrite the paragraph in a way that blends the two styles. Share your paragraphs with a classmate and discuss which versions are most effective and why.

2. Find something you've written for a course, and study it to see whether you've used any of your own everyday expressions, any words or structures that are not "academic." If by chance you don't find any, see if there's a place or two where shifting into more casual or unexpected language would help you make a point, get your reader's attention, or just add liveliness to your text. Be sure to keep your audience and purpose in mind, and use language that will be appropriate to both.

3. Below is a short passage from Stephanie Owen and Isabel Sawhill's report, "Should Everyone Go to College?" Use one of the translation templates on page 143 to translate the academic language in the underlined sentence into everyday language. Compare your response with a classmate.

We all know that, on average, college graduates make significantly more money over their lifetimes than those with only a high school education. What gets less attention is the fact that not all college degrees or college graduates are equal. <u>There is enormous variation in the so-called return to education depending on factors such as institution attended, field of study, whether a student graduates, and post-graduation occupation.</u>

4. Find a reading on **theysayiblog.com** that blends academic and everyday styles, such as James Hatch's 2019 essay, "My Semester with the Snowflakes." Identify a sentence or passage where you see the author mixing everyday and academic language. Explain how this blending affects the overall argument. How did you react as a reader?

ELEVEN

"BUT DON'T GET ME WRONG"
The Art of Metacommentary

——◻——

When we tell people that we are writing a chapter on the art of metacommentary, they often give us a puzzled look and tell us that they have no idea what "metacommentary" is. "We know what commentary is," they'll sometimes say, "but what does it mean when it's *meta?*" Our answer is that whether or not they know the term, they practice the art of metacommentary on a daily basis whenever they make a point of explaining something they've said or written: "What I meant to say was _____," "My point was not _____, but _____," or "You're probably not going to like what I'm about to say, but _____." In such cases, they are not offering new points but telling an audience how to interpret what they have already said or are about to say. In short, then, metacommentary is a way of commenting on your claims and telling others how—and how not—to think about them.

It may help to think of metacommentary as being like the chorus in a Greek play that stands to the side of the drama unfolding on the stage and explains its meaning to the audience—or like a voice-over narrator who comments on and explains the action in a television show or movie. Think of metacommentary as a sort of second text that stands alongside your main text and explains what it means. In the main text you say something; in the metatext you guide your readers in interpreting and processing what you've said.

What we are suggesting, then, is that you think of your text as two texts joined at the hip: a main text in which you make your argument and another in which you "work" your ideas, distinguishing your views from others they may be confused with, anticipating and answering objections, connecting one point to another, explaining why your claim might be controversial, and so forth. The figure below demonstrates what we mean.

THE MAIN TEXT SAYS SOMETHING. THE METATEXT TELLS READERS HOW—AND HOW NOT—TO THINK ABOUT IT.

USE METACOMMENTARY TO CLARIFY
AND ELABORATE

But why do you need metacommentary to tell readers what you mean and guide them through your text? Can't you just clearly say what you mean up front? The answer is that no matter how clear and precise your writing is, readers can still fail to understand it in any number of ways. Even the best writers can provoke reactions in readers that they didn't intend, and even good readers can get lost in a complicated argument or fail to see how one point connects with another. Readers may also fail to see what follows from your argument, or they may follow your reasoning and examples yet fail to see the larger conclusion you draw from them. They may fail to see your argument's overall significance or mistake what you are saying for a related argument that they have heard before but that you want to distance yourself from. As a result, no matter how straightforward a writer you are, readers still need you to help them grasp what you really mean. Because the written word is prone to so much mischief and can be interpreted in so many different ways, we need metacommentary to keep misinterpretations and other communication misfires at bay.

Another reason to master the art of metacommentary is that it will help you develop your ideas and generate more text. If you have ever had trouble producing the required number of pages for a writing project, metacommentary can help you add both length and depth to your writing. We've seen many students who try to produce a five-page paper sputter to a halt at two or three pages, complaining they've said everything they can think of about their topic. "I've stated my thesis and presented my reasons and evidence," students have told us. "What else is there to do?" It's almost as if such writers have generated a thesis and don't know what to do with it. When these students learn to use metacommentary, however, they get more out of their ideas and write longer, more substantial texts. In sum, metacommentary can help you extract the full potential from your ideas, drawing out important implications, explaining ideas from different perspectives, and so forth.

So even when you may think you've said everything possible in an argument, try inserting the following types of metacommentary:

▸ In other words, <u>she doesn't realize how right she is</u>.

▸ What _____ really means is _____.

▸ My point is not _____ but _____.

▸ Ultimately, then, my goal is to demonstrate that _____.

Ideally, such metacommentary should help you recognize some implications of your ideas that you didn't initially realize were there.

Let's look at how the cultural critic Neil Postman uses metacommentary in the following passage describing the shift in American culture when it began to move from print and reading to television and movies:

It is my intention in this book to show that a great . . . shift has taken place in America, with the result that the content of much of our public discourse has become dangerous nonsense. *With this in view, my task in the chapters ahead is* straightforward. *I must, first, demonstrate* how, under the governance of the printing

press, discourse in America was different from what it is now—
generally coherent, serious and rational; *and then* how, under the
governance of television, it has become shriveled and absurd.
But to avoid the possibility that my analysis will be interpreted as
standard-brand academic whimpering, a kind of elitist complaint
against "junk" on television, *I must first explain that . . .* I appreciate junk as much as the next fellow, *and I know full well that*
the printing press has generated enough of it to fill the Grand
Canyon to overflowing. Television is not old enough to have
matched printing's output of junk.

NEIL POSTMAN, *Amusing Ourselves to Death:*
Public Discourse in the Age of Show Business

To see what we mean by metacommentary, look at the phrases
above that we have italicized. With these moves, Postman
essentially stands apart from his main ideas to help readers
follow and understand what he is arguing.

> He previews what he will argue: *It is my intention in this book*
> *to show . . .*

> He spells out how he will make his argument: *With this in*
> *view, my task in the chapters ahead is . . . I must, first, dem-*
> *onstrate . . . and then . . .*

> He distinguishes his argument from other arguments it may
> easily be confused with: *But to avoid the possibility that my*
> *analysis will be interpreted as . . . I must first explain that . . .*

TITLES AS METACOMMENTARY

Even the title of Postman's book, *Amusing Ourselves to Death:*
Public Discourse in the Age of Show Business, functions as a form of

metacommentary since, like all titles, it stands apart from the text itself and tells readers the book's main point: that the very pleasure provided by contemporary show business is destructive.

Titles, in fact, are one of the most important forms of metacommentary, functioning rather like carnival barkers telling passersby what they can expect if they go inside. Subtitles, too, function as metacommentary, further explaining or elaborating on the main title. The subtitle of this book, for example, not only explains that it is about "the moves that matter in academic writing" but also indicates that "they say / I say" is one of these moves. Thinking of a title as metacommentary can actually help you develop sharper titles, ones that, like Postman's, give readers a hint of what your argument will be. Contrast such titles with unhelpfully open-ended ones, like "Shakespeare" or "Steroids" or "English Essay" or essays with no titles at all. Essays with vague titles (or no titles) send the message that the writer has simply not bothered to reflect on what is being said and is uninterested in guiding or orienting readers.

USE OTHER MOVES AS METACOMMENTARY

Many of the other moves covered in this book function as metacommentary: entertaining objections, adding transitions, framing quotations, answering "so what?" and "who cares?" When you entertain objections, you stand outside of your text and imagine what a critic might say; when you add transitions, you essentially explain the relationship between various claims. And when you answer the "so what?" and "who cares?" questions, you look beyond your central argument and explain who should be interested in it and why.

TEMPLATES FOR INTRODUCING
METACOMMENTARY

TO WARD OFF POTENTIAL MISUNDERSTANDINGS

The following moves help you differentiate certain views from
ones they might be mistaken for:

▸ Essentially, I am arguing not that <u>we should give up the policy</u>
  but that we should monitor effects far more closely.

▸ This is not to say _____, but rather _____.

▸ X is concerned less with _____ than with _____.

TO ELABORATE ON A PREVIOUS IDEA

The following moves elaborate on a previous point, saying to
readers: "In case you didn't get it the first time, I'll try saying
the same thing in a different way."

▸ In other words, _____.

▸ To put it another way, _____.

▸ What X is saying here is that _____.

TO PROVIDE A ROAD MAP TO YOUR TEXT

This move orients readers, clarifying where you have been and
where you are going—and making it easier for them to process
and follow your text:

▸ Chapter 2 explores _____, while Chapter 3 examines
  _____.

▸ Having just argued that _____, I want now to complicate
  the point by _____.

The Art of Metacommentary

TO MOVE FROM A GENERAL CLAIM TO A SPECIFIC EXAMPLE

These moves help you explain a general point by providing a concrete example that illustrates what you're saying:

▸ For example, _____.

▸ _____, for instance, demonstrates _____.

▸ Consider _____, for example.

▸ To take a case in point, _____.

TO INDICATE THAT A CLAIM IS MORE, LESS, OR EQUALLY IMPORTANT

The following templates help you give relative emphasis to the claim that you are introducing, showing whether that claim is of more or less weight than the previous one or equal to it:

▸ Even more important, _____.

▸ But above all, _____.

▸ Incidentally, we will briefly note, _____.

▸ Just as important, _____.

▸ Equally, _____.

▸ Finally, _____.

TO EXPLAIN A CLAIM WHEN YOU ANTICIPATE OBJECTIONS

Here's a template to help you anticipate and respond to possible objections:

Chapter 6 has more templates for anticipating objections.

▸ Although some readers may object that _____, I would answer that _____.

TO GUIDE READERS TO YOUR MOST GENERAL POINT

These moves show that you are wrapping things up and tying up various subpoints previously made:

▶ In sum, then, _____.

▶ My conclusion, then, is that _____.

▶ In short, _____.

In this chapter we have tried to show that the most persuasive writing often doubles back and comments on its own claims in ways that help readers negotiate and process them. Instead of simply piling claim upon claim, effective writers are constantly "stage-managing" how their claims will be received. It's true, of course, that to be persuasive a text has to have strong claims to argue in the first place. But even the strongest arguments will flounder unless writers use metacommentary to prevent potential misreadings and make their arguments shine.

Exercises

1. Complete each of the following metacommentary templates in any way that makes sense:

   a. In making a case for raising the minimum wage, I am not saying that _____.

   b. But my argument will do more than prove that one particular industrial chemical has certain toxic properties. In this essay, I will also _____.

   c. My point about the national obsession with sports reinforces the belief held by many _____ that _____.

d. I believe, therefore, that the war is completely unjustified. But let me back up and explain how I arrived at this conclusion: _____. In this way, I came to believe that this war is a big mistake.

2. Read the following passage from Pau Gasol's 2018 essay, "An Open Letter about Female Coaches." You can find the link to the full essay on **theysayiblog.com**. Underline where Gasol uses the moves of metacommentary to guide his readers through the main text of his argument. Does the author use any of the chapter's templates (see p. 160)? How do you think the author's use of metacommentary enhances (or harms) his writing?

> The reason I wanted to start by telling you about my parents, is that their story makes me think about today's NBA. Specifically about how, in the 72-year history of the league, there has never been a female head coach. Even more specifically, it makes me think of Becky Hammon: a coach who has been the topic of much conversation lately, and who I've had the opportunity to play for in San Antonio.
>
> But if you think I'm writing this to argue why Becky is qualified to be an NBA head coach . . . well, you're mistaken. That part is obvious: One, she was an accomplished player—with an elite point guard's mind for the game. And two, she has been a successful assistant for arguably the greatest coach in the game. What more do you need? But like I said—I'm not here to make that argument. Arguing on Coach Hammon's behalf would feel patronizing. To me, it would be strange if NBA teams were not interested in her as a head coach.

3. Read over the draft of an essay, and try the following:

   a. Locate a passage that needs more clarification or elaboration. Revise it using the metacommentary templates included in this chapter.

   b. Add in "road map" metacommentary to help your reader follow your text, using the templates on page 160.

   c. Compose a title and subtitle that function as metacommentary on your whole argument.

TWELVE

"WHAT I REALLY WANT TO SAY IS"

Revising Substantially

———◼———

ONE OF THE MOST common frustrations teachers have—we've had it, too—is that students do not revise in any substantial way. As one of our colleagues put it, "I ask my classes to do a substantial revision of an essay they've turned in, emphasis on the word 'substantial,' but invariably little is changed in what I get back. Students hand in the original essay with a word changed here and there, a few spelling errors corrected, and a comma or two added. . . . I feel like all my advice is for nothing." We suspect, however, that in most cases when students do merely superficial revisions, it's not because they are indifferent or lazy, as some teachers may assume, but because they aren't sure what a good revision looks like. Like even many seasoned writers, these students would *like* to revise more thoroughly, but when they reread what they've written, they have trouble seeing where it can be improved—and how. What they lack is not just a reliable picture in their head of what their draft *could* be but also reliable strategies for getting there. In this chapter, we supply ten such revision strategies and a revision checklist (see pp. 180–85) that are designed to work in virtually any academic setting, regardless of assignment, instructor, discipline, or course.

1. THINK GLOBALLY

Perhaps the best strategy for revising your writing in a substantial way is to think globally, as we might put it, about your draft. This involves stepping back from your writing and looking at the big picture, asking yourself what, finally, you are trying to say. You might ask: Do I have a central argument, or do I just ramble and talk *about* my subject? And if I do have a central argument, does that argument make sense? Is it coherent and unified, or do I go off on tangents or even contradict myself? Do I logically link the parts, tying them together with clear connections between them all, developing a continuous line of argument over my essay's entire length? Does my evidence match my central argument and, as we put it in our revision checklist, is it clear what is motivating my argument—why it needs to be made in the first place? That is, do I present my argument as an entry into some larger conversation or debate, as a response to something "they say"? Have I included the strongest possible objections that can be made against my argument or answered any counterarguments in a superficial way? In the end, might any such counterarguments I address be more convincing to readers—or even to me—than my own argument?

It was big questions like these that inspired a student several years ago to radically revise an essay she'd written on the Iraq War, transforming it from a series of disconnected observations about the war into a sharply focused critique of the view that the war promoted democracy. Her first draft had been a mere collection of scattered claims, all presented as if they were of equal importance: Iraq had no weapons of mass destruction. The United States has the strongest military. Saddam Hussein was evil. Many Americans and Iraqis were killed. The war increased terrorism. And so forth. But her final draft nicely subordinated all its points to a larger "they say/I say" thesis: though Saddam Hussein is an evil dictator, it makes no sense to wage war on Iraq's innocent people. The final version was virtually a different essay.

We open with this suggestion to think globally not just because it is perhaps the central way to substantially revise an essay but also because it is so frequently neglected. Because writing is often associated with local, sentence-level mechanics and grammar, some writers picture revision as a small-scale matter of dotting an occasional "i" and crossing an occasional "t." What often gets overlooked, as writing expert Nancy Sommers points out, are "strategies for handling the whole essay," ones that would help writers "reorder lines of reasoning or ask questions about their purposes and readers." It would be as if a jewelry appraiser were to assess a gem only by studying its smallest, microscopic details and never holding it back to form an overall impression.

Revising globally, then, may mean changing the way we think. It asks us to move beyond microlevel edits, beyond merely tweaking or refining an existing argument. At its best, revision is a messy process that often helps us discover what our argument is in the first place. In fact, a good way to test how

substantial your revisions are is to ask how much you learned about your argument through the revision process.

2. BUT STILL SWEAT THE SMALL STUFF

But just because the global level is very important in revising, it doesn't mean that local, surface-level issues—word choice, sentence structure, grammar, style, and so forth—aren't very important too. After all, everything you write is composed of countless small-scale decisions, and if you improve enough of them your next draft has a chance of constituting a significant revision. Also, it is always possible that changing just a single word will help you radically resee your central argument and lead to major, global changes. So while we suggest you think of global revisions as more important than microlevel ones, in practice the two levels are deeply interdependent. Although writers are often told to start out by focusing on their big idea—getting that big idea down on paper and only at a later stage worrying about small-scale mechanics—seasoned writers often move back and forth between the two levels throughout the revision process.

To see how we sweat the small stuff, consider the photo on the facing page of revisions we made on our last paragraph, none of which significantly alter the paragraph's central point. The central point—about the importance of small edits and their connection to big edits—is recognizable from the one draft to the other. And yet we like to think that, taken together, these edits make the passage much more readable. The mere decision alone to move this section up in the chapter and make it the second strategy listed has a big impact. The reader no longer needs to struggle to recall what we'd said several items back about thinking globally. We now have just said it.

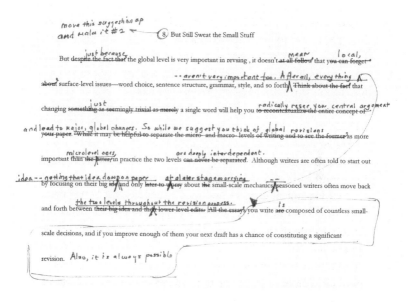

The messiness of the revision process.

3. READ YOUR OWN WRITING

But it is difficult to make any revisions, global or local, unless you do something even more fundamental, which is simply to read what you've written and then ideally reread and reread it again. It is very hard to set the revision process in motion if you don't do at least one initial read-through of your draft, and then do as many additional read-throughs as needed to get a solid grasp of the material with which you're dealing. As Donald Murray explains in *A Writer Teaches Writing*, "The writer reads and rereads and rereads, standing far back and reading quickly from a distance, moving in close and reading slowly line-by-line, reading again and again. . . ."

But why, you might wonder, should you read your own writing? You, after all, are the one who wrote it, so if anyone must know what your text says, shouldn't it be you? The answer is that, precisely because you're the author, you're too close to your text to know what it says. As writers, we tend to be so invested in what we've written that we need to find ways of stepping back from our text to gain some critical distance.

Perhaps the central way of gaining such distance is by reading the draft from an outsider's perspective—as if, instead of being the author, you were some other person who is on the lookout for logical glitches and inconsistencies, for better ways of stating a point, for parts that are hard to follow, for claims and subclaims that need more explanation, or for how your argument might be vulnerable to critique. You might also try reading your text aloud to yourself—or even try using text-to-speech technology on your computer or phone. And it never hurts, if you have time, to set your draft aside for a few days so that when you return to it you can reread it with fresh eyes.

4. AND HAVE OTHERS READ YOUR WRITING, TOO

Of course there are other ways to get critical distance on your work and see it from an outsider's perspective. One of the best ways is to show your work to someone who is willing to read it—a fellow student, family member, friend, or tutor—and ask for feedback. Teachers, in fact, may ask you to pair up with another student to comment on each other's work. It's a great way to get a sense of audience: how your text will be processed and received when it goes out into the world. In seeking out such readers, we often naturally gravitate toward those who share our opinions and predilections. But don't underestimate the value of readers who may know little about your subject or disagree with your position. Often, the more readers differ from you, the more likely they will be able to see things that you yourself could not have thought of.

5. GO BACK TO THE TEXT

While developing a deep familiarity with your own writing is essential in any revision process, developing a deep familiarity with your sources is also very important. It's surprising how often errors are introduced when we haven't read the text we're responding to carefully enough and start writing about it before we really understand it. It's also surprising how often errors are introduced when we fail to check and double-check our quotations against the originals and thus mistranscribe them in our texts. If we are right that the most persuasive writing responds to something that others have said, then writing that misquotes or misrepresents what those others say, as we suggested in Chapter 2 (see particularly our comments on the "closest cliché syndrome"), will be built on a false foundation.

If you're anything like us, however, you might not like going back to your source. At times we don't want to go back to a source because we don't want to take the time to unpack its difficult, challenging language. At other times, we don't want to return to a source because we fear, deep down, that it doesn't quite say what we want it to say. When this happens, there is always a danger of creating a straw man: distorting what an author says in order to pursue our own agenda, transforming the author into a mere projection of ourselves. In this respect, accurately representing what "they say" is not just an intellectual obligation but a moral one as well.

As an example, let's turn to Rosa, a student who wanted to write an essay defending the practice of meditation. In her first draft, Rosa made a strong case that meditation promotes democratic politics, but she misconstrued her essay's central source, a scholarly article by Dean Mathiowetz that reads:

Meditation Is Good for Nothing

Does meditation bring political benefits in the sense of strengthening citizenship or democracy? Taking the Zen phrase "meditation doesn't work—it's good for nothing" as my point of departure . . . I argue that meditation can foster significant dimensions of democratic citizenship. . . .

Mathiowetz's argument here is that meditation can in fact "foster significant dimensions of democratic citizenship"—or, as he goes on to claim, that, paradoxically, because "meditation . . . is good for nothing," it can help citizens and politicians detach from their self-interested passions and biases and find common ground. Yet Rosa presented Mathiowetz as saying that meditation is literally "good for nothing" and has no political or civic benefits.

When Rosa realized her mistake, she was inspired to do a revision. And the following week, she produced a much improved draft that opens as follows:

Many people think that meditation is a waste of time. According to these skeptics, meditation is a useless activity that is only for self-absorbed flakes who have no concern for the give-and-take of politics. But I disagree. As Dean Mathiowetz argues, the very uselessness of meditation makes it a valuable political tool. It can make us less polarized—better able to listen to one another and move beyond our rigid political views, and more committed to the common good.

In this way, Rosa was able to continue using Mathiowetz as a central source in her essay but without distorting his position. Instead of casting him as a naysayer in her essay who opposes meditation, she now presents Mathiowetz as the pro-meditation ally he really is.

6. DOES YOUR EXAMPLE SAY WHAT YOU SAY IT SAYS?

Offering an example to support your argument is such a natural, familiar part of writing that it may seem easy. And yet providing examples is often a challenge, largely because of the kind of disconnection issues we discussed in Chapter 9. When giving an example—which might take the form of a statistic, a quotation, evidence, or a story or anecdote—writers often discover that the example gets away from them. That is, the example they provide turns out not to support the point they want it to support and may even contradict it. So in revising your drafts, pay special attention to whether your example actually supports your argument, whether your example and what it is supposed to exemplify are united.

A student named Jacob needed help with this issue in an essay he'd written about how, as his title put it, "We All Need to Become More Green." In an attempt to provide a model example of someone who, in Jacob's words, has admirably "stopped using toxic, traditional household cleaners" that harm the environment, Jacob cites the case of his mother:

> My mother is a perfect example. She cares a lot about the environment and has always opposed chemicals. She frequently uses cleaning products in our house that are environmentally friendly but claims they never work. She once spent almost a hundred dollars on eco-friendly cleaners for our house but ended up throwing most of them out and returning to the toxic products she's always used. Nothing ever changes. She keeps using the old-fashioned cleaners but complaining about them.

Although each sentence here is admirably clear, Jacob ran into the classic problem of his thesis being out of sync with his example. Instead of showing that we should all stop using toxic cleaners, the story of his mother actually shows just how hard giving up such cleaners can be.

With Jacob's permission, his instructor circulated his essay to his class and asked how it might be revised. One student proposed that Jacob modify his thesis so that it asserts not just that we should all be more green, but that, to echo Kermit the Frog, "it's not easy being green," which, the student added, might be a fun new title for Jacob's essay. In his next draft, however, Jacob did decide to modify his argument, but in a different way by claiming that nobody, not even his deeply committed mother, will ever be able to become fully green if they don't lower their expectations about cleanliness.

7. KEEP ASKING "AS OPPOSED TO WHAT?"

Throughout this book we suggest that writers start "with what others are saying," as the subtitle of Chapter 1 puts it, and that they use this "they say" to motivate their "I say." But writers often neglect this important rhetorical move. They get so caught up in making their claims that they forget even the truest, most accurate, and well-supported claim will seem pointless if they fail to answer the all-important "as opposed to what?" or "who says otherwise?" question.

We sometimes forget to ask these questions ourselves. For example, it was only after years of writing and rewriting this very book that we realized there was an important "they say" or "as opposed to what?" contrast buried in our manuscript that we needed to draw out. At the end of a passage describing our templates as "one of the novel features of this book," we'd written:

> This book offers model templates to help you put key principles of writing directly into practice.

When we reread this sentence, we felt that it was missing something, that it sounded flat and uninspired. But why? After experimenting with different versions of the sentence, none of which seemed to help, we realized we weren't following our own advice. "There's no 'they say' here," Cathy announced. "Nothing we push off against, no 'as opposed to what.'" With this in mind, we embarked on another round of revisions and eventually came up with the following contrast, which now appears on page 2 of this edition:

> <u>Instead of focusing solely on abstract principles of writing, then,</u> this book offers model templates to help you put those principles directly into practice.

Why did we prefer this version? Because its new material, which we've underlined, not only establishes that we offer templates but also indicates why: to depart from and, we hope, improve upon writing instruction that focuses only on "abstract principles."

Had this sentence been all we changed, however, it would not have amounted to the type of "substantial" revision we've been saying is so important. But as often happens in the revision process, this one revision led to several others, setting in motion a series of revisions that significantly transformed our core argument. As we went back and reread the parts of the book we'd already written, we found several ways to extend the contrast we draw above between our templates and more abstract approaches. In the preface and introduction, we added two sections—"OK—but Templates?," and "What This Book Doesn't Do"—which help us further explain our template-based approach by contrasting it with what it isn't.

8. MOVE IT UP!

In her memoir *The Vanity Fair Diaries*, the magazine's former editor, Tina Brown, describes "the rewarding moment" in editing a manuscript:

> when you see that the whole thing should start on page nine and flip the penultimate paragraph to the top of the piece, and all you want to do is call the writer immediately and tell him or her why.

Brown's premise here is simple: *where* you say something matters, and the more important the point, the more it needs to be moved to "the top of the piece," where it will better get your reader's attention and infuse all you say that follows.

Imagine, after all, how frustrating it is for readers to have to slog through a lengthy text that doesn't state what its big point is until the very end, which is precisely what happens in Charles R. Morris's 333-page book, *A Rabble of Dead Money: The Great Crash and the Global Depression: 1929–1939*. Although Morris demonstrates impressive knowledge of the Great Depression and its historical era, he doesn't declare his central argument—that, contrary to what most people assume, "the 1929 stock market crash . . . did not cause the Depression"—until page 313. Had Morris foregrounded this point early in the book and used it to structure all that followed, readers wouldn't have been left wondering where he was going for the first three hundred pages: "Why is Morris telling us this?" "What's his big point?" "And this matters because . . . ?"

Delays of this kind are so common among writers that journalists long ago coined a term for it: "burying the lead" (or "lede," as it is sometimes spelled). Because writing is not a smoothly linear process of adding one perfectly polished paragraph on top of another until the last word is written, writers often don't know what their most important, or "lead," point will be until late in the writing process. As our cartoon on page 167 suggests, it is common for writers to start out thinking that their big idea will be one thing, only to realize later, just as they think their work is finished, that a different point needs to take center stage. When this happens, the best remedy, as Brown suggests, is to "flip" that point up "to the top of the piece," near the opening, and edit the rest so that your belatedly discovered argument informs your entire text from start to finish.

9. TAKE YOUR "UH-OH" MOMENTS SERIOUSLY

In our view, the best writers are always on the lookout for places in their writing that take their argument in the wrong direction. Especially when reading their work with a skeptical eye, as we suggested earlier, these self-critical writers keep looking for unanticipated implications in their writing that, for one reason or another, they are not comfortable with. As you reread your drafts, then, we suggest that you listen for any little voices in your head that say, "Uh-oh, what have I done? As I was arguing _____, I accidentally suggested _____." "Uh-oh" moments, as they might be called, can often be upsetting. But if you're willing to put in the time and to experiment with different solutions, you can head off such problems in your draft and possibly even turn them to your advantage.

Gerald had several such "uh-oh" moments as he was writing "Hidden Intellectualism" (see p. 309), in which he makes the counterintuitive claim that schools should be organized like sports. One, for instance, came when he was arguing that the worlds of academic intellectual culture and of popular sports are more similar than one might assume. He had written:

> [T]he real intellectual world, the one that existed in the big world beyond school, is organized very much like the world of team sports, with rival texts, rival interpretations and evaluations of texts, . . . and elaborate team competitions in which "fans" of writers, intellectual systems, methodologies, and -isms contend against one another.

"Oh, no," Gerald thought to himself as he reread this passage. "Couldn't someone misunderstand me? Couldn't someone think that in saying schools should be organized like sports, I'm promoting the ugly side of sports, the side that's filled with petty one-upmanship and, at times, even violence? How can I argue that schools should imitate the contentious domain of sports when schools already have too much small-minded and destructive competition?"

For a while, Gerald was disturbed enough by thoughts like these that he was tempted to simply eliminate the comparison he makes between sports and school. But after wrestling with the problem, he realized that he was defending sports not at their worst but at their best. As a result, the next chance he got, Gerald sat down with his manuscript and added the following new material, which explains that sports not only promote rivalry but

> also satisfy the thirst for community. When you entered sports debates, you became part of a community that was not limited to your family and friends, but was national and public.

In this way, Gerald was able to use his "uh-oh" moment to enhance his argument. What began as a serious problem ended up helping him discover an aspect of his own argument that he hadn't seen before: that schooling should emulate not the uglier side of sports but the side that encourages camaraderie and broad, public excitement.

10. DON'T LET THE MESS SHOW

At several points in this chapter we have suggested that revising your writing in a global, substantial way is often a messy undertaking. In this final section, however, we want to suggest that to create a coherent, unified, and reader-friendly text, you need to *hide* this very mess. In other words, when you find any problems in your text, you need to do what is often a lot of hard work to correct them and make it look as if they never existed. If, for instance, you find a problem with your thesis, you need to not only reframe your thesis but also make sure that all your supporting claims, evidence, and examples, as we suggested above, match that thesis, erasing any confusing disconnects between your thesis and the rest of your text. Along similar lines, if you find that a section of your text doesn't make sense, you need to revise it until it does or eliminate that section altogether, making sure that the material that had preceded and followed the deleted material is well stitched together. And for a final example, if you realize that your best argument is buried too far back in your essay, you need not only to "move it up," as we suggested above, but also revise your entire draft so that it looks as if that best argument is what you had originally planned to say.

Joseph M. Williams and Lawrence McEnerney, writing experts, make a version of this point:

> If you find that the sentence from your conclusion is more insightful than the one from your introduction, then you have to revise your introduction to make it seem that you had this sentence in mind all along (even though when you started drafting the paper you may have had no idea how you were going to end it).

This advice holds true, we think, not just for introductions and conclusions but for virtually every part of a text. Even if you discover that your best claim appears mid-essay, you need to engage in a little smoke and mirrors, revising in a way that makes "it seem that you had" this claim in mind from the very outset, even though you hadn't.

A REVISION CHECKLIST

The checklist that follows is keyed both to this chapter on revision and to the writing advice throughout this book. It is composed of a series of questions designed to help you when rereading and revising your drafts.

Is Your Revision Really Substantial?

Look over the revisions you've made to your draft before turning it in and ask yourself if you have made enough changes to seriously improve it. If you've merely changed a few words or phrases, then you probably haven't addressed these larger issues: How coherent is your argument? Does your argument enter in dialogue with a motivating "they say"? Does your argument address a naysayer's counterargument? Is your argument consistent or contradictory?

Did you reread your draft several times and perhaps show it to other readers for feedback? If so, do you adequately respond to any concerns these readers raised, including ones possibly expressed to you by your instructor or a classmate?

Are the parts of your composition in the most effective order, or do some need to be moved? If you rearranged any of your text, have you revised the remaining material to avoid letting the "mess" show? (See pp. 179–80.)

How Well Do You Represent What Others Say?

Do you start with what "they say"? If not, try revising to do so. See pages 23–28 for templates that can help.

Is it clear what is motivating your argument—why it needs to be made in the first place? If not, see pages 23–27 for templates that can help.

Do you summarize what others have said? If so, have you represented their views accurately—and adequately? Can you improve your summaries, perhaps by going back to the text and rereading the source you're summarizing?

Do you quote others? Have you carefully checked your quotations against the original sources? Do you frame each quotation in a way that integrates it into your text, explaining the quotation in your own words, and have you carefully considered whether the quotation actually supports your argument? (See pp. 49–51 for tips on creating a "quotation sandwich.")

Look at the verbs you use to introduce summaries and quotations, and consider how well they fit the action you're describing. If you've used all-purpose signal verbs such as X "said" or "believes," are there other such phrases that might be more precise, such as X "complains" or "predicts"? (See pp. 43–44 for a list of such signal verbs.)

Have you documented all of the sources you mention, both in parenthetical notations in the body of your text and at the end in a works-cited or references list?

Do you remind readers of the "they say" you're responding to throughout your text, or do you get off track and inadvertently start responding to a different "they say"? Can you revise so as to respond more continuously throughout the entire length of your text? (See pp. 27–28 for advice on using return sentences to keep your argument focused.)

How Effective Is What *You* Say?

Is it clear how you are responding to your "they say"? Is it clear what your position is—*agree, disagree, or a combination of both—or* might readers be unsure and need clarification? Do you use signal verbs that fit your position and clear language ("I question whether . . ." or "I'm of two minds about . . .")? (See Chapter 4 for three ways to respond and Chapter 5 for help in distinguishing the "I say" from "they say.")

If you disagree with the "they say" you're responding to, do you give reasons why in a way that moves the conversation forward, or do you merely contradict the "they say"? If you agree with the "they say," do you "agree with a difference," adding something of your own to the conversation? (For help with this move, see p. 66.) And finally, if you both agree and disagree with your "they say," do you do so without contradicting yourself or seeming evasive? (See Chapter 4 for help in responding in these three different ways.)

Are your "I say" and "they say" clearly connected? Do your argument and the argument you are responding to address the same issue, or does a switch occur that takes you on a tangent? Do you use the same key terms for explaining both? (See p. 132 for our discussion of key terms.)

What reasons—evidence, data, or examples—do you offer to support your "I say"? Do your reasons actually support your position, or is there a mismatch between them? Could a naysayer use your reasons against you to support a contrary position, and if so, could you defend your reasoning by summarizing and answering this objection? (See Chapter 6 for tips on doing so.)

Will readers be able to distinguish what you say from what others say? Do you use voice markers ("My own view, however, is . . ." or "Skeptics, however, would disagree . . .") to mark the shift from the views of others to your own view and back? (See Chapter 5 for advice about using voice markers to make that distinction clear.)

Have You Introduced Any Naysayers?

Have you acknowledged likely objections to your argument? If so, have you represented these objections fairly—and responded to them persuasively? *If not,* think about what other perspectives exist on your topic, and incorporate them into your draft. (See Chapter 6 for tips on planting and responding to naysayers in your text.)

Have You Used Metacommentary?

How well, if at all, do you stand back from your writing and clarify what you do and don't mean? Might your argument be improved if you did a better job of explaining what you mean—or *don't* mean— with phrases like "in other words," "don't get me wrong," or "what I'm really trying to say here is . . ." (See Chapter 11 for examples of how to reinforce your argument with metacommentary.)

Do you have a helpful title? Does your title merely identify your topic, or does it successfully point to the position you take on that topic? Is your title lively and engaging, and might a subtitle help indicate your position?

Have You Tied It All Together?

Can readers follow your argument from one sentence, paragraph, and section to the next? Can readers see how each successive point is joined together in service of your overall argument? Are there any tangents that need to be brought in line with your larger train of thought or perhaps eliminated altogether?

Do you use transition phrases like "however," "in addition," and "in other words," which clarify how your ideas relate to one another? Are these phrases the right ones for your purposes—or do you use "however," say, when you really mean "also" or "in addition"? (See pp. 127–28 for a list of transitions.)

Do you use pointing words like "this" and "that," which help you gesture backward in your text and lead readers from one point to the next? If so, is it always clear what "this" and "that" refer to, or do you need to add nouns (e.g., "this book" or "this tendency to exaggerate") to avoid ambiguity? (See pp. 130–32 for tips on using pointing words to connect parts of your argument.)

Have you used what we call "repetition with a difference" to help connect parts of your argument? That is, do you succeed in *saying the same thing but in a slightly different way each time, which helps you move your argument forward and avoid being monotonous?* (See pp. 134–36 for help with this move.)

Have You Shown Why Your Argument Matters?

Do you make clear why your argument is important—and why your readers should care? Might your draft be improved by using templates like "My critique here is important because _____" or "The stakes in how we answer this question are high, given that _____"? (See Chapter 8 for advice on addressing the "so what?" and "who cares?" questions.)

Exercises

1. Read over a draft of your writing, and think about it globally. Explain to yourself the "big picture" of your argument using the following template: "Aha! Now I see! What I'm really trying to say is not, as I initially thought, _____ but _____." Use your response to write yourself a revision plan. Name two important things you need to do so that your argument matches what you're "really trying to say."

2. Read over a draft of your writing, paying particular attention to how you use sources.

   a. Go back to your sources to check how accurately you are using them. Confirm that your summaries and paraphrases are fair representations of the sources' arguments. Have you transcribed your quotations correctly? Have you properly cited all your sources?

   b. Look critically at the examples—quotations, evidence, anecdotes, and so forth—that you use to support your claims. Ask yourself, "Does this example support my argument?" Revise your writing to unify your argument and examples.

3. Read a draft of your writing out loud or listen to it using text-to-speech technology.

   a. As you read or listen, mark the places in the text that are hard to follow. Then go back to these places and revise them. Could you use better transitions? Might metacommentary help? Could you use more voice markers, such as "In Smith's opinion . . ." or "She argues . . ."?

b. As you read or listen, also mark the places in the text where you find yourself saying "uh-oh" because your words or their implications don't reflect your underlying intentions. Then go back to these "uh-oh" moments to clarify your intentions. Consider using a template like "This is not to suggest . . . It is, however, to suggest . . ."

THIRTEEN

"I TAKE YOUR POINT"

Entering Class Discussions

———※———

HAVE YOU EVER been in a class discussion that feels less like a genuine meeting of the minds than like a series of discrete, disconnected monologues? You make a comment, say, that seems provocative to you, but the classmate who speaks after you makes no reference to what you said, instead going off in an entirely different direction. Then the classmate who speaks next makes no reference either to you or to anyone else, making it seem as if everyone in the conversation is more interested in their own ideas than in actually conversing with anyone else.

We like to think that the principles this book advances can help improve class discussions, which increasingly include various forms of online communication. Particularly important for class discussion is the point that our own ideas become more cogent and powerful the more responsive we are to others and the more we frame our claims not in isolation but as responses to what others before us have said. Ultimately, then, a good face-to-face classroom discussion (or online communication) doesn't just happen spontaneously. It requires the same sorts of disciplined moves and practices used in many writing situations, particularly that of identifying to what and to whom you are responding.

FRAME YOUR COMMENTS AS A RESPONSE TO SOMETHING THAT HAS ALREADY BEEN SAID

The single most important thing you need to do when joining a class discussion is to link what you are about to say to something that has already been said.

▸ I really liked Aaron's point about <u>the two sides being closer than they seem</u>. I'd add that <u>both seem rather moderate</u>.

▸ I take your point, Nadia, that _____. Still . . .

▸ Though Kayla and Ryan seem to be at odds about _____, they may actually not be all that far apart.

In framing your comments this way, it is usually best to name both the person and the idea you're responding to. If you name the person alone ("I agree with Aaron because _____"), it may not be clear to listeners what part of what Aaron said you are referring to. Conversely, if you only summarize what Aaron said without naming him, you'll probably leave your classmates wondering whose comments you're referring to.

But won't you sound stilted and deeply redundant in class if you try to restate the point your classmate just made? After all, in the case of the first template above, the entire class will have just heard Aaron's point about the two sides being closer than they seem. Why, then, would you need to restate it?

We agree that in oral situations it does often sound artificial to restate what others just said precisely because they just said it. It would be awkward if on being asked to pass the salt at lunch, one were to reply: "If I understand you correctly, you have asked me to pass the salt. Yes, I can, and here it is." But in oral discussions about complicated issues that are open to multiple interpretations, we usually do need to resummarize what others have said to make sure that everyone is on the same page. Since Aaron may have made several points when he spoke and may have been followed by other commentators, the class will probably need you to summarize which point of his you are referring to. And even if Aaron made only one point, restating that point is helpful not only to remind the group what his point was (since some may have missed or forgotten it) but also to make sure that he, you, and others have interpreted his point in the same way.

TO CHANGE THE SUBJECT, INDICATE EXPLICITLY THAT YOU ARE DOING SO

It is fine to try to change the conversation's direction. There's just one catch: you need to make clear to listeners that this is what you are doing. For example:

▶ So far we have been talking about <u>the characters in the film</u>. But isn't the real issue here <u>the cinematography</u>?

▶ I'd like to change the subject to one that hasn't yet been addressed.

You can try to change the subject without indicating that you are doing so. But you risk that your comment will come across as irrelevant rather than as a thoughtful contribution that moves the conversation forward.

BE EVEN MORE EXPLICIT
THAN YOU WOULD BE IN WRITING

Because listeners in an oral discussion can't go back and reread what you just said, they are more easily overloaded than are readers of a print text. For this reason, in a class discussion you will do well to take some extra steps to help listeners follow your train of thought. (1) When you make a comment, limit yourself to one point only, though you can elaborate on this point, fleshing it out with examples and evidence. If you feel you must make two points, either unite them under one larger umbrella point, or make one point first and save the other for later. Trying to bundle two or more claims into one comment can result in neither getting the attention it deserves. (2) Use metacommentary to highlight your key point so that listeners can readily grasp it.

▸ **In other words, what I'm trying to get at here is _____ .**

▸ **My point is this: _____ .**

▸ **My point, though, is not _____ but _____ .**

▸ **This distinction is important because _____ .**

Exercises

1. Choose a text you've read in class, and discuss the text's argument in a small group. Use these questions to start your conversation:

   a. Whom (or what) is the writer responding to?

    b. What perspectives does the writer include, and what perspectives are missing?

    c. Why does this argument matter?

2. Listen carefully to a class discussion, either in this class or another one of your courses. Notice what moves from this chapter your classmates and your instructor make:

    a. How do they frame their comments to link their ideas to something that has already been said?

    b. How do they change the direction of the conversation?

    c. How do they use metacommentary to clarify their points?

Reflect on the conversation as a whole. Were the people in the conversation responsive to one another's ideas, or did the conversation feel more like a series of unconnected points? Explain one strategy from this chapter that would improve class discussions.

3. In your next class discussion, try using use these strategies to help your classmates follow your ideas:

    a. Write down your thoughts before you say them.

    b. Limit yourself to just one point per comment.

    c. Use metacommentary to highlight your key idea.

How did these strategies help clarify your ideas? How did they help you listen more attentively to others? How did they invite others to respond? What was challenging about this exercise?

FOURTEEN

"WHAT'S MOTIVATING THIS WRITER?"

Reading for the Conversation

"WHAT IS THE AUTHOR'S ARGUMENT? What is the author trying to say?" For many years, these were the first questions we would ask our classes in a discussion of an assigned reading. The discussion that resulted was often halting, as our students struggled to get a handle on the argument, but eventually, after some awkward silences, the class would come up with something we could all agree was an accurate summary of the author's main thesis. Even after we'd gotten over that hurdle, however, the discussion would often still seem forced and would limp along as we all struggled with the question that naturally arose next: now that we had determined what the author was saying, what did we ourselves have to say?

For a long time we didn't worry much about these halting discussions, justifying them to ourselves as the predictable result of assigning difficult, challenging readings. Several years ago, however, as we started writing this book and began thinking about writing as the art of entering conversations, we latched on to the idea of leading with some different questions: "What other argument(s) is the writer responding to?" "Is the writer disagreeing or agreeing with something, and if so, what?" "What is motivating the writer's argument?" "Are there other ideas that you have encountered in this class or elsewhere that might be pertinent?" The results were often striking. The discussions that followed tended to be far livelier and to draw in a greater number of students. We were still asking students to look for the main argument, but we were now asking them to see that argument as a response to some other argument that provoked it, gave it a reason for being, and helped all of us see why we should care about it.

What had happened, we realized, was that by changing the opening question, we changed the way our students approached reading and perhaps the way they thought about academic work in general. Instead of thinking of the argument of a text as an isolated entity, they now thought of that argument as one that responded to and provoked other arguments. Since they were now dealing not with *one* argument but at least *two* (the author's argument and the one[s] being responded to), they now had alternative ways of seeing the topic at hand. This meant that instead of just trying to understand the view presented by the author, they were more able to question that view intelligently and engage in the type of discussion and debate that is the hallmark of a college education. In our discussions, animated debates often arose between students who found the author's argument convincing and others who were more convinced by the view it was challenging. In the best of these debates, the binary positions would be questioned by other students, who suggested each was too simple, that both might be right or that a third alternative was possible. Still other students might object that the discussion thus far had missed the author's real point and suggest that we all go back to the text and pay closer attention to what it actually said.

We eventually realized that the move from reading for the author's argument in isolation to reading for how the author's argument is in conversation with the arguments of others helps readers become active, critical readers rather than passive recipients of knowledge. On some level, reading for the conversation is more rigorous and demanding than reading for what one author says. It asks that you determine not only what the author thinks but also how what the author thinks fits with what others think and ultimately with what you yourself think. Yet on another level, reading this way is a lot simpler and more familiar than reading for the thesis alone, since it returns writing to the familiar, everyday act of communicating with other people about real issues.

DECIPHERING THE CONVERSATION

We suggest, then, that when assigned a reading, you imagine the author not as sitting alone in an empty room hunched over a desk or staring at a screen but as sitting in a crowded coffee shop talking to and engaging with others who are making claims. In other words, imagine an ongoing, multisided conversation in which all participants (including the author) are trying to persuade others to agree or at least to take their positions seriously.

The trick in reading for the conversation is to figure out *what views the author is responding to* and *what the author's own argument is*—or, to put it in the terms used in this book, to determine the "they say" and how the author responds to it. One of the challenges in reading for the "they say" and "I say" can be figuring out which is which, since it may not be obvious when writers are summarizing others and when they are speaking for themselves. Readers need to be alert for any changes in voice that a writer might make, since instead of using explicit road-mapping phrases like "although many believe," authors may simply summarize the view that they want to engage with and indicate only subtly that it is not their own.

Consider the opening to an article by David Zinczenko:

> If ever there were a newspaper headline custom-made for Jay Leno's* monologue, this was it. Kids taking on McDonald's this week, suing the company for making them fat. Isn't that like middle-aged men suing Porsche for making them get speeding tickets? Whatever happened to personal responsibility?
>
> I tend to sympathize with these portly fast-food patrons, though. Maybe that's because I used to be one of them.
>
> DAVID ZINCZENKO, "Don't Blame the Eater"

Whenever we teach this passage, some students inevitably assume that Zinczenko must be espousing the view expressed in his first paragraph: that suing McDonald's is ridiculous. When their reading is challenged by their classmates, these students point to the page and reply, "Look. It's right here on the page. This is what Zinczenko wrote. These are his exact words." The assumption these students are making is that if something appears on the page, the author must endorse it. In fact, however, we ventriloquize views that we don't believe in, and may in fact passionately disagree with, all the time. The central clues that Zinczenko disagrees with the view expressed in his opening paragraph come in the second paragraph, when he finally offers a first-person

See Chapter 6 for more discussion of naysayers.

*Jay Leno Comedian and former host of NBC's *The Tonight Show.*

declaration and uses a contrastive transition, "though," thereby resolving any questions about where he stands.

WHEN THE "THEY SAY" IS UNSTATED

Another challenge can be identifying the "they say" when it is not explicitly identified. Whereas Zinczenko offers an up-front summary of the view he is responding to, other writers assume that their readers are so familiar with these views that they need not name or summarize them. In such cases, you the reader have to reconstruct the unstated "they say" that is motivating the text through a process of inference.

See, for instance, if you can reconstruct the position that Tamara Draut is challenging in the opening paragraph of her essay "The Growing College Gap":

> "The first in her family to graduate from college." How many times have we heard that phrase, or one like it, used to describe a successful American with a modest background? In today's United States, a four-year degree has become the all-but-official ticket to middle-class security. But if your parents don't have much money or higher education in their own right, the road to college—and beyond—looks increasingly treacherous. Despite a sharp increase in the proportion of high school graduates going on to some form of postsecondary education, socio-economic status continues to exert a powerful influence on college admission and completion; in fact, gaps in enrollment by class and race, after declining in the 1960s and 1970s, are once again as wide as they were thirty years ago, and getting wider, even as college has become far more crucial to lifetime fortunes.
>
> TAMARA DRAUT, "The Growing College Gap"

You might think that the "they say" here is embedded in the third sentence: they say (or we all think) that a four-year degree is "the all-but-official ticket to middle-class security," and you might assume that Draut will go on to disagree.

If you read the passage this way, however, you would be mistaken. Draut is not questioning whether a college degree has become the "ticket to middle-class security" but whether most Americans can obtain that ticket, whether college is within the financial reach of most American families. You may have been thrown off by the "but" following the statement that college has become a prerequisite for middle-class security. However, unlike the "though" in Zinczenko's opening, this "but" does not signal that Draut will be disagreeing with the view she has just summarized, a view that in fact she takes as a given. What Draut disagrees with is that this ticket to middle-class security is still readily available to the middle and working classes.

Were one to imagine Draut in a room talking with others with strong views on this topic, one would need to picture her challenging not those who think college is a ticket to financial security (something she agrees with and takes for granted) but those who think the doors of college are open to anyone willing to put forth the effort to walk through them. The view that Draut is challenging, then, is not summarized in her opening. Instead, she assumes that readers are already so familiar with this view that it need not be stated.

Draut's example suggests that in texts where the central "they say" is not immediately identified, you have to construct it yourself based on the clues the text provides. You have to start by locating the writer's thesis and then imagine some of the arguments that might be made against it. What would it look like to disagree with this view? In Draut's case, it is relatively easy to construct a counterargument: it is the familiar faith in the

American Dream of equal opportunity when it comes to access to college. Figuring out the counterargument not only reveals what motivated Draut as a writer but also helps you respond to her essay as an active, critical reader. Constructing this counterargument can also help you recognize how Draut challenges your own views, questioning opinions that you previously took for granted.

WHEN THE "THEY SAY" IS ABOUT SOMETHING "NOBODY HAS TALKED ABOUT"

Another challenge in reading for the conversation is that writers sometimes build their arguments by responding to a *lack* of discussion. These writers build their case not by playing off views that can be identified (like faith in the American Dream or the idea that we are responsible for our body weight) but by pointing to something others have overlooked. As the writing theorists John M. Swales and Christine B. Feak point out, one effective way to "create a research space" and "establish a niche" in the academic world is "by indicating a gap in . . . previous research." Much research in the sciences and humanities takes this "Nobody has noticed X" form.

In such cases, the writer may be responding to scientists, for example, who have overlooked an obscure plant that offers insights into global warming or to literary critics who have been so busy focusing on the lead character in a play that they have overlooked something important about the minor characters.

READING PARTICULARLY CHALLENGING TEXTS

Sometimes it is difficult to figure out the views that writers are responding to, not because these writers do not identify those views but because their language and the concepts they are dealing with are particularly challenging. Consider, for instance, the first two sentences of *Gender Trouble: Feminism and the Subversion of Identity*, a book by the feminist philosopher and literary theorist Judith Butler, thought by many to be a particularly difficult academic writer:

> Contemporary feminist debates over the meaning of gender lead time and again to a certain sense of trouble, as if the indeterminacy of gender might eventually culminate in the failure of feminism. Perhaps trouble need not carry such a negative valence.
>
> JUDITH BUTLER, *Gender Trouble:*
> *Feminism and the Subversion of Identity*

There are many reasons readers may stumble over this relatively short passage, not the least of which is that Butler does not explicitly indicate where her own view begins and the view she is responding to ends. Unlike Zinczenko, Butler does not use the first-person "I" or a phrase such as "in my own view" to show that the position in the second sentence is her own. Nor does Butler offer a clear transition such as "but" or "however" at the start of the second sentence to indicate, as Zinczenko does with "though," that in the second sentence she is questioning the argument she has summarized in the first. And finally, like many academic writers, Butler uses abstract, challenging words that many readers may need to look up, like "indeterminacy" (the quality of being impossible to define or pin down), "culminate" (finally result in), and "negative valence" (a term borrowed from chemistry, roughly denoting "negative significance" or "meaning"). For all these reasons, we can imagine many readers feeling intimidated before they reach the third sentence of Butler's book.

But readers who break down this passage into its essential parts will find that it is actually a lucid piece of writing that conforms to the classic "they say / I say" pattern. Though it can be difficult to spot the clashing arguments in the two sentences, close analysis reveals that the first sentence offers a way of looking at a certain type of "trouble" in the realm of feminist politics that is being challenged in the second.

To understand difficult passages of this kind, you need to translate them into your own words—to build a bridge, in effect, between the passage's unfamiliar terms and ones more familiar to you. Building such a bridge should help you connect what you already know to what the author is saying—and will then help you move from reading to writing, providing you with some of the language you will need to summarize the text. One major challenge in translating the author's words into your own, however, is to stay true to what the author is actually saying, avoiding what we call "the closest cliché syndrome," in which one mistakes a commonplace idea for an author's more complex one (mistaking Butler's critique of the concept of "woman," for instance, for the common idea that women must have equal rights). The work of complex writers like Butler, who frequently challenge conventional thinking, cannot always be collapsed into the types of ideas most of us are already familiar with. Therefore, when you translate, do not try to fit the ideas of such writers into your preexisting beliefs, but instead allow your own views to be challenged. In building a bridge to the writers you read, it is often necessary to meet those writers more than halfway.

For more on translating, see Chapter 10.

For more on the closest cliché syndrome, see Chapter 2.

So what, then, does Butler's opening say? Translating Butler's words into terms that are easier to understand, we can see that the first sentence says that for many feminists today, "the indeterminacy of gender"—the inability to define the essence of sexual identity—spells the end of feminism; that for many feminists the inability to define "gender," presumably the building block of the feminist movement, means serious "trouble" for feminist politics. In contrast, the second sentence suggests that this same "trouble" need not be thought of in such "negative" terms, that the inability to define femininity, or "gender trouble" as Butler calls it in her book's title, may not be such a bad thing—and, as she goes on to argue in the pages that follow, may even be something that feminist activists can profit from. In other words, Butler suggests, highlighting uncertainties about masculinity and femininity can be a powerful feminist tool.

Pulling all these inferences together, then, the opening sentences can be translated as follows: "While many contemporary feminists believe that uncertainty about what it means to be a woman will undermine feminist politics, I, Judith Butler, believe that this uncertainty can actually help strengthen feminist politics." Translating Butler's point into our own book's basic move: "They say that if we cannot define 'woman,' feminism is in big trouble. But I say that this type of trouble is precisely what feminism needs." Despite its difficulty, then, we hope you agree that this initially intimidating passage does make sense if you stay with it.

We hope it is clear that critical reading is a two-way street. It is just as much about being open to the way that writers can challenge you, maybe even transform you, as it is about questioning those writers. And if you translate a writer's argument into your own words as you read, you should allow the text to take you outside the ideas that you already hold and to introduce you to new terms and concepts. Even if you end up disagreeing with an author, you first have to show that you have really listened to what is being said, have fully grasped the arguments, and can accurately summarize those arguments. Without such deep, attentive listening, any critique you make will be superficial and decidedly *uncritical*. It will be a critique that says more about you than about the writer or idea you're supposedly responding to.

In this chapter we have tried to show that reading for the conversation means looking not just for the thesis of a text in isolation but for the view or views that motivate that thesis—the "they say." We have also tried to show that reading for the conversation means being alert for the different strategies writers use to engage the view(s) that are motivating them, since not all writers engage other perspectives in the same way. Some writers explicitly identify and summarize a view they are responding to at the outset of their text and then return to it frequently as their text unfolds. Some refer only obliquely to a view that is motivating them, assuming that readers will be able to reconstruct that view on their own. Other writers may not explicitly distinguish their own view from the views they are questioning in ways that all of us find clear, leaving some readers to wonder whether a given view is the writer's own or one that is being challenged. And some writers push off against the "they say" that is motivating them in a challenging academic language that requires readers to translate what they are saying into more accessible, everyday terms. In sum, then, though most persuasive writers do follow a conversational "they say / I say" pattern, they do so in a great variety of ways. What this means for readers is that they need to be armed with various strategies for detecting the conversations in what they read, even when those conversations are not self-evident.

Exercises

1. Read Michelle Alexander's "The New Jim Crow" (pp. 330–43). Use the strategies described in this chapter to examine the conversation at the heart of her essay. Write a paragraph explaining what is motivating Alexander. What views of the US criminal justice system—and American culture—does Alexander think need correcting?

2. Annotate the concluding section of Michelle Alexander's essay, found on pages 330–43. Write "TS" in the margins where you see Alexander summarizing a "they say." Write "IS" in the margins where you see her asserting her own "I say" position. Circle the voice markers you see in the text.

3. Read over a draft of your own writing, and choose an important text you rely on in it. Reread that text, and then do the following:

   a. Ask yourself, "What view is motivating the author of this text?" Highlight where you see the writer naming or hinting at this motivating viewpoint.

   b. Examine how you use the text to motivate your own argument. Have you presented its argument thoroughly and accurately? Have you aligned the text clearly with your own "I say" position, showing whether it supports your position, challenges it, or some combination of both? If not, revise how you frame, summarize, or interpret this source accordingly.

FIFTEEN

"BUT AS SEVERAL SOURCES SUGGEST"

Research as Conversation

———▣———

So, YOU'VE BEEN ASKED to write a research essay. What exactly does that mean? What is your instructor asking you to do?

The best answer to these questions, of course, will always come from your instructors and from any assignment prompt or prompts that they may provide. Although most instructors will want a traditional paper or essay, some will want a webpage, podcast, or a poster that includes a visual component and may even be produced collaboratively with your classmates. Yet other instructors will urge you to produce what is often referred to as a "literature review," in which you summarize a variety of sources on a topic ("literature," in this case, referring not to poems and novels but to published commentary, such as the literature on the French Revolution). Chances are, however, if you've been assigned this book, your instructor will want whatever final project you produce to follow our "they say / I say" model. In our opinion, even the best literature reviews are not just disconnected summaries of various sources but coherent, unified documents that highlight the connections among these sources, framing—and very often entering—the conversation among them. As a result, though we speak throughout this chapter about "the research essay," we hope you'll be able to translate what we say about the conversational pattern at the heart of such essays to any alternative versions of the genre you may be producing. Regardless of what form it takes, the research essay, as we conceive it, is always about entering into conversation with others.

This might mean rethinking some common assumptions. In high school, you may have been asked to write research essays that involve reading various sources on a topic, learning as much as you could about it, and then reporting on what you learned in an essay or oral report. As a result, you may have formed the impression that the research essay is a kind of "data dump," as it is often called, in which you gather a lot of data or information and then dump it into some prescribed number of pages. College-level research, however, as compositionist Joseph Bizup points out, generally means *doing something* with the information you gather, which for us above all means using it to take a stance in response to other researchers. "Sources," in this model, are not merely storehouses of information that you cite, usually to support a thesis, but conversationalists like you who hold views that need to be challenged, agreed with, or some combination of both (for more on these three ways of responding, see Chapter 4). For this reason, we believe that the best research essays rely on the same "they say / I say" format that we've been describing for academic writing in general.

That being said, it does not follow that the college research essay and your standard college writing assignment are one and the same. As we illustrate below, the research paper poses special challenges, one of which has to do with its greater length; in most courses, including first-year writing, it is usually the longest paper you'll be asked to write. How do you fill all those pages? How do you develop an argument or thesis that you can focus on over your essay's entire length? And what about all the sources (articles, book chapters, and so forth) you need to find? How do you find sources that are relevant and credible? How do you select sources from among the often overwhelming number available on the internet? And perhaps most pressing of all, how do you find sources that you can fit together or synthesize as part of a common dialogue or debate?

Given how daunting such challenges can be, we have broken them down into the following issues, to be addressed one at a time.

DEVELOP A GOOD RESEARCH QUESTION

One big challenge of the research essay is navigating the sheer volume of sources that the internet makes available on almost any topic you want to write about. Students often come to our offices in a panic, having found many more sources than they can possibly read in a single semester. We reassure them, however, that they don't have to read everything that's been written on their topic, that they aren't expected to become experts on the subject (though nobody will complain if they do). Their goal instead should be to use a certain number of sources to develop some fundamental skills of intellectual inquiry, the central one of which, as we said before, is to enter a debate or conversation, terms that, as we suggest in our preface, are deeply related.

But still, students will ask, which sources do we focus on? How do we reduce a huge pile of sources to a manageable number? Our answer is pretty much the same one most writing instructors will give you: by coming up with a good research question. A good research question will help you cut through the clutter by identifying which sources are most important to you and how you'll approach them.

But what is a good research question?

In our view, you probably won't be surprised to hear, a good research question identifies a controversy, posing an issue that people can agree or disagree about. In other words, a good research question does more than identify a general topic, about which everything—and, hence, ultimately nothing—can be said. Instead, it focuses on a debate or conversation that both narrows down your sources and helps you integrate or synthesize those sources under a common umbrella issue. Consider these examples:

▸ Why did X happen? Was it, as _____ argues, because of _____ or, as _____ contends, because of _____?

▸ What should we do about X? Should we _____, as _____ urges, or _____, as _____ argues?

▸ Is X as harmful as _____ insists, or does it have benefits, as _____ claims?

▸ Is it true, as some assert, that _____?

▸ What is the relationship between _____ and _____? Is it X, as most assume, or could it be Y, as one source suggests?

In addition, good research questions often come by tapping into your own personal interests:

▸ Throughout the many years that I have taken an interest in _____, I, probably like most people, have assumed that _____. When I researched the topic for this essay, however, I was surprised to discover that _____.

▸ X argues _____. In my experience, however, _____.

Templates like these are tailor-made for sources, helping you put writers who may not even mention one another into a dialogue as part of a common conversation. But remember, a good research question is not something you can nail down once and for all at the start of your project. It is something you revise, refine, and in some cases radically alter as you work with your sources and better identify the unifying issue that you and they are concerned with.

To appreciate how important a research question is, consider how a hypothetical research paper that lacks one might open:

Robotics

Robotics is a very interesting topic in today's society. According to author X, human beings since time immemorial have been making tools to help them accomplish tasks, and in many respects artificial intelligence and robotics are no different. Authors Y and Z suggest that many companies are exploring robotics for ways it can help them make more money, and robots are a central concern in a lot of literature, film, and popular culture. The classic novel *Frankenstein* is basically about a robot. One study by author Z shows that young people take a special interest in robots, but many older people do, too.

Authors have touched on many different aspects of robotics. For example . . .

The problem with research papers like this is that they are untethered to any specific question or issue and therefore tend to lack direction, coming across as dumping grounds or grab bags of information without any unifying thread. As a result, such papers often take the form of a series of "and then" statements with references to sources sprinkled in—not unlike the "list summaries" we complained about in Chapter 2.

A controversial question or issue can remedy this type of unfocused writing. Compare, for example, the opening above with the opening to an essay reproduced in full at the end of this chapter by student writer Jason Smith:

> In recent years, many commentators have suggested that robots will take over most jobs in the next fifty years and leave the human workforce out in the cold. Experts even argue that this takeover is already happening. This paper challenges this alarmist way of thinking. The evidence, I argue, suggests that robots are not eliminating human jobs. In fact, they are creating new jobs.
>
> JASON SMITH, *Roe Butt, Cy Borg, Ann Droid:*
> *Hint, They're Not Taking Your Job*

Note here that Smith addresses the same topic—robots—as the hypothetical writer above, but he narrows it to the question of whether robots are likely to replace human workers. As a result, everything in this opening, as in the remainder of Smith's essay, is quietly devoted to this controversial question. Smith's title alone indicates that he is not going to just *talk about* robots but instead enter a conversation over whether or not robots should be feared.

You might also note here that Smith does not state his research question explicitly. But some exemplary writers do, as the environmental journalist Ben Adler illustrates when, in his very title, he asks, "Banning Plastic Bags Is Great for the World, Right? Not So Fast." In this way, Adler reaches out directly to his readers and draws them in, helping them invest in the conversation he's entering.

LET ONE GOOD SOURCE LEAD TO ANOTHER

Thus far we've suggested that a controversial question is central to academic research. But here you might wonder where a controversial question comes from. How do you find a question or issue that different people—you and your sources—disagree about? By looking in your sources themselves.

Sources frequently respond to other sources, either to confirm what those other sources are saying, contradict it, or some combination of both, as in:

▸ **X is far too pessimistic in her prediction that _____ .**

▸ **Authors X and Y focus on the wrong issue. The issue is not _____ but _____ .**

▸ **I agree with X in her critique of the view that _____ , but _____ .**

In such ways, sources are connected together in an intertextual network of conversation that the best researchers are always alert for. One major challenge of the research paper is to locate one of these conversations in your sources and then frame and enter that conversation.

This is no easy task. Nevertheless, you may be heartened to know that a single source alone can point you in the right direction. That is, just one effective source can provide you with a controversial issue or question that you can use in your own paper—as long as you appropriately credit the source, of course. If you're interested in writing about the environmental or green movement, for instance, you wouldn't have to go very far in Adler's article alone to find such a controversy, since Adler starts identifying positions he agrees and disagrees with as early as his third paragraph. You could also track down some of these sources—which online writing often makes easy when it provides clickable links—and read them next. You might also want to search to see if any of the sources Adler mentions extended the conversation by responding to Adler after his article was published, perhaps by using the Cited By function, which we discuss below (p. 215).

Using one source in this way to find other sources actually has a name. It's called "citation chaining" (or "reference mining") and involves following the trail of a conversation or debate from one source to another, in much the same way as you might follow a trail of bread crumbs. To start such a chain, you might ask questions like these: "In the material I have read, whom are the authors in dialogue with? Who are their 'they says'? What other sources are mentioned in this material that I might follow up on? Are there other texts these sources refer to that could be useful to me?"

BEWARE OF CONFIRMATION BIAS

Before you start searching for sources, though, it is important to understand what you're searching for—and *not* searching for. You're not just looking for sources that support your own viewpoint. Sure, you'll need some, or even many, sources that support your beliefs. But if you look only for the sources that you agree with, you will miss one of the central points of research—and of education itself—which is to get outside yourself and learn from different perspectives. Put another way, you could fall prey to so-called confirmation bias, the tendency to seek out and emphasize whatever confirms your preexisting beliefs and to ignore complicating and contradictory evidence.

Tips for Avoiding Confirmation Bias

- Try searching journal databases (like *JSTOR* for the humanities or *EBSCO* for the sciences) instead of relying solely on the internet search engine you usually use. This is an important step, because the most commonly used search engines prioritize results based on what they have learned about you from previous searches and are thus prone to reinforcing what you already believe. For this reason, when you do use your favorite search engine, try scrolling down in the list of entries that come up rather than relying solely on the first one or two that appear.

- Seek out sources with a variety of perspectives. Do all your sources agree or toe the same general line? Do they come from the same websites, journals, or group of authors?

- If you have trouble finding opposing points of view, try returning to the sources you agree with to see if they mention authors they differ from.

- Become your own naysayer. Ask yourself, "If I had to challenge or critique my own argument, what would I say? What is the strongest objection that could be made against my position?"

- But above all else, be sure to treat other perspectives with an open mind. Play the "believing game," as we discuss in Chapter 2, in which you try to understand what they are saying on their own terms before rushing to judgment.

APPRECIATE SCHOLARLY SOURCES

Some students might shy away from scholarly sources since they are usually a harder read than their nonscholarly counterparts. But such sources have many benefits, not least of which that they make chaining or tracking conversations relatively easy.

Unlike most popular and journalistic sources, academic sources provide all the citation information you need to track down any source or sources that have been referred to. That is, scholarly sources are scholarly precisely because they draw so heavily on other sources and include key elements like works-cited pages, references, or bibliographies that tell you exactly where those other sources can be found.

Our goal here, however, is not to cover all the ins-and-outs of scholarly documentation (MLA and APA style, endnotes, footnotes, parenthetical notes, works-cited lists, and so forth). Nor is our goal to explain how these distinctive documentation features of academic writing differ from one discipline to another. There are many excellent writers' handbooks and websites out there that provide this type of intricate instruction. And yet our discussion of research would be incomplete if it didn't underscore how helpful it is that scholarly writers tell you exactly which sources they are responding to in any particular passage and that they end their publications with all the documentation information you need to track these sources down.

See Appendix, "Citing What 'They Say.'"

In this way, scholarly, academic writers (like you!) are remarkably transparent, taking pains to identify their sources in ways that popular, journalistic, and literary writers do not. So, for instance, when Michelle Alexander, in the excerpt included in this book from *The New Jim Crow: Mass Incarceration in the Age of Colorblindness*, cites studies, she includes note numbers that direct readers to the precise studies she's referring to. One of her sentences on page 356, for instance, runs as follows:

Studies show that people of all colors *use and sell* illegal drugs at remarkably similar rates.[9]

To locate these studies, all you need to do is flip to the end of Alexander's text and look for endnote 9, which cites several reports, such as the US Department of Health and Human Services and the National Household Survey on Drug Abuse. So, for example, if you were examining illegal drug use in your community compared to national averages, you could turn to the sources cited by Alexander for relevant data. Through devices like these, scholarly writers are remarkably transparent, inviting any reader to independently assess the conversation that they are engaged in.

But looking inside a scholarly source is not the only way to piece together or "chain" a debate or conversation. Because it is unlikely that any one scholarly source will be the last word in a published conversation, you might want to find out if any other sources have responded to your source, something you can do by using the handy Cited By or Cited Reference functions provided by *Google Scholar*, and journal repositories like *JSTOR* or *EBSCO*. For example, when we keyed in "Michelle Alexander, *The New Jim Crow*" into *Google Scholar*, here's what we got:

Librarians are usually more than happy to help you use this function. But the upshot is that, the number to the right of "Cited by" tells you that Alexander's book has inspired a tremendous amount of discussion, having been cited in no less than 15,171 other publications—far too many sources for you to possibly sort through. But no need to despair. By clicking on the "Cited by" link itself, you can do a more focused search by checking the box, "Search within citing articles," and then entering into the new search bar keywords tailored to your particular interests, as in: "presidential election, voter suppression, Black Lives Matter, voter identification laws." When we keyed in these more precise terms, we were able to reduce our list of 15,000+ publications to 2,910 results. And when we sorted by date, selecting, for example, only articles published "Since 2023," we further reduced that number to an even more manageable 294 that can be scanned for relevant titles.

EVALUATE YOUR SOURCES

Whether a source converges around a common question or issue is only one consideration when evaluating a source. Another factor is whether a source is reliable or not, which is often difficult to determine. Even as the internet greatly expands the amount of knowledge available to us, it is notoriously susceptible to misinformation and propaganda that look like objective fact. In their research article, "Lateral Reading: Reading Less and Learning More When Evaluating Digital Information," Sam Wineburg and Sarah McGrew of the Stanford History Education Group, found that even professional historians accustomed to online searches "often fell victim to easily manipulated features of websites such as official-looking logos and domain names."

So even as the internet has made academic research easier in many ways, it makes it hard to tell if what you are looking at is or isn't reliable. How are you to sort out one type of text from the other? How can you tell whether a source you're looking at has been discredited? One common answer is to restrict your searches to a type of scholarly writing we discussed earlier: the type that appears in academic journals and university presses that rely on the peer-review process of only publishing submissions that have been approved by other expert scholars.

Despite its merits, however, this approach excludes such indispensable venues as the *New York Times* and the *Wall Street Journal*, and general interest magazines like *Harper's* and the *Atlantic*, not to mention many popular books and most of what appears on the internet. Limiting yourself only to peer-reviewed sources is especially difficult when writing about current events and contemporary issues, which tend to be the purview of news periodicals.

For this reason, you might want to know about a second approach for determining whether a source is credible: the strategy that Wineburg and McGrew recommend of "reading laterally," which involves cross-checking all sources. Wineburg and McGrew suggest that in doing online research, we imitate professional fact-checkers, who tend to be more adept than even experienced academics at evaluating web sources. While most researchers, according to Wineburg and McGrew, "read vertically, staying within a website to evaluate its reliability," fact-checkers "read laterally," looking not just at what the source itself says but at what other sources say about it, too. In contrast to vertical readers, these savvy researchers are able to more accurately determine whether any group sponsors the website and who might have a financial stake in its claims.

Fact-checkers are also able to more accurately assess whether a website has a bias that needs to be taken into account and whether it promotes suspicious information.

Tips for Researching Like a Fact-Checker

- Open a browser tab and window and type in the website's name along with key terms like "funding," "credibility," and "bias." Hit Search and see what comes up.

- Go to the *Wikipedia* pages for the authors or website you're investigating, and consider following up on the links at the bottom of the page under "References," "Notes and References," and "Internal Links."

- Cross-check any claims presented by the source that strike you as improbable. In other words, when you come across claims that sound suspect, try investigating further to see if the claim is supported or refuted by other sources. That one source treats as factual what another source treats as questionable can, after all, be an excellent starting point for a paper.

- And again, if you're using a popular search engine, be sure not to rely exclusively on the first two or three results that come up but to scroll down to the lower items. Remember that the results given in nonscholarly search engines are based on your previous searches and are designed to get clicks.

If we could add anything to Wineburg and McGrew's suggestions here, it would be to not underestimate how interesting in itself reading laterally like this can be. You may just find that investigating whether a given source is reliable is so fascinating that you just have to make it the central question that your research paper addresses, as in:

▶ **While many observers seem to find website X trustworthy, others are suspicious of X because of _____ . I, however, am of two minds about this site and argue that we need to use this website with great caution.**

▶ **X challenges the reliability of Blog Y on the grounds that _____ . My own view is _____ .**

Templates like these can form the basis of a dynamite research paper. After all, throughout this chapter we have insisted that strong research writing requires a good controversial question, and it is hard to think of a controversial question that is better and more fundamental than whether the sources we rely on can be trusted.

DON'T LET ALL THOSE VOICES DERAIL YOU

Avoiding tangents is important in any piece of writing. As we explained in Chapter 9, regardless of the nature of the assignment, you need to stay focused throughout the entire length of your paper.

And yet, as we suggested at the start of this chapter, staying focused throughout a research paper can be especially challenging. This is not just because the research paper is relatively long but also because it requires you to synthesize a large number of sources that rarely come prepackaged in a ready-made conversation. In some cases, the sources you collect will not directly mention or address the others, and most will have an agenda that differs from your own. As a result, it can be difficult to reduce all your sources to a common conversation or issue and all too easy to let them throw you off track.

To see how one student manages to stay focused on his central research question over the full course of his research paper, let's return to the essay by student writer Jason Smith (pp. 224–33). As we noted earlier, Smith does an excellent job stating his central question—whether or not robots threaten to eliminate human jobs—at the start of his essay and even in his title. What we now want to note is that he does an equally good job staying focused on this issue while piloting through numerous sources.

On page 227, for instance, Smith opens one of his paragraphs with the following:

> A second alarming view of robots taking home the paycheck comes from . . . McKinsey Quarterly. . . .

This topic sentence, which introduces a new article, may look unremarkably simple. Nevertheless, this sentence does something that is actually quite difficult: it puts this new article in dialogue not only with the previous article that Smith had just addressed but also with the controversial question that Smith established in his opening paragraph a full three pages earlier. How can we tell that this sentence makes all these connections? In part because it relies on the same key terms, or their synonyms and antonyms, that Smith has already established in his preceding pages: terms like "robots," "alarmist," "fear," "taking over," "paycheck," "work," "employments," "workforce," and "jobs." Even the seemingly inconsequential word "second" makes connections, suggesting a parallel between this "second" article and the previous one that Smith addressed, suggesting that both adopt an "alarming view of robots taking home the paycheck." If you need help with such moves, you might want to do the exercises below, which are designed to help.

In this chapter, we've given you, we hope, some useful tips on how to write the college research essay. But as the chapter draws to a conclusion, we'd like to step back from this how-to discussion and say a word about what such research, as we see it, is essentially all about. For some students, the research essay may seem to be just one more pointless hoop that some authority is asking them to jump through. But for us, it's the highest expression of the conversational approach to writing that we discuss in this book, an opportunity to take off the training wheels and contribute to a conversation that instead of being preestablished by your instructor, you independently find and frame yourself. In this way, the academic research essay is far from merely academic in the negative sense. It is a chance to practice a set of skills that you can use the rest of your life: going out into the community, finding a space for yourself, and making a contribution of your own.

Exercises

1. Read Ayana Elizabeth Johnson's 2020 essay, "To Save the Climate, Look to the Oceans," on **theysayiblog.com** in light of the techniques addressed in this chapter. Working with a partner or a small group, answer the following questions:

   a. What do you take Johnson's central research question to be? What debate does that question frame or set up? Choose one of the templates from this chapter that corresponds with Johnson's question and then state that question using the template's language.

b. Look at the sources Johnson includes in her essay, which are hyperlinked, and analyze what Johnson does with each one. Does the source support or challenge her position? And how do you know? How does Johnson synthesize that source into her essay's central debate question?

c. Choose one of the sources Johnson includes and read it "laterally," as the term is used in this chapter, to evaluate its credibility. "Fact-check" the source to determine its commitments and biases. In the end, do you think the source is reliable? Why or why not?

d. Use *Google Scholar* to determine who has cited Johnson's essay and what conversations or debates her essay is part of. How might you enter this conversation in a research essay of your own?

2. Take a section of Johnson's essay and annotate it in the same ways that we annotated Jason Smith's essay (pp. 224–33). Identify as many "moves that matter" as you can, noting, for instance, how Johnson

- entertains counterarguments

- sets up a debate or conversation

- synthesizes sources to a common issue

- uses transition terms

- uses pointing words

- uses voice markers

- repeats herself with a difference

- includes metacommentary

- develops a constellation of key terms and phrases

- frames, or "sandwiches," quotations

3. To get going on a research essay, try the following steps:

Decide on a general topic for your essay, and then, working with a classmate, use the templates on page 208 to come up with at least two different research questions that address that topic. Analyze each question with your classmate, weighing its strengths and weaknesses until you decide which question you prefer.

Then, having decided on a question, continue working with your partner to develop a list of eight to ten key terms and phrases that you can use both in your paper itself and to search for sources on the internet.

After you've gathered your sources and written a draft of your paper, have a classmate read your draft to determine if it exhibits any of the confirmation bias discussed in this chapter. Do you use sources only to support your position, or do you bring in a variety of perspectives, including those of naysayers? Do other perspectives come to mind that could—or should— also be included in your text? Work together to either track down sources that represent any excluded perspectives or come up with language of your own to represent them, as in, "It is sometimes said that . . ."

Finally, have your partner evaluate how well you integrate or synthesize your sources. Are all your sources aligned with one another and with your essay's central debate question or issue? Can you come up with strategies to heighten the alignment and eliminate any misalignment?

Roe Butt, Cy Borg, Ann Droid: Hint, They're Not Taking Your Job

JASON SMITH

IN RECENT YEARS, many commentators have suggested that robots will take over most jobs in the next fifty years and leave the human workforce out in the cold. Experts even argue that this takeover is already happening. This paper challenges this alarmist way of thinking. The evidence, I argue, suggests that robots are not eliminating human jobs. In fact, they are creating new jobs. Throughout history, such innovative tools didn't end work but increased it.

JASON SMITH wrote this essay for his first-year writing course at Atlantic Cape Community College, where he is pursuing a general studies associate's degree in science. This essay was nominated for the Norton Writer's Prize and is documented in MLA style.

To be sure, in periods when innovations take hold, workers tend to fear their own dislocation. For example, as researcher James Lacey notes, during the industrialization of the French silk industry, "French weavers threw their wooden shoes (sabots) into textile machines to make them break down. (Thus the term sabotage.)" However, it is likely that those displaced workers found other jobs—as auto mechanics, gas station attendants, and car makers, for example—just as those who worked in carriage houses and were replaced by the automobile did. Changes happen in every industry over time: the airplane replaced the train, for example, and lightbulbs replaced the need for the candlemaker, but in every era, many displaced workers found new professions. A well-defined pattern is beginning to emerge here—all technological advances bring with them new opportunities.

> Makes a concession to the "they say" that actually bolsters his "I say."

Predictions about the downfall of the workforce due to technological innovation have been happening for nearly a century. Jeff Borland notes that "in the 1930s, John Maynard Keynes envisaged that innovations such as electricity would produce a world where people spent most of their time on leisure." Later, during the 1930s, as Richard Freeman notes, "US President Franklin D. Roosevelt blamed unemployment on his country's failure to employ the surplus labor created by the efficiency of its industrial processes." He also points out

> Summarizes some "they say" sources from the past.

that "in the early 1960s, widespread fears that automation was eliminating thousands of jobs per week led the Kennedy and Johnson administrations to examine the link between productivity growth and employment." Despite those worries and failed projections, studies through the 1960s, '70s, '80s, and '90s (which includes the advent of computers) proclaimed the demise of work.

Two more recent studies demonstrate contemporary arguments for the impact robots will have on our future. *Race against the Machine*, a book by Erik Brynjolfsson and Andrew McAfee, focuses on the results of their study of the recovery from the Great Recession of 2008. In his TED talk based on the book, McAfee uses a chart that presents a dramatic correlation between productivity and the labor force and notes that his research with coauthor Brynjolfsson reveals that from 2008 through 2011, while the US working-age population increased, the actual number of available jobs declined, even though the economy was recovering during that time frame and productivity actually increased. Their inevitable conclusion, according to McAfee, is that robots are already replacing the human workforce.

However, the data gathered in *Race against the Machine* is shortsighted. Had the study continued only three more years, the authors would have seen the graph's job curve return to normal values. After any recession, the rebound in

Previews the first of two "they say" sources to be addressed.

Answers this first "they say," integrating sources.

employment has always taken longer than the rebound in the GDP, for several reasons. Manufacturers reduce their inventories, which makes it look like fewer people are producing more. In a recession, the remaining workers always find ways to pick up the slack left behind by laid-off workers, often through the use of overtime, which is cheaper in the short run than hiring new workers or rehiring those laid off. Once again, the greater productivity stems from existing workers, not automation. The most recent recession, moreover, produced some unusual employment data. Part-time workers are not counted as full-time employees, yet their work output is included in the overall productivity numbers.

A second alarming view of robots taking home the paycheck comes from Michael Chui, James Manyika, and Mehdi Miremadi in a *McKinsey Quarterly* article titled "Where Machines Could Replace Humans—and Where They Can't." They write: "Last year, we showed that currently demonstrated technologies could automate 45 percent of the activities people are paid to perform and that about 60 percent of all occupations could see 30 percent or more of their constituent activities automated, again with technologies available today." The problem with this report is its use of probability for its logic: just because a thing *can* be done does not mean it *will* be done. As Gillian B. White points out in her reporting on

> Summarizes and answers the second "they say," integrating yet more sources.

a study by two economists, "The authors note that just because an industry can automate doesn't mean that it will." Costs in every case must be examined, as well as return on investment. Theoretical predictions only go so far; there is a real-world cost/benefit analysis that must be applied to each of these possible robot advancements. In addition, Chui, Manyika, and Miremadi overlook arguments that it will require more humans to maintain and build robots than they replace (Metz).

In fact, convincing, well-researched papers that examine data over a much greater time span find there is no evidence of a robot takeover. These studies indicate that the opposite is true. For example, Jeff Borland and Michael Coelli, two Australian researchers, published an exhaustive study in 2017 that found that

> (i) the total amount of work available [in Australia] has not decreased following the introduction of computer-based technologies; and (ii) the pace of structural change and job turnover in the labor market has not accelerated with the increasing application of computer-based technologies. A review of recent studies that claim computer-based technologies may be about to cause widespread job destruction establishes several major flaws with these predictions. (377)

Continues to answer this second "they say," integrating even more sources.

Borland and Coelli found that fears about job losses have happened often throughout history: "Our suggested explanation for why techno-phobia has such a grip on popular imagination is a human bias to believe that 'we live in special times'" (377). In other words, we think that our particular era is unique—that now is truly the time that robots will take over our jobs—but such a scenario doesn't come to pass.

There are more practical reasons why robots will not replace humans in many fields, especially those areas of work that require direct interaction with humans. In his *Tech.Co* article "5 Reasons Why Robots Will Never Fully Replace Humans," Lanre Onibalusi notes that robots cannot "understand irrational thought," cannot "understand context," and "lack creative problem solving" abilities and that "people prefer to talk with a human." Additionally, as Ryan Nakashima reports, behind almost every form of robotization is an army of technocrats. This army of workers is considered the "dirty little secret" behind the artificially intelligent robot. Whether it be the hundreds of programmers or the vast numbers of call-center operators required to carry the load, robots require human helpers. It seems that robots simply cannot understand context, and enormous numbers of analysts are required to try to reteach an automated system every time it fails to understand a request

Engages more sources in support of the "I say."

from a customer (Nakashima). In fact, according to a recent *New York Times* article, grocery retailers who have started using robots report that "the robots are good for their workers. They free up employees from mundane and sometimes injury-prone jobs like unloading delivery trucks to focus on more fulfilling tasks like helping customers" (Corkery). In this case, as in others, robots help increase productivity rather than replace humans.

Some of these alarmists argue that as robots become smarter, laws must be instituted to guard against a massive upheaval, or even elimination, of the human workforce. The problem with this preemptive approach is that no one can possibly imagine where or when those laws should exist or how to apply them. The normal course of events is to first have solid evidence that some event is "bad" and later proceed to legislate. For example, those who oppose self-driving cars, another kind of robot, call for governmental restrictions on them, but before such vehicles are on the road, there's no reason to fear them. In fact, they require human help. Many have heard of the self-driving truck that hauled two thousand cases of beer 120 miles in Colorado without a driver at the wheel (Isaac). What was not revealed was that there was a full police escort for the entire route and that the vehicle was incapable of negotiating the on- and off-ramps. I will admit that during the writing of this paper,

Addresses a final naysayer.

a self-driving-car fatality did occur when an Arizona woman was struck and killed by a driverless vehicle owned by Uber. Uber immediately suspended all driverless test vehicles in the United States and Canada, and the following week Nvidia suspended all tests with the same product (Sage). Perhaps here is an example of a worthy event triggering the possibility of new laws, but an overall ban on automation itself in the workforce seems hasty.

As Jeff Borland has astutely observed, "The tale of new technologies causing the death of work is the prophecy that keeps on giving." It is sensational, alarmist, and grossly premature. I agree with those who believe society should not worry about robots taking away all the jobs. Most of the predictions for the future are countered by past facts. The reality is that all new technologies bring about new avenues of invention, experimentation, and work and that much of the new technology requires the intervention of humans. It is therefore unnecessary for governments to regulate robots to protect jobs.

> Succinctly recaps the essay's "I say" position.

WORKS CITED

Borland, Jeff. "Why We Are Still Convinced Robots Will Take
    Our Jobs despite the Evidence." *The Conversation*, 25 Nov.
    2017, theconversation.com/why-we-are-still-convinced
    -robots-will-take-our-jobs-despite-the-evidence-87188.
    Accessed 4 Apr. 2018.

Borland, Jeff, and Michael Coelli. "Are Robots Taking Our
    Jobs?" *The Australian Economic Review*, vol. 50, no. 4, 2017,
    pp. 377–97. *Wiley Online Library*, doi:10.1111/1467-8462.12245.
    Accessed 4 Apr. 2018.

Brynjolfsson, Erik, and Andrew McAfee. *Race against the Machine*.
    Digital Frontier Press, 2011.

Chui, Michael, James Manyika, and Mehdi Miremadi. "Where
    Machines Could Replace Humans—and Where They Can't
    (Yet)." *McKinsey Quarterly*, July 2016, www.mckinsey.com
    /business-functions/digital-mckinsey/our-insights/where
    -machines-could-replace-humans-and-where-they-cant-yet.
    Accessed 4 Apr. 2018.

Corkery, Michael. "Should Robots Have a Face?" *The New York
    Times*, 26 Feb. 2020, www.nytimes.com/2020/02/26/business
    /robots-retail-jobs.html. Accessed 4 April 2018.

Freeman, Richard B. "Who Owns the Robots Rules the World."
    IZA World of Labor, May 2015, wol.iza.org/articles/who-owns
    -the-robots-rules-the-world/long. Accessed 3 Apr. 2018.

Isaac, Mike. "Self-Driving Truck's First Mission: A 120-Mile Beer
    Run." *The New York Times*, 25 Oct. 2016, www.nytimes
    .com/2016/10/26/technology/self-driving-trucks-first-mission-a
    -beer-run.html. Accessed 4 Apr. 2018.

Lacey, James. "Re: Should Governments Limit Corporations'
    Abilities to Replace Human Workers with Technology?"
    Quora, 1 Jan. 2017, www.quora.com/Should-governments
    -limit-corporations-abilities-to-replace-human-workers-with
    -technology. Accessed 3 Apr. 2018.

McAfee, Andrew. "Race against the Machine." *YouTube*,
    TedxBoston, 17 July 2012, www.youtube.com
    /watch?v=QfMGyCk3XTw. Accessed 3 Apr. 2018.

Metz, Cade. "Robots Will Steal Our Jobs, but They'll Give Us
    New Ones." *Wired*, 24 Aug. 2015, wired.com/2015/08/robots
    -will-steal-jobs-theyll-give-us-new-ones. Accessed 4 Apr. 2018.
Nakashima, Ryan. "AI's Dirty Little Secret: It's Powered by
    People." *AP News*, 5 Mar. 2018, apnews.com/1f58465e55d643
    ea84e51713f35ad214. Accessed 4 Apr. 2018.
Onibalusi, Lanre. "5 Reasons Why Robots Will Never Fully Replace
    Humans." *Tech.Co*, 2 Aug. 2017, tech.co/robots-replace-humans
    -work-2017-08. Accessed 4 Apr. 2018.
Sage, Alexandria, and Sonam Rai. "Nvidia Halts Self-Driving
    Tests in Wake of Uber Accident." *Reuters*, 27 Mar. 2018,
    www.reuters.com/article/us-autos-selfdriving-nvidia
    /nvidia-halts-self-driving-tests-in-wake-of-uber-accident
    -idUSKBN1H32E0. Accessed 4 Apr. 2018.
White, Gillian B. "How Many Robots Does It Take to Replace a
    Human Job?" *The Atlantic*, 30 Mar. 2017, www.theatlantic
    .com/business/archive/2017/03/work-automation/521364.
    Accessed 4 Apr. 2018.

SIXTEEN

"ON CLOSER EXAMINATION"

Entering Conversations about Literature

———□———

IN CHINUA ACHEBE'S NOVEL *Things Fall Apart*, Okonkwo, the main character, is a tragic hero.

So what? Who cares?

Why does this typical way of opening an essay on a literary work leave readers wondering, "Why are you telling me this?" Because, in our view, such statements leave it unclear who would say otherwise. Would anyone deny that the main character of Achebe's novel is a tragic hero? Is there some other view of the subject that this writer is responding to? Since no such alternative interpretation is indicated, the reader thinks, "OK, Okonkwo is a tragic hero—as opposed to what?"

Now compare this opening with another possible one:

> Several members of our class have argued that Okonkwo, the main character of *Things Fall Apart*, represents what we now call "toxic masculinity." My own view, however, is that, while it is true that Okonkwo commits violent acts spurred by his need not to be seen as weak, he is ultimately a tragic hero—a deeply flawed but ultimately sympathetic figure.

We hope you agree that the second version, which responds to what someone else says about Okonkwo, makes for more engaging writing than the first. Since the first version fails to present itself as a response to any alternative view of its subject, it comes at readers out of the blue, leaving them wondering why it needs to be said at all.

As we stress in this book, it is the views of others and our desire to respond to these views that gives our writing its underlying motivation and helps readers see why what we say matters, why others should care, and why we need to say it in the first place. In this chapter we suggest that this same principle applies to writing about literature. Literary critics, after all, don't make assertions about literary works out of the blue. Rather, they contribute to discussions and debates about the meaning and significance of literary works, some of which may continue for years and even centuries.

Indeed, this commitment to discussion animates most literature courses, in which students discuss and debate assigned works in class before writing papers about them. The premise is that engaging with classmates and teachers enables us to make discoveries about the work that we might not arrive at in simply reading the work alone.

We suggest that you think of writing about literature as a natural extension of such in-class discussions, listening carefully to others and using what they say to set up and motivate what you have to say.

START WITH WHAT OTHERS ARE SAYING

But in writing about literature, where do views to respond to—"they say"s—come from? Many sources. Published literary criticism is perhaps the most obvious:

▸ Critic X complains that author Y's story is compromised by their _____ perspective. While there's some truth to this critique, I argue that critic X overlooks _____.

▸ According to critic A, novel X suggests _____. I agree, but would add that _____.

But the view that you respond to in writing about literature can be far closer to home than published literary criticism. As our opening example illustrates, it can be something said about the literary work by a classmate or teacher:

▸ Several members of our class have suggested that the final message of play X is _____. I agree up to a point, but I still think that _____.

Another tactic is to start with something you yourself thought about the work that on second thought you now want to revise:

▸ On first reading play Z, I thought it was an uncritical celebration of _____. After rereading the play and discussing it in class, however, I see that it is more critical of _____ than I originally thought.

You can even respond to something that hasn't actually been said about the work but might hypothetically be said:

▸ It might be said that poem Y is chiefly about _____. But the problem with this reading, in my view, is _____.

▸ Though religious readers might be tempted to analyze poem X as a parable about _____, a closer examination suggests that the poem is in fact _____.

Sometimes the "they say" that you respond to in writing about a literary work can be found in the work itself, as distinct from what some critic or other reader has said *about* the work. Much great literary criticism responds directly to the literary work, summarizing some aspect of the work's form or content and then assessing it, in much the same way you can do in response to a persuasive essay:

▸ **Ultimately, as I read it, *The Scarlet Letter* seems to say _____. I have trouble accepting this proposition, however, on the grounds that _____.**

One of the more powerful ways of responding to a literary work is to address any contradictions or inconsistencies:

▸ **At the beginning of the poem, we encounter the generalization, seemingly introducing the poem's message, that "_____." But this statement is then contradicted by the suggestion made later in the poem that "_____." This opens up a significant inconsistency in the text: is it suggesting _____ or, on the contrary, _____?**

▸ **At several places in novel X, author Y leads us to understand that the story's central point is that _____. Yet elsewhere the text suggests _____, indicating that Y may be ambivalent on this issue.**

If you review the above templates, you'll notice that each does what a good discussion, lecture, or essay does: it makes an argument about some aspect of a work that can be interpreted in various ways. Instead of just making a claim about the work in isolation—character X is a tragic hero; sonnet Y is about the loss of a loved one—these templates put one claim as a response to another, making clear what motivated the argument to begin with. They thus act as conversation starters that can invite or even provoke other readers to respond with their own interpretations and judgments.

FIGURING OUT
WHAT A LITERARY WORK "MEANS"

In order to enter conversations and debates about literature, you need to meet the time-honored challenge of being able to read and make sense of literary works, understanding and analyzing what the text says. On the one hand, like the types of persuasive essays we focus on throughout this book, literary works make arguments their authors want to convey, things they are for and against, ideas they want to endorse or condemn. On the other hand, discovering "the argument" of a literary work—what it's "saying"—can be a special challenge because, unlike persuasive essays, literary works usually do not spell out their arguments explicitly. Though poets, novelists, and playwrights may have the same level of conviction as persuasive writers, rarely do they step out from behind the pages of their texts and say, "OK, folks, this is what it all means. What I'm trying to say in a nutshell is _____." That is, since literary texts do not include an explicit thesis statement identifying their main point, it's left up to us as readers to figure it out.

Because literary works tend to avoid such explicitness, their meanings often need to be teased out from the clues they provide: from the dialogue between characters, the plot, the imagery and symbolism, and the kind of language the author uses. In fact, it is this absence of overt argument that makes literature so endlessly debatable—and explains why scholars and critics argue so much about what literary works mean in ways similar to the classroom discussions that you have likely participated in as a student.

The Elusive Literary Author

Indeed, not even the use of the first-person "I" in a literary work is an indication that you have located the author's own position or stance, as it usually is in an essay. When Kelly Coryell, for example, in her essay "All Words Matter" (pp. 344–57) writes, "I've never understood the popular saying 'Sticks and stones may break my bones but words will never hurt me,'" we can be confident that the "I" is Coryell herself and that the position she expresses is her own and informs everything else in her essay. But we cannot assume that the "I" who addresses us in a work of fiction or poetry is necessarily the author, for the person who "I" refers to is a fictional character—and one who may be unreliable and untrustworthy.

Take, for example, the first sentence of Edgar Allan Poe's short story "The Cask of Amontillado":

> The thousand injuries of Fortunato I had borne as I best could, but when he ventured upon insult I vowed revenge.

As soon becomes clear in the story, the "I" who speaks as the narrator here is not Poe himself but an insanely vengeful murderer whose words must be seen through to get at the point of Poe's story.

Instead of a readily identifiable position, literary works often present the perspectives of a number of different characters and leave it to readers to determine which if any speaks for the author. Thus when we encounter the seemingly eloquent lines in *Hamlet* "To thine own self be true, . . . / And canst thou not be false to any man," we can't assume, as we might if we encountered this statement in an essay, that it represents the author's own view. For these words are uttered by Polonius, a character whom Shakespeare presents as a tedious, cliché-spouting bore—not someone he leads us to trust. After all, part of Hamlet's problem is that it's not clear to him what being "true" to his own self would require him to do.

This elusive quality of literary texts helps explain why some of our students complain about the challenge of finding the "hidden meaning," as they sometimes call it, let alone summarizing that meaning in the way assignments often require. Sure, some students say, they enjoy reading literature for pleasure. But analyzing literature in school for its "meaning" or "symbolism"—that's another matter. Some even say that the requirement that they hunt for meanings and symbols robs literature of its fun.

In fact, as most students come to recognize, analyzing meanings, symbols, and other elements should enhance rather than stifle the pleasure we get from reading literature. But it can indeed be hard to figure out what literary works mean. How do we determine the point of a story or poem when the author, unlike an essayist like Coryell, does not tell us explicitly what they are trying to say? How do you go from a fictional event or poetic image (a woman pondering her wallpaper design, two roads that diverge in the woods) or from a dialogue between fictional characters ("You your best thing, Sethe. You are.") to what these events, images, or lines of dialogue mean?

Look for Conflict *in* the Work

There is no simple recipe for figuring out what a literary work means, but one tactic that seems to help our own students is to look for the conflict or debate in the literary work itself and then ask what the text is leading us to think about that conflict. Asking these questions—what is the conflict in the work and which side, if any, should we favor?—will help you think about and formulate a position on what the work means. And since such claims are often ones that literary scholars argue about, thinking about the conflict *in* a literary work will often lead you to discussions and debates *about* the work that you can then respond to in your writing. Because literary authors don't tell us explicitly what the text means, it's always going to be *arguable*—and your task in writing about a literary work is to argue for what *you* think it means. Here are two templates to help get you started responding to other interpretations:

▸ **It might be argued that in the clash between characters X and Y in play Z, the author wants us to favor character Y, since she is presented as the play's heroine. I contend, however, that _____ .**

▸ **Several critics seem to assume that poem X endorses the values of discipline and rationality represented by the image of _____ over those of play and emotion represented by the image of _____ . I agree, but with the following caveat: that the poem ultimately sees both values as equally important and even suggests that ideally they should complement one another.**

This tactic of looking for the conflicts in literary works is part of a long tradition of critical thought that sees conflict as central to literature. In ancient Greece, Aristotle argued that conflict between characters or forces underlies the plots of tragic dramas such as *Oedipus*. Indeed, the ancient Greek word *agon*, which means antagonism, conflict, or debate, leaves its traces in the term "protagonist," the hero or leading character of a narrative work who comes into conflict with other characters or with the fates. And Plato noted the pervasiveness of conflict in literature when he banished poets from his ideal community on the grounds that their works depict endless conflict and division.

This emphasis on the centrality of conflict in literature has been echoed by modern theorists like the New Critics of the 1940s and '50s, who focused on such tensions and paradoxes as good and evil or innocence and experience—and more recently by poststructuralists and political theorists who see literature engaging in conflicts—both external and internal—related to gender, racial, and sexual identities. Writers today continue to recognize conflict as the engine of good storytelling. As the Hollywood screenwriter Robert McKee puts it, "Nothing moves forward in a story except through conflict."

Building on this idea that conflict is central to literature, we suggest the following four questions to help you understand and formulate your own position on any literary work:

1. What is the central conflict?
2. Which side—if any—does the text seem to favor?
3. What's your evidence? How might others interpret the evidence differently?
4. What's your opinion of the text?

WHAT IS THE CENTRAL CONFLICT?

Conflicts tend to manifest themselves in different ways in different literary genres. In works that take a narrative or story form (novels, short stories, and plays), the central conflict will often be represented in an actual debate between characters. These debates between characters will often reflect larger questions and debates in the society or historical era in which they were written, over such issues as the responsibility of rulers, the consequences of capitalism and consumerism, or the struggle for gender equality. Sometimes these debates will be located within an individual character, appearing as a struggle in someone caught between conflicting or incompatible choices. Whatever form they may take, these debates can provide you with points of entry into the issues raised by the work, its historical context, and its author's vision of the world.

One narrative work that lends itself to such an approach is Flannery O'Connor's 1961 short story "Everything That Rises Must Converge." The story presents a running debate between a mother and her son, Julian, about the civil rights movement for racial equality that had erupted in the American South at the time the story was written, with Julian defending the outlook of this movement and his mother defending the South's traditional racial hierarchy. The story raises the debatable question of which character we should side with: Julian, his mother, both, or neither?

WHICH SIDE—IF ANY—DOES THE TEXT SEEM TO FAVOR?

When we teach this story, most of our students first assume the story sides with Julian's outlook, which to them as northern, urban college students in the twenty-first century seems the obviously enlightened position. Who, after all, could fail to see that the mother's views are backward and racist? As our class discussions unfold, however, most students come to reject this view as a misreading, one based more on their own views than on what's in the text. Sooner or later, someone points out that in several places Julian is presented in highly critical ways—and that his apparently progressive sympathy for racial integration rests on arid intellectual abstractions and a hypocritical lack of self-knowledge, in contrast with his mother's heartfelt loyalty to her roots. Eventually another possible interpretation surfaces, that both characters suffer from a common malady: that they're living in a mental bubble that keeps them from being able to see themselves as they really are.

The writing assignment we often give builds on this class discussion by offering students the following template for thinking about which character, if any, the text leads them to favor:

▸ **Some might argue that when it comes to the conflict between Julian and his mother over _____, our sympathies should lie with _____. My own view is that _____.**

WHAT'S YOUR EVIDENCE?

In entering the types of discussions and debates modeled by the above template, how do you determine where your "sympathies should lie"? More generally, how do you arrive at and justify an interpretation of what a literary text says?

The answer lies in the *evidence* provided by the work: its images, dialogue, plot, historical references, tone, stylistic details, and so forth.

It is important to remember, however, that evidence is not set in stone. Students sometimes assume that there exists some fixed code that unlocks the meaning of literary works, symbols, images, and other evidence. A character dies? This must mean that he or she is being condemned. A stairway appears? A symbol for upward mobility. A garden? Must be something sexual.

But evidence itself is open to interpretation and thus to debate. The mother's death in O'Connor's story, for instance, *could* be seen as evidence that we are supposed to disapprove of her as someone whose racial views are regressive and on the way out. On the other hand, her death may instead be evidence that she is to be seen as a heroic martyr too good for this cruel, harsh world. What a character's death means, then, depends on how that character is treated in the work, positively or negatively, which in turn may be subject to debate.

As we've repeatedly emphasized in this book, others will often disagree with you and may even use the same evidence you do to support interpretations that are contrary to your own. As with other objects of study, literary works are like the famous ambiguous drawing that can be seen as either a duck or a rabbit, depending how one views it.

Since the same piece of evidence in a literary work will often support differing, even opposing interpretations, you need to argue for what you think the evidence shows—and to acknowledge that others may read that evidence differently.

In writing about literature, then, you need to show that the evidence you are citing supports your interpretation and to anticipate other alternative ones:

▸ **Although some might read the metaphor of _____ in this poem as evidence that, for author X, modern technology undermines community traditions and values, I see it as _____.**

To present evidence in such a "they say / I say" way, you need to be alert for how others may read the work differently than you—and even use this very same evidence in support of an opposing interpretation:

▸ **Some might claim that evidence X suggests _____, but I argue that, on the contrary, it suggests _____.**

▸ **I agree with my classmate _____ that the image of _____ in novel Y is evidence of childhood innocence that has been lost. Unlike _____, however, I think this loss of innocence is to be read not as a tragic event but as a necessary, even helpful, stage in human development.**

Are Some Interpretations Simply Wrong?

No matter how flexible and open to debate evidence might be, not all interpretations we arrive at using that evidence are equally valid. And some interpretations are simply unsupported by that evidence. Let us illustrate.

As we noted earlier, some of our students first favored Julian over his mother. One student, let's call her Jasmine, cited as evidence a passage early in the story in which Julian is compared to Saint Sebastian, a Christian martyr who is said to have exhibited exceptional faith under extreme suffering and persecution. As the mother stood preparing for Julian to take her to her weekly swimming class, Julian is described as standing "pinned to the door frame, waiting like Saint Sebastian for the arrows to begin piercing him."

Thinking this passage proves that Julian is the more sympathetic character, Jasmine pointed to other evidence as well, including the following passage:

> [Julian] was free of prejudice and unafraid to face facts. Most miraculous of all, instead of being blinded by love for [his mother] as she was for him, he had cut himself emotionally free of her and could see her with complete objectivity. He was not dominated by his mother.

Citing passages like this in her essay, Jasmine concluded: "Julian represents the future of society, a nonracist and an educated thinker."

After rereading the story, however, and hearing other students' views, Jasmine came to realize that the passages she had cited—comparing Julian to a saint, suggesting that he is racially progressive, and that he is "free of" his mother and "objective" about her—were all intended ironically. Julian congratulates *himself* for being saint-like, free of prejudice, and objective, but the story ultimately implies that he deludes himself.

How did the supporters of the ironic reading convince Jasmine to revise her initial reading—to see it as wrong, unsupported by the evidence? First, they pointed to the glaring discrepancy between the situations and kinds of suffering endured by Julian and Saint Sebastian. Could anyone be serious, they asked, in comparing something as mundane as being forced to wait a few minutes to go to the YMCA to a martyr dying for his faith? No, they answered, and the jarring incongruity of the events being compared, they argued, suggests that Julian, far from saint-like, is presented in this passage as an impatient, ungrateful, undutiful son. In addition, students pointed out that the gap between Julian's self-image as a progressive man of "complete objectivity" and "facts," "free of [his mother]," and the blubbering young man crying "Mama, Mama!" with "guilt and sorrow" at the end of the story suggests that Julian's righteous, high-minded image of himself is not to be taken at face value.

At this point you may be wondering, How can we say that some interpretations of literature must be ruled out as *wrong*? Isn't the great thing about interpreting literary works—in contrast to scientific texts—that there are no wrong answers? Are we saying that there is one "correct" way to read a literary work—the one way the work itself tells us we "should" read it?

No, we aren't saying that there is only one way to read a literary work. If we believed there were, we would not be offering a method of literary analysis based on multiple interpretations and debate. But yes, acknowledging that literary interpretations are open to debate is not to say that a work can mean anything we want it to mean, as if all interpretations are equally good. In our view, and that of most literature teachers, some interpretations are better than others—more persuasively reasoned and better grounded in the evidence of the text.

If we maintain that all interpretations are equally valid, we risk confusing the perspective of the work's author with our own, as did the students who confused their own views on the civil rights movement of the 1960s with Flannery O'Connor's. Such misreadings are reminiscent of what we call "the closest cliché syndrome," where what's summarized is not the view the author actually expresses but a familiar cliché—or, in O'Connor's case, a certain social belief—that the writer believes and mistakenly assumes the author must too. The view that there are no wrong answers in literary interpretation encourages a kind of solipsism that erases the difference between us and others and transforms everything we encounter into a version of ourselves.

See p. 35 for more on the closest cliché syndrome.

As the literary theorist Robert Scholes puts it, reading, conceived "as a submission to the intentions of another is the first step" to understanding what a literary work is saying. For "if we do not postulate the existence of [an author] behind the verbal text," we will "simply project our own subjective modes of thought and desire upon the text." In other words, unless we do the best we can to get at what authors are saying, we will never truly recognize their ideas except as some version of our own. Scholes acknowledges that good reading often involves going beyond the author's intention, pointing out contradictions and ideological blind spots, but he argues that we must recognize the author's intention *before* we can try to see beyond it in these ways.

WHAT'S YOUR OPINION OF THE TEXT?

In accord with the principle that we must try to understand the text on its own terms before responding to it, we have thus far in this chapter focused on how to understand and unpack what literary texts say and do. Our approach to get at what they say involves looking for the central conflict in the work and then asking yourself how the author uses various types of evidence (characters, dialogue, imagery, events, plot, etc.) to guide you in thinking about that conflict. Ultimately, your job as a reader of literature is to be open to a work as its author presents it, or else your reading will fail to see what makes that work worth reading and thinking about.

But once you have reached a good understanding of the work, it is time to allow your own opinion to come into play. Offering your own interpretation of a work and opening that interpretation to response are crucial steps in any act of literary analysis, but they are not the end of the process. The final step involves offering your own insight into or critique of the work and its vision, assessing whether, as you see it, it is morally justified or questionable, unified or contradictory, historically regressive or progressive, and so forth. For example:

> Though she is one of the most respected Southern authors of the American literary canon, Flannery O'Connor continually deni-grates the one character in her 1961 story who represents the civil rights movement and in so doing disparages progressive ideas that I believe deserve a far more sympathetic hearing.

Offering a critique, however, doesn't necessarily mean finding fault:

> Some criticize O'Connor's story by suggesting that it has a politi-cally regressive agenda. But I see the story as a laudable critique of politics as such. In my view, O'Connor's story rightly criticizes the polarization of political conflicts—North vs. South, liberal vs. conservative, and the like—and suggests that they need to come together: to "converge," as O'Connor's title implies, through reli-gious love, understanding, and forgiveness.

We realize that the prospect of critiquing a literary work can be daunting. Indeed, simply stating what you think an author is saying can be intimidating, since it means going out on a limb, asserting something about highly respected figures—works that are often complex, contradictory, and connected to larger historical movements. Nevertheless, if you can master these challenges, you may find that figuring out what a literary work is saying, offering an opinion about it, and entering into conversation and debate with others about such questions is what makes literature matter. And if you do it well, what *you* say will invite its own response: your "I say" will become someone else's "they say," and the conversation will go on and on.

SEVENTEEN

"THE DATA SUGGEST"

Writing in the Sciences

CHRISTOPHER GILLEN

———⌐◲⌐———

CHARLES DARWIN DESCRIBED *On the Origin of Species* as "one long argument." In *Dialogue Concerning the Two Chief World Systems*, Galileo Galilei cast his argument for a sun-centered solar system as a series of conversations. As these historical examples show, scientific writing is fundamentally argumentative. Like all academic writers, scientists make and defend claims. They address disagreements and explore unanswered questions. They propose novel mechanisms and new theories. And they advance certain explanations and reject others. Though their vocabulary may be more technical and their emphasis more numerical, science writers use the same

———

CHRISTOPHER GILLEN is a professor of biology at Kenyon College and the faculty director of the Kenyon Institute in Biomedical and Scientific Writing. He teaches courses in animal physiology, biology of exercise, and introductory biology, all stressing the critical reading of primary research articles.

rhetorical moves as other academic writers. Consider the following example from a book about the laws of physics:

> The common refrain that is heard in elementary discussions of quantum mechanics is that a physical object is in some sense both a wave and a particle, with its wave nature apparent when you measure a wave property such as wavelength, and its particle nature apparent when you measure a particle property such as position. But this is, at best, misleading and, at worst, wrong.
>
> V. J. Stenger, *The Comprehensible Cosmos*

The "they say / I say" structure of this passage is unmistakable: they say that objects have properties of both waves and particles; I say they are wrong. This example is not a lonely argumentative passage cherry-picked from an otherwise non-argumentative text. Rather, Stenger's entire book makes the argument that is foreshadowed by its title, *The Comprehensible Cosmos*: that although some might see the universe as hopelessly complex, it is essentially understandable.

Here's another argumentative passage, this one from a research article about the role of lactic acid in muscle fatigue:

> In contrast to the often suggested role for acidosis as a cause of muscle fatigue, it is shown that in muscles where force was depressed by high $[K^+]_o$, acidification by lactic acid produced a pronounced recovery of force.
>
> O. B. Nielsen, F. de Paoli, and K. Overgaard, "Protective Effects of Lactic Acid on Force Production in Rat Skeletal Muscle," *Journal of Physiology*

In other words: many scientists think that lactic acid causes muscle fatigue, but our evidence shows that it actually promotes recovery. Notice that the authors frame their claim with a version of the "they say / I say" formula: "Although previous work suggests _____ , our data argue _____ ." This basic move and its many variations are widespread in scientific writing. The essential argumentative moves taught in this book transcend disciplines, and the sciences are no exception. The examples in this chapter were written by professional scientists, but they show moves that are appropriate in any writing that addresses scientific issues.

Despite the importance of argument in scientific writing, newcomers to the genre often see it solely as a means for communicating uncontroversial, objective facts. It's easy to see how this view arises. The objective tone of scientific writing can obscure its argumentative nature, and many textbooks reinforce a nonargumentative vision of science when they focus on accepted conclusions and ignore ongoing controversies. And because science writers base their arguments on empirical data, a good portion of many scientific texts *does* serve the purpose of delivering uncontested facts.

However, scientific writing often does more than just report facts. Data are crucial to scientific argumentation, but they are by no means the end of the story. Given important new data, scientists assess their quality, draw conclusions from them, and ponder their implications. They synthesize the new data with existing information, propose novel theories, and design the next experiments. In short, scientific progress depends on the insight and creativity that scientists bring to their data. The thrill of doing science, and writing about it, comes from the ongoing struggle to use data to better understand our world.

START WITH THE DATA

Data are the fundamental currency of scientific argument. Scientists develop hypotheses from existing data and then test those by comparing their predictions to new experimental data. Summarizing data is therefore a basic move in science writing. Because data can often be interpreted in different ways, describing the data opens the door to critical analysis, creating opportunities to critique previous interpretations and develop new ones.

Describing data requires more than simply reporting numbers and conclusions. Rather than jumping straight to the punch line—to what X concluded—it is important first to describe the hypotheses, methods, and results that led to the conclusion: "To test the hypothesis that _____, X measured _____ and found that _____. Therefore, X concluded _____." In the following sections, we explore the three key rhetorical moves for describing the data that underpin a scientific argument: presenting the prevailing theories, explaining methodologies, and summarizing findings.

Present the Prevailing Theories

Readers must understand the prevailing theories that a study responds to before they can fully appreciate the details. So before diving into specifics, place the work in context by describing the prevailing theories and hypotheses. In the following passage from a journal article about insect respiration, the authors discuss an explanation for discontinuous gas exchange (DGC), a phenomenon where insects periodically close valves on their breathing tubes:

See how a computer scientist describes a prevailing theory on p. 368.

> Lighton (1996, 1998; see also Lighton and Berrigan, 1995) noted the prevalence of DGC in fossorial insects, which inhabit microclimates where CO_2 levels may be relatively high. Consequently, Lighton proposed the chthonic hypothesis, which suggests that

DGC originated as a mechanism to improve gas exchange while at the same time minimizing respiratory water loss.

A. G. GIBBS AND R. A. JOHNSON, "The Role of Discontinuous Gas Exchange in Insects: The Chthonic Hypothesis Does Not Hold Water," *Journal of Experimental Biology*

Notice that Gibbs and Johnson not only describe Lighton's hypothesis but also recap the evidence that supports it. By presenting this evidence, Gibbs and Johnson set the stage for engaging with Lighton's ideas. For example, they might question the chthonic hypothesis by pointing out shortcomings of the data or flaws in its interpretation. Or they might suggest new approaches that could verify the hypothesis. The point is that by incorporating a discussion of experimental findings into their summary of Lighton's hypothesis, Gibbs and Johnson open the door to a conversation with Lighton.

Here are some templates for presenting the data that underpin prevailing explanations:

▶ **Experiments showing _____ and _____ have led scientists to propose _____.**

▶ **Although most scientists attribute _____ to _____, X's result _____ leads to the possibility that _____.**

Explain the Methods

Even as we've argued that scientific arguments hinge on data, it's important to note that the quality of data varies depending on how they were collected. Data obtained with sloppy techniques or poorly designed experiments could lead to faulty conclusions. Therefore, it's crucial to explain the methods used to collect data. In order for readers to evaluate a method, you'll need to indicate its purpose, as the following passage from a journal article about the evolution of bird digestive systems demonstrates:

> To test the hypothesis that flowerpiercers have converged with hummingbirds in digestive traits, we compared the activity of intestinal enzymes and the gut nominal area of cinnamon-bellied flowerpiercers (*Diglossa baritula*) with those of eleven hummingbird species.
>
> J. E. SCHONDUBE AND C. MARTINEZ DEL RIO,
> "Sugar and Protein Digestion in Flowerpiercers and
> Hummingbirds: A Comparative Test of Adaptive Convergence,"
> *Journal of Comparative Physiology*

You need to indicate purpose whether describing your own work or that of others. Here are a couple of templates for doing so:

- ▸ **Smith and colleagues evaluated _____ to determine whether _____ .**

- ▸ **Because _____ does not account for _____ , we instead used _____ .**

Summarize the Findings

Scientific data often come in the form of numbers. Your task when presenting numerical data is to provide the context readers need to understand the numbers—by giving supporting information and making comparisons. In the following passage from a book about the interaction between organisms and their environments, Turner uses numerical data to support an argument about the role of the sun's energy on Earth:

> The potential rate of energy transfer from the Sun to Earth is prodigious—about 600 W m^{-2}, averaged throughout the year. Of this, only a relatively small fraction, on the order of 1–2 percent,

is captured by green plants. The rest, if it is not reflected back into space, is available to do other things. The excess can be considerable: although some natural surfaces reflect as much as 95% of the incoming solar beam, many natural surfaces reflect much less (Table 3.2), on average about 15–20 percent. The remaining absorbed energy is then capable of doing work, like heating up surfaces, moving water and air masses around to drive weather and climate, evaporating water, and so forth.

J. S. Turner, *The Extended Organism*

Turner supports his point that a huge amount of the sun's energy is directly converted to work on Earth by quoting an actual value (600) with units of measurement (W m^{-2}, watts per square meter). Readers need the units to evaluate the value; 600 watts per square inch is very different from 600 W m^{-2}. Turner then makes comparisons using percent values, saying that only 1 to 2 percent of the total energy that reaches Earth is trapped by plants. Finally, Turner describes the data's variability by reporting comparisons as ranges—1 to 2 percent and 15 to 20 percent—rather than single values.

Supporting information—such as units of measurement, sample size (*n*), and amount of variability—helps readers assess the data. In general, the reliability of data improves as its sample size increases and its variability decreases. Supporting information can be concisely presented as:

▶ _____ ± _____ *(mean ± variability)* _____ *(units)*,
n = _____ *(sample size)*.

For example: before training, resting heart rate of the subjects was 56 ± 7 beats per minute, *n* = 12. Here's another way to give supporting information:

▸ We measured _____ (*sample size*) subjects, and the average response was _____ (*mean with units*), with a range of _____ (*lower value*) to _____ (*upper value*).

To help readers understand the data, make comparisons with values from the same study or from other similar work. Here are some templates for making comparisons:

▸ Before training, average running speed was _____ ± _____ kilometers per hour, _____ kilometers per hour slower than running speed after training.

▸ We found athletes' heart rates to be _____ ± _____ % lower than nonathletes'.

▸ The subjects in X's study completed the maze in _____ ± _____ seconds, _____ seconds slower than those in Y's study.

You will sometimes need to present qualitative data, such as that found in some images and photographs, which cannot be reduced to numbers. Qualitative data must be described precisely with words. In the passage below from a review article about connections between cellular protein localization and cell growth, the author describes the exact locations of three proteins, Scrib, Dlg, and Lgl:

> Epithelial cells accumulate different proteins on their apical (top) and basolateral (bottom) surfaces. . . . Scrib and Dlg are localized at the septate junctions along the lateral cell surface, whereas Lgl coats vesicles that are found both in the cytoplasm and "docked" at the lateral surface of the cell.

> M. PEIFER, "Travel Bulletin—Traffic Jams Cause Tumors," *Science*

EXPLAIN WHAT THE DATA MEAN

Once you summarize experiments and results, you need to say what the data mean. Consider the following passage from a study in which scientists fertilized plots of tropical rainforest with nitrogen (N) and/or phosphorus (P):

> Although our data suggest that the mechanisms driving the observed respiratory responses to increased N and P may be different, the large CO_2 losses stimulated by N and P fertilization suggest that knowledge of such patterns and their effects on soil CO_2 efflux is critical for understanding the role of tropical forests in a rapidly changing global C [carbon] cycle.
>
> C. C. CLEVELAND AND A. R. TOWNSEND, "Nutrient Additions to a Tropical Rain Forest Drive Substantial Soil Carbon Dioxide Losses to the Atmosphere,"
> *Proceedings of the National Academy of Sciences*

Notice that in discussing the implications of their data, Cleveland and Townsend use language—including the verbs "suggest" and "may be"—that denotes their level of confidence in what they say about the data.

Whether you are summarizing what others say about their data or offering your own interpretation, pay attention to the verbs that connect data to interpretations.

To signify a moderate level of confidence:

▸ **The data *suggest / hint / imply* _____ .**

To express a greater degree of certainty:

▸ **Our results *show / demonstrate* _____ .**

Almost never will you use the verb "prove" in reference to a single study, because even very powerful evidence generally falls short of proof unless other studies support the same conclusion.

Scientific consensus arises when multiple studies point toward the same conclusion; conversely, contradictions among studies often signal research questions that need further work. For these reasons, you may need to compare one study's findings to those of another study. Here, too, you'll need to choose your verbs carefully:

▶ Our data *support / confirm / verify* the work of X by showing that _____.

▶ By demonstrating _____, X's work *extends* the findings of Y.

▶ The results of X *contradict / refute* Y's conclusion that _____.

▶ X's findings *call into question* the widely accepted theory that _____.

▶ Our data *are consistent with* X's hypothesis that _____.

MAKE YOUR OWN ARGUMENTS

Now we turn toward the part of scientific writing where you express your own opinions. One challenge is that the statements of other scientists about their methods and results usually must be accepted. You probably can't argue, for example, that "X and Y claim to have studied six elephants, but I think they actually only studied four." However, it might be fair to say, "X and Y studied only six elephants, and this small sample size casts doubts on their conclusions." The second statement doesn't question what the scientists did or found but instead examines how the findings are interpreted.

When developing your own arguments—the "I say"—you will often start by assessing the interpretations of other scientists. Consider the following example from a review article about the beneficial acclimation hypothesis (BAH), the idea that organisms exposed to a particular environment become better suited to that environment than unexposed animals:

> To the surprise of most physiologists, all empirical examinations of the BAH have rejected its generality. However, we suggest that these examinations are neither direct nor complete tests of the functional benefit of acclimation.
>
> R. S. WILSON AND C. E. FRANKLIN, "Testing the Beneficial Acclimation Hypothesis," *Trends in Ecology & Evolution*

Wilson and Franklin use a version of the "twist it" move: they acknowledge the data collected by other physiologists but question how those data have been interpreted, creating an opportunity to offer their own interpretation.

For more on the "twist it" move, see p. 64.

You might ask whether we should question how other scientists interpret their own work. Having conducted a study, aren't they in the best position to evaluate it? Perhaps, but as the above example demonstrates, other scientists might see the work from a different perspective or through more objective eyes. And, in fact, the culture of science depends on vigorous debate in which scientists defend their own findings and challenge those of others—a give-and-take that helps improve science's reliability. So expressing a critical view about someone else's work is an integral part of the scientific process. Let's examine some of the basic moves for entering scientific conversations: agreeing, with a difference; disagreeing and explaining why; simultaneously agreeing and disagreeing; anticipating objections; and saying why it matters.

Agree, but with a Difference

Scientific research passes through several levels of critical analysis before being published. Scientists get feedback when they discuss work with colleagues, present findings at conferences, and receive reviews of their manuscripts. So the juiciest debates may have been resolved before publication, and you may find little to disagree with in the published literature of a research field. Yet even if you agree with what you've read, there are still ways to join the conversation—and reasons to do so.

One approach is to suggest that further work should be done:

▸ **Now that _____ has been established, scientists will likely turn their attention toward _____ .**

▸ **X's work leads to the question of _____ . Therefore, we investigated _____ .**

▸ **To see whether these findings apply to _____ , we propose to _____ .**

Another way to agree and at the same time jump into the conversation is to concur with a finding and then propose a mechanism that explains it. In the following sentence from a review article about dietary deficiencies, the author agrees with a previous finding and offers a probable explanation:

Inadequate dietary intakes of vitamins and minerals are widespread, most likely due to excessive consumption of energy-rich, micronutrient-poor, refined food.

B. AMES, "Low Micronutrient Intake
May Accelerate the Degenerative Diseases of Aging through
Allocation of Scarce Micronutrients by Triage,"
Proceedings of the National Academy of Sciences

Here are some templates for explaining an experimental result:

▸ **One explanation for X's finding of _____ is that _____.**
  An alternative explanation is _____.

▸ **The difference between _____ and _____ is probably**
  due to _____.

Disagree—and Explain Why

Although scientific consensus is common, healthy disagreement is not unusual. While measurements conducted by different teams of scientists under the same conditions should produce the same result, scientists often disagree about which techniques are most appropriate, how well an experimental design tests a hypothesis, and how results should be interpreted. To illustrate such disagreement, let's return to the debate about whether or not lactic acid is beneficial during exercise. In the following passage, Lamb and Stephenson are responding to work by Kristensen and colleagues, which argues that lactic acid might be beneficial to resting muscle but not to active muscle:

> The argument put forward by Kristensen and colleagues (12) . . .
> is not valid because it is based on observations made with isolated
> whole soleus muscles that were stimulated at such a high rate that
> >60% of the preparation would have rapidly become completely
> anoxic (4). . . . Furthermore, there is no reason to expect that adding
> more H^+ to that already being generated by the muscle activity
> should in any way be advantageous. It is a bit like opening up the
> carburetor on a car to let in too much air or throwing gasoline

over the engine and then concluding that air and gasoline are deleterious to engine performance.

G. D. Lamb and D. G. Stephenson,
"Point: Lactic Acid Accumulation Is an Advantage during
Muscle Activity," *Journal of Applied Physiology*

Lamb and Stephenson bring experimental detail to bear on their disagreement with Kristensen and colleagues. First, they criticize methodology, arguing that the high muscle stimulation rate used by Kristensen and colleagues created very low oxygen levels (anoxia). They also criticize the logic of the experimental design, arguing that adding more acid (H^+) to a muscle that is already producing it isn't informative. It's also worth noting how they drive home their point, likening Kristensen and colleagues' methodology to flooding an engine with air or gasoline. Even in technical scientific writing, you don't need to set aside your own voice completely.

In considering the work of others, look for instances where the experimental design and methodology fail to adequately test a hypothesis:

▸ **The work of Y and Z appears to show that _____, but their experimental design does not control for _____.**

Also, consider the possibility that results do not lead to the stated conclusions:

▸ **While X and Y claim that _____, their finding of _____ actually shows that _____.**

OK, But . . .

Science tends to progress incrementally. New work may refine or extend previous work but doesn't often completely overturn it.

For this reason, science writers frequently agree up to a point and then express some disagreement. In the following example from a commentary about methods for assessing how proteins interact, the authors acknowledge the value of the two-hybrid studies, but they also point out their shortcomings:

> The two-hybrid studies that produced the protein interaction map for *D. melanogaster* (12) provide a valuable genome-wide view of protein interactions but have a number of shortcomings (13). Even if the protein-protein interactions were determined with high accuracy, the resulting network would still require careful interpretation to extract its underlying biological meaning. Specifically, the map is a representation of all possible interactions, but one would only expect some fraction to be operating at any given time.
>
> J. J. Rice, A. Kershenbaum, and G. Stolovitzky,
> "Lasting Impressions: Motifs in Protein-Protein Maps
> May Provide Footprints of Evolutionary Events,"
> *Proceedings of the National Academy of Sciences*

Delineating the boundaries or limitations of a study is a good way to agree up to a point. Here are templates for doing so:

▸ While X's work clearly demonstrates _____, _____ will be required before we can determine whether _____.

▸ Although Y and Z present firm evidence for _____, their data cannot be used to argue that _____.

▸ In summary, our studies show that _____, but the issue of _____ remains unresolved.

Anticipate Objections

Skepticism is a key ingredient in the scientific process. Before an explanation is accepted, scientists demand convincing evidence and assess whether alternative explanations have been thoroughly explored, so it's essential that scientists consider possible objections to their ideas before presenting them. In the following example from a book about the origin of the universe, Tyson and Goldsmith first admit that some might doubt the existence of the poorly understood "dark matter" that physicists have proposed, and then they go on to respond to the skeptics:

> Unrelenting skeptics might compare the dark matter of today with the hypothetical, now defunct "ether," proposed centuries ago as the weightless, transparent medium through which light moved. . . . But dark matter ignorance differs fundamentally from ether ignorance. While ether amounted to a placeholder for our incomplete understanding, the existence of dark matter derives not from mere presumption but from the observed effects of its gravity on visible matter.

N. D. TYSON AND D. GOLDSMITH,
Origins: Fourteen Billion Years of Cosmic Evolution

Anticipating objections in your own writing will help you clarify and address potential criticisms. Consider objections to your overall approach, as well as to specific aspects of your interpretations. Here are some templates for doing so:

▸ **Scientists who take a _____ (*reductionist / integrative / biochemical / computational / statistical*) approach might view our results differently.**

▸ This interpretation of the data might be criticized by X, who has argued that _____.

▸ Some may argue that this experimental design fails to account for _____.

Say Why It Matters

Though individual studies can be narrowly focused, science ultimately seeks to answer big questions and produce useful technologies. So it's essential when you enter a scientific conversation to say why the work—and your arguments about it—matter. The following passage from a commentary on a research article notes two implications of work that evaluated the shape of electron orbitals:

> The classic textbook shape of electron orbitals has now been directly observed. As well as confirming the established theory, this work may be a first step to understanding high-temperature superconductivity.
>
> C. J. HUMPHREYS, "Electrons Seen in Orbit," *Nature*

Humphreys argues that the study confirms an established theory and that it may lead to better understanding in another area. When thinking about the broad significance of a study, consider both the practical applications and the impact on future scientific work:

▸ These results open the door to studies that _____.

▸ The methodologies developed by X will be useful for _____.

▸ Our findings are the first step toward _____.

▸ **Further work in this area may lead to the development of**
   _____ .

READING AS A WAY OF ENTERING
SCIENTIFIC CONVERSATIONS

In science, as in other disciplines, you'll often start with work done by others, and therefore you will need to critically evaluate their work. To that end, you'll need to probe how well their data support their interpretations. Doing so will lead you toward your own interpretations—your ticket into an ongoing scientific conversation. Here are some questions that will help you read and respond to scientific research:

How well do the methods test the hypothesis?

- Is the sample size adequate?

- Is the experimental design valid? Were the proper controls performed?

- What are the limitations of the methodology?

- Are other techniques available?

How fairly have the results been interpreted?

- How well do the results support the stated conclusion?

- Has the data's variability been adequately considered?

- Do other findings verify (or contradict) the conclusion?

- What other experiments could test the conclusion?

What are the broader implications of the work, and why does it matter?

- Can the results be generalized beyond the system that was studied?

- What are the work's practical implications?

- What questions arise from the work?

- Which experiments should be done next?

The examples in this chapter show that scientists do more than simply collect facts; they also interpret those facts and make arguments about their meaning. On the frontiers of science, where we are probing questions that are just beyond our capacity to answer, the data are inevitably incomplete and controversy is to be expected. Writing about science presents the opportunity to add your own arguments to the ongoing discussion.

EIGHTEEN

"ANALYZE THIS"

Writing in the Social Sciences

ERIN ACKERMAN

SOCIAL SCIENCE is the study of people—how they behave and relate to one another, and the organizations and institutions that facilitate these interactions. People are complicated, so any study of human behavior is at best partial, taking into account some elements of what people do and why, but not always explaining those actions definitively. As a result, it is the subject of constant conversation and argument.

Consider some of the topics studied in the social sciences: minimum wage laws, immigration policy, health care, what causes aggressive behavior, employment discrimination. Got an opinion on any of these topics? You aren't alone. But in the writing you do as a student of the social sciences, you need to write about more

ERIN ACKERMAN is the social sciences librarian at the College of New Jersey and formerly taught political science at John Jay College, City University of New York. Her research and teaching interests include American law and politics, women and law, and information literacy in the social sciences.

than just your opinions. Good writing in the social sciences, as in other academic disciplines, requires that you demonstrate that you have examined what you think and why. The best way to do that is to bring your views into conversation with those expressed by others and to test what you and others think against a review of evidence. In other words, you'll need to start with what others say and then present what you say as a response.

Consider the following example from an op-ed in the *New York Times* by two psychology professors:

> Is video game addiction a real thing?
>
> It's certainly common to hear parents complain that their children are "addicted" to video games. Some researchers even claim that these games are comparable to illegal drugs in terms of their influence on the brain—that they are "digital heroin" (the neuroscientist Peter C. Whybrow) or "digital pharmakeia" (the neuroscientist Andrew Doan). The American Psychiatric Association has identified internet gaming disorder as a possible psychiatric illness, and the World Health Organization has proposed including "gaming disorder" in its catalog of mental diseases, along with drug and alcohol addiction.
>
> This is all terribly misguided. Playing video games is not addictive in any meaningful sense. It is normal behavior that, while perhaps in many cases a waste of time, is not damaging or disruptive of lives in the way drug or alcohol use can be.
>
> Christopher J. Ferguson and Patrick Markey,
"Video Games Aren't Addictive"

In other words, "they" (parents, other researchers, health organizations) say that the video games are addictive, whereas Ferguson and Markey disagree. In the rest of the op-ed, they argue that video game critics have misinterpreted the evidence and are not being very precise with what counts as "addiction."

This chapter explores some of the basic moves social science writers make. Writing in the social sciences often takes the form of a research paper that generally includes several core components: a strong introduction and thesis, a literature review, and the writer's own analysis, including presentation of evidence/data and consideration of implications. The introduction sets out the thesis, or point, of the paper, briefly explaining the topic or question you are investigating and previewing what you will say in your paper and how it fits into the preexisting conversation. The literature review summarizes what has already been said on your topic. Your analysis allows you to present evidence (the information, or data, about human behavior that you are measuring or testing against what other people have said), to explain the conclusions you have drawn based on your investigation, and to discuss the implications of your research. Do you agree, disagree, or some combination of both with what has been said by others? What reasons can you give for why you feel that way? And so what? Who should be interested in what you have to say, and why?

You may get other types of writing assignments in the social sciences, such as preparing a policy memo, writing a legal brief, or designing a grant or research proposal. While there may be differences from the research papers in terms of the format and audience for these assignments, the purposes of sections of the research paper and the moves discussed here will help you with those assignments as well.

THE INTRODUCTION AND THESIS: "THIS PAPER CHALLENGES . . ."

Your introduction sets forth what you plan to say in your essay. You might evaluate the work of earlier scholars or certain widely held assumptions and find them incorrect when measured against new events or data. Alternatively, you might point out that an author's work is largely correct but that it could use some qualifications or be extended in some way. Or you might identify a gap in our knowledge—we know a great deal about topic X but almost nothing about some other closely related topic. In each of these instances, your introduction needs to cover both "they say" and "I say" perspectives. If you stop after the "they say," your readers won't know what you are bringing to the conversation. Similarly, if you were to jump right to the "I say" portion of your argument, readers might wonder why you need to say anything at all.

Sometimes you join the conversation at a point where the discussion seems settled. One or more views about a topic have become so widely accepted among a group of scholars or society at large that these views are essentially the conventional way of thinking about the topic. You may wish to offer new reasons to support this interpretation, or you may wish to call these standard views into question. To do so, you must first introduce and iden-tify these widely held beliefs and then present your own view. In fact, much of the writing in the social sciences takes the form of calling into question that which we think we already know. Consider the following example from an article in the *Journal of Economic Perspectives*:

Fifteen years ago, Milton Friedman's 1957 treatise *A Theory of the Consumption Function* seemed badly dated. Dynamic optimization theory had not been employed much in economics when Friedman wrote, and utility theory was still comparatively primitive, so his statement of the "permanent income hypothesis" never actually specified a formal mathematical model of behavior derived explicitly from utility maximization. . . . [W]hen other economists subsequently found multiperiod maximizing models that could be solved explicitly, the implications of those models differed sharply from Friedman's intuitive description of his "model." Furthermore, empirical tests in the 1970s and 1980s often rejected these rigorous versions of the permanent income hypothesis in favor of an alternative hypothesis that many households simply spent all of their current income.

Today, with the benefit of a further round of mathematical (and computational) advances, Friedman's (1957) original analysis looks more prescient than primitive.

> CHRISTOPHER D. CARROLL, "A Theory of Consumption
> Function, with and without Liquidity Constraints,"
> *Journal of Economic Perspectives*

This introduction makes clear that Carroll will defend Milton Friedman against some major criticisms of his work. Carroll mentions what has been said about Friedman's work and then goes on to say that the critiques turn out to be wrong and to suggest that Friedman's work reemerges as persuasive. A template of Carroll's introduction might look something like this: "Economics research in the last fifteen years suggested Friedman's 1957 treatise was _____ because _____. In other words, they say that Friedman's work is not accurate because of _____, _____, and _____. Recent research convinces me, however, that Friedman's work makes sense."

In some cases, however, there may not be a strong consensus among experts on a topic. You might enter the ongoing debate by casting your vote with one side or another or by offering an alternative view. In the following example, Sheri Berman identifies two competing accounts of how to explain world events in the twentieth century and then puts forth a third view:

Conventional wisdom about twentieth-century ideologies rests on two simple narratives. One focuses on the struggle for dominance between democracy and its alternatives. . . . The other narrative focuses on the competition between free-market capitalism and its rivals. . . . Both of these narratives obviously contain some truth. . . . Yet both only tell part of the story, which is why their common conclusion—neoliberalism as the "end of History"—is unsatisfying and misleading.

What the two conventional narratives fail to mention is that a third struggle was also going on: between those ideologies that believed in the primacy of economics and those that believed in the primacy of politics.

SHERI BERMAN, "The Primacy of Economics versus the Primacy of Politics: Understanding the Ideological Dynamics of the Twentieth Century," *Perspectives on Politics*

After identifying the two competing narratives, Berman suggests a third view—and later goes on to argue that this third view explains current debates over globalization. A template for this type of introduction might look something like this: "In recent discussions of _____, a controversial aspect has been _____. On the one hand, some argue that _____. On the other hand, others argue that _____. Neither of these arguments, however, considers the alternative view that _____."

Given the complexity of many of the issues studied in the social sciences, however, you may sometimes agree *and* disagree with existing views—pointing out things that you believe are correct or have merit, while disagreeing with or refining other points. In the example below, anthropologist Sally Engle Merry agrees with another scholar about something that is a key trait of modern society but argues that this trait has a different origin than the other author identifies:

For more on different ways of responding, see Chapter 4.

Although I agree with Rose that an increasing emphasis on governing the soul is characteristic of modern society, I see the transformation not as evolutionary but as the product of social mobilization and political struggle.

> SALLY ENGLE MERRY, "Rights, Religion, and Community:
> Approaches to Violence against Women in the
> Context of Globalization," *Law and Society Review*

Here are some templates for agreeing and disagreeing:

▸ **Although I agree with X up to a point, I cannot accept his overall conclusion that _____ .**

▸ **Although I disagree with X on _____ and _____ , I agree with her conclusion that _____ .**

▸ **Political scientists studying _____ have argued that it is caused by _____ . While _____ contributes to the problem, _____ is also an important factor.**

▸ **While noting _____ , I contend _____ .**

In the process of examining people from different angles, social scientists sometimes identify gaps—areas that have not been explored in previous research.

In the following example, several sociologists identify such a gap:

Family scholars have long argued that the study of dating deserves more attention (Klemer, 1971), as dating is an important part of the life course at any age and often a precursor to marriage (Levesque & Caron, 2004). . . .

The central research questions we seek to answer with this study are whether and how the significance of particular dating rituals are patterned by gender and race simultaneously. We use a racially diverse data set of traditional-aged college students from a variety of college contexts. Understanding gender and racial differences in the assessment of dating rituals helps us explore the extent to which relationship activities are given similar importance across institutional and cultural lines. Most of the studies that inform our knowledge of dating and relationships are unable to draw conclusions regarding racial differences because the sample is Caucasian (e.g., Bogle, 2008), or primarily so (e.g., Manning & Smock, 2005). Race has been recently argued to be an often-overlooked variable in studies examining social psychological processes because of the prevalence of sample limitations as well as habitual oversight in the literature (Hunt, Jackson, Powell, & Steelman, 2000). Additionally, a failure to examine both gender and race prevents assessment of whether gendered beliefs are shared across groups. Gauging the extent of differences in beliefs among different population subgroups is critical to advancing the study of relationship dynamics (see Weaver & Ganong, 2004).

PAMELA BRABOY JACKSON, SIBYL KLEINER,
CLAUDIA GEIST, AND KARA CEBULKO, "Conventions of Courtship:
Gender and Race Differences in the Significance of Dating Rituals,"
Journal of Family Issues

Jackson and her coauthors note that while other scholars have said that studying dating is important and have examined some aspects of dating, we have little information about whether attitudes about dating activities (such as sexual intimacy, gift exchange, and meeting the family) vary across groups by gender and race. Their study aims to fill this gap in our understanding of relationships.

Here are some templates for introducing gaps in the existing research:

▸ **Studies of X have indicated _____ . It is not clear, however, that this conclusion applies to _____ .**

▸ **_____ often take for granted that _____ . Few have investigated this assumption, however.**

▸ **X's work tells us a great deal about _____ . Can this work be generalized to _____ ?**

▸ **Our understanding of _____ remains incomplete because previous work has not examined _____ .**

Again, a good introduction indicates what you have to say in the larger context of what others have said. Throughout the rest of your paper, you will move back and forth between the "they say" and the "I say," adding more details.

THE LITERATURE REVIEW:
"PRIOR RESEARCH INDICATES . . ."

The point of a literature review is to establish the state of knowledge on your topic. Before you (and your reader) can properly consider an issue, you need to understand the conversation about your topic that has already taken place (and is likely still in progress). In the literature review, you explain what "they say" in more detail, summarizing, paraphrasing, or quoting the viewpoints to which you are responding. But you need to balance what they are saying with your own focus. You need to characterize someone else's work fairly and accurately but set up the points you yourself want to make by selecting the details that are relevant to your own perspective and observations.

It is common in the social sciences to summarize several arguments in a single paragraph or even a single sentence, grouping several sources together by their important ideas or other attributes. The example below cites some key findings and conclusions of psychological research that should be of interest to motivated college students looking to improve their academic performance:

> Some people may associate sacrificing hours of sleep with being studious, but the reality is that sleep deprivation can hurt your cognitive functioning without your being aware of it (e.g., becoming worse at paying attention and remembering things; Goel, Rao, Durmer, & Dinges, 2009; Pilcher & Walters, 1997).... Sleep affects learning and memory by organizing and consolidating memories from the day (Diekelmann & Born, 2010; Rasch & Born, 2013), which can lead to better problem-solving ability and creativity (Verleger, Rose, Wagner, Yordanova, & Kolev, 2013).
>
> ADAM L. PUTNAM, VICTOR W. SUNGKHASETTEE, AND
> HENRY L. ROEDIGER, III, "Optimizing Learning in College:
> Tips from Cognitive Psychology," *Perspectives on
> Psychological Science*

A template for this paragraph might look like this: "Students believe _____, but researchers disagree because _____. According to researchers, negative consequences of sleep deprivation include _____. The research shows that a positive effect of sleep is _____, which improves _____."

Such summaries are brief, bringing together relevant arguments by several scholars to provide an overview of scholarly work on a particular topic. In writing such a summary, you need to ask yourself how the authors themselves might describe their positions and also consider what in their work is relevant for the point you wish to make. This kind of summary is especially appropriate when you have a large amount of research material on a topic and want to identify the major strands of a debate or to show how the work of one author builds on that of another. Here are some templates for overview summaries:

▸ In addressing the question of _____, researchers have considered several explanations for _____. X argues that _____. According to Y and Z, another plausible explanation is _____.

▸ What is the effect of _____ on _____? Previous work on _____ by X and by Y and Z supports _____.

▸ Scholars point to the role of _____ in _____.

▸ Existing research on _____ presents convincing evidence of _____.

Sometimes you may need to say more about the works you cite. On a midterm or final exam, for example, you may need to demonstrate that you have a deep familiarity with a particular work. And in some disciplines of the social sciences, longer, more detailed literature reviews are the standard. Your instructor and any assigned articles are your best guides for the length and level of detail of your literature review. Other times, the work of certain authors is especially important for your argument, and therefore you need to provide more details to explain what these authors have said. See how political scientists Hahrie Han and Lisa Argyle, in a report for the Ford Foundation, summarize an argument that is central to their investigation of improving democratic participation:

> [A]t the root of declining rates of participation is the sense that people do not feel like their participation matters. People do not feel like they have any real reason or opportunity to exercise voice in the political process. People's sense of agency is in decline, especially given negative or incomplete experiences of government in their lives.
>
> This lack of caring comes as no surprise when we examine research showing that most people have negative or, at best, incomplete experiences of the role of government in their lives. Suzanne Mettler, for instance, finds that many middle-class people who benefit from different government programs—ranging from education savings accounts to welfare to tax credits—believe that they "have not used a government social program." In addition, other scholars find a trend towards increasing privatization of public goods and political processes in the twenty-first century. As a result, government is what Mettler calls a "submerged state," since the role of government in people's lives is effectively submerged from view.
>
> HAHRIE HAN AND LISA ARGYLE, "A Program Review of the Promoting Electoral Reform and Democratic Participation (PERDP) Initiative of the Ford Foundation"

Note that Han and Argyle start by identifying the broad problem of lack of participation and then explain how Mettler's work describes how middle-class people may be unaware of the role of government in their lives, leading Mettler to argue for the idea of the "submerged state."

You may want to include direct quotations of what others have said, as Han and Argyle do. Using exact words helps you demonstrate that you are representing the author fairly. But you cannot simply insert a quotation; you need to explain to your readers what it means for your point. Consider the following example drawn from a political science book on the debate over tort reform:

> The essence of *agenda setting* was well enunciated by E. E. Schattschneider: "In politics as in everything else, it makes a great difference whose game we play" (1960, 47). In short, the ability to define or control the rules, terms, or perceived options in a contest over policy greatly affects the prospects for winning.
>
> WILLIAM HALTOM AND MICHAEL MCCANN,
Distorting the Law: Politics, Media, and the Litigation Crisis

Notice how Haltom and McCann first quote Schattschneider and then explain in their own words how political agenda setting can be thought of as a game, with winners and losers.

Remember that whenever you summarize, quote, or paraphrase the work of others, credit must be given in the form of a citation to the original work. The words may be your own, but if the idea comes from someone else you must give credit to the original work. There are several formats for documenting sources. Consult your instructor for help choosing which citation style to use.

THE ANALYSIS

The literature review covers what others have said on your topic. The analysis allows you to present and support your own response. In the introduction you indicate whether you agree, disagree, or some combination of both with what others have said. You will want to expand on how you have formed your opinion and why others should care about your topic.

"The Data Indicate . . ."

The social sciences use evidence to develop and test explanations. This evidence is often referred to as data. Data can be quantitative or qualitative and can come from a number of sources. You might use statistics related to GDP growth, unemployment, voting rates, or demographics. You might report results from an experiment or simulation. Or you could use surveys, interviews, or other first-person accounts.

Regardless of the type of data used, it is important to do three things: define your data, indicate where you got the data, and then say what you have done with your data. For a chapter in their book assessing media coverage of female candidates, political scientists Danny Hayes and Jennifer Lawless explain how they assembled a data set:

> From the perspective of campaign professionals and voters, local newspaper coverage remains the most important news source during House campaigns....
>
> We began by selecting the appropriate newspaper for each House race in 2010 and 2014.... [W]e identified every news story during the thirty days leading up to the election that mentioned at least one of the two major-party candidates....
>
> Our data collection efforts produced 10,375 stories about 1,550 candidates who received at least some local news coverage in either the 2010 or 2014 midterms....
>
> Coders read the full text of each article and recorded several pieces of information. First, they tracked the number of times a candidate's sex or gender was mentioned.... Second, we recorded the number of explicit references to candidate traits, both positive and negative (e.g., "capable" and "ineffective")....
>
> Third, we tracked every time an issue was mentioned in connection with a candidate.... We then classified issues in two ways:

(1) We assigned each issue to one of the eight broad categories...
and (2) we classified a subset of the topics as "women's" or "men's"
issues.

> Danny Hayes and Jennifer L. Lawless, *Women on the Run:*
> *Gender, Media, and Political Campaigns in a Polarized Era*

Hayes and Lawless explain how they collected their data—local
newspaper coverage of congressional candidates—and explain
how they coded and classified the coverage to allow them to
perform statistical analysis of the news pieces. While you probably won't collect 10,000-plus news items for a class project, you
could collect information (such as media coverage, interview
responses, or legal briefs) and analyze and sort them to identify
patterns such as repeated words and ideas.

If your data are quantitative, you also need to explain
them. Sociologist Jonathan Horowitz's research concludes
that job quality influences personal assessments of well-being
by "improving social life, altering class identification, affecting
physical health, and increasing amounts of leisure time." See
how he introduces the data he analyzes:

> In this study, I use data from the General Social Survey (GSS) and
> structural equation modeling to test relationships between job qual-
> ity and subjective well-being. The GSS is a nationally representative
> sample of adults in the United States that asks a large number of
> questions about experiences at work (Smith et al., 2010). In particu-
> lar, the GSS introduced a new battery of questions titled "Quality
> of Working Life" in 2002 (and repeated in 2006 and 2010) which
> includes multiple questions about several job quality dimensions.
>
> > Jonathan Horowitz, "Dimensions of Job Quality,
> > Mechanisms, and Subjective Well-Being in the United States,"
> > *Sociological Forum*

Here are some templates for discussing data:

▸ **In order to test the hypothesis that _____, we assessed _____. Our calculations suggest _____.**

▸ **I used _____ to investigate _____. The results of this investigation indicate _____.**

"But Others May Object . . ."

No matter how strongly your data support your argument, there are almost surely other perspectives (and thus other data) that you need to acknowledge. By considering possible objections to your argument and taking them seriously, you demonstrate that you've done your work and that you're aware of other perspectives—and most important, you present your own argument as part of an ongoing conversation.

See p. 330 for a selection from *The New Jim Crow*. See how law professor Michelle Alexander acknowledges that there may be objections to her argument describing trends in mass incarceration as the "New Jim Crow."

> Some might argue that as disturbing as this system appears to be, there is nothing particularly new about mass incarceration; it is merely a continuation of past drug wars and biased law enforcement practices. Racial bias in our criminal justice system is simply an old problem that has gotten worse, and the social excommunication of "criminals" has a long history; it is not a recent invention. There is some merit to this argument.
>
> MICHELLE ALEXANDER, *The New Jim Crow: Mass Incarceration in the Age of Colorblindness*

Alexander imagines a conversation with people who might be skeptical about her argument, particularly her claim that this represents a "new" development. And she responds that they are correct, to a point. After acknowledging her agreement with the assessment of historical racial bias in the criminal justice system, she goes on in the rest of her chapter to explain that the expanded scope and consequences of contemporary mass incarceration have caused dramatic differences in society.

Someone may object because there are related phenomena that your analysis does not explain or because you do not have the right data to investigate a particular question. Or perhaps someone may object to assumptions underlying your argument or how you handled your data. Here are some templates for considering naysayers:

▸ _____ might object that _____.

▸ Is my claim realistic? I have argued _____, but readers may question _____.

▸ My explanation accounts for _____ but does not explain _____. This is because _____.

"Why Should We Care?"

Who should care about your research, and why? Since the social sciences attempt to explain human behavior, it is important to consider how your research affects the assumptions we make about human behavior. In addition, you might offer recommendations for how other social scientists might continue to explore an issue, or what actions policy makers should take.

In the following example, sociologist Devah Pager identifies the implications of her study of the way having a criminal record affects a person applying for jobs:

> [I]n terms of policy implications, this research has troubling conclusions. In our frenzy of locking people up, our "crime control"

policies may in fact exacerbate the very conditions that lead to crime in the first place. Research consistently shows that finding quality steady employment is one of the strongest predictors of desistance from crime (Shover 1996; Sampson & Laub 1993; Uggen 2000). The fact that a criminal record severely limits employment opportunities—particularly among blacks—suggests that these individuals are left with few viable alternatives.

> DEVAH PAGER, "The Mark of a Criminal Record,"
> *American Journal of Sociology*

Pager's conclusion that a criminal record negatively affects employment chances creates a vicious circle, she says: steady employment discourages recidivism, but a criminal record makes it harder to get a job.

In answering the "so what?" question, you need to explain why your readers should care. Although sometimes the implications of your work may be so broad that they would be of interest to almost anyone, it's never a bad idea to identify explicitly any groups of people who will find your work important.

Templates for establishing why your claims matter:

▸ **X is important because** _____ .

▸ **Ultimately, what is at stake here is** _____ .

▸ **The finding that** _____ **should be of interest to** _____ **because** _____ .

As noted at the beginning of this chapter, the complexity of people allows us to look at their behavior from many different viewpoints. Much has been, and will be, said about how and why people do the things they do. As a result, we can look at writing in the social sciences as an ongoing conversation. When you join this conversation, the "they say / I say" framework will help you figure out what has already been said ("they say") and what you can add ("I say"). The components of social science writing presented in this chapter are tools to help you join that conversation.

NINETEEN

"HELP ME UNDERSTAND…"

When Your "They Say" Is a Bot

—◻—

A COLLEAGUE OF ours recently asked us how generative AI tools like ChatGPT can be used with this textbook—how, that is, they can help students make the signature move of the academic world: entering into conversation or debate with what "they say." It was a good question, and we didn't have an immediate answer. After giving it some thought, however, and working more closely with these new technologies, we realized that an answer was needed. The result is this chapter. While these supersmart chatbots are sometimes thought of as a conversational search engine, we show how, if used responsibly, they can help you make the kinds of analytic, argumentative moves that this book addresses, and so, in this chapter, we provide model prompts or templates for moving chatbots in this "they say / I say" direction, as in:

▸ **I am writing an essay in which I want to argue _____ and could use some help thinking through my argument. Can you help me identify who says or might say otherwise—what views my own argument might be seen as a response to?**

But before saying more about using generative AI tools in the service of this kind of academic critical thinking, we need to address some basic points about how to use them responsibly.

Most important, your instructor likely has a policy on the use of chatbots, so be sure to read your course syllabus carefully and check with your instructor if you're in any doubt. And don't be surprised if your instructor asks you not only to follow citation guidelines but also to submit a transcript or record of any interactions you had with generative AI in writing your paper so that your work with the technology can be assessed as part of the final written product. You may also be asked to do more in-class writing, in part to give your instructor a sense of your unique style and concerns as a writer but also to provide a benchmark against which any take-home writing assignments can be compared. Along similar lines, you may also be asked to draw more on personal experiences in your writing and in class discussions, which can help reassure readers that you're the one who wrote your paper and not some distant machine technology. See Chapter 7, "In My Experience."

REVEAL, DON'T CONCEAL

It's hard to explain the sheer excitement of using these new generative AI tools to anyone who hasn't yet used them. These programs rely on Large Language Models (LLMs)—predictive engines—that draw on gigantic storehouses of data and are often described as having learned from these datasets how to respond to human prompts and questions in literate, grammatical (even polite!) language. When we first tried our hand at these chatbots, we kept saying things like "Wow," and "Look at this! Did you know that these bots can _____?" Not only do chatbots draw on enormous swaths of data and produce coherent, logical writing but they also do all this in a matter of mere seconds, answering the prompts you give them in real time and thus creating the illusion of real, human-to-human conversation. Furthering this illusion, these advanced technologies have the capacity to remember what you said in earlier parts of the conversation, meaning that you can develop a powerful train of thought with them over time, and keep directing and redirecting them in the direction you want.

Is it any wonder then, that worldwide debates are raging about whether and how generative AI should be regulated—including in the domain of education? After all, as you probably already know, it can be very tempting for students to turn in an AI-generated text as their own, to simply change a word or two and put their name on it. But the central message we want to offer on this topic is: *don't.* It's no more acceptable to submit the work of a bot as your own than it is to submit the work of another person as your own. Ultimately, plagiarizing is not only a way of cheating the academic system but also of cheating yourself, since it denies you the chance to develop the independent intellectual skills that you go to college to learn.

That having been said, there may be occasions when you find chatbots helpful in your writing process—if, that is, your instructor allows it, and if, as our section heading suggests, you reveal rather than conceal that you are doing so, giving credit where credit is due by following documentation guidelines, which we summarize in an appendix at the back of this book ("Citing What 'They Say'").

A good rule of thumb, then, is to be transparent in your use of generative AI, citing it as you would any other source or collaborator, as in:

▸ **When asked why _____, ChatGPT responded, "_____."**

In addition, to show that you played a significantly active role directing or prompting the bot, you might write:

▸ **Working collaboratively with BARD over a series of twenty prompts (see** this link **to the transcript of these exchanges), the bot and I came up with the following interpretation: "_____."**

▸ **After a series of prompts (see the chat history in my Works Cited page), BING was able to explain the concept clearly: "_____."**

To quote a chatbot's answers, you may want to consult not only our appendix on citation but also Chapter 3, "The Art of Quoting." And though it could go without saying, you may also want to avoid sharing significant quantities of original writing with today's chatbots, which are owned by private corporations that are free to do almost whatever they want with information they collect on us.

FACT OR FICTION?

In addition to exercising caution uploading your original writing to any AI tool, caution is called for when using chatbots as sources you quote, because they are prone to what are commonly called "hallucinations" in which they fabricate (or "hallucinate") facts. Anyone who has ever worked with these technologies can see pretty quickly that they not only make factual errors but also do so in such a convincingly authoritative tone that these errors can be easy to miss.

Consider what happened when a first-year student at the State University of New York was using a chatbot to investigate the role of masculinity in the Spider Man movies, and the bot she was using wrote at great length about an article by T. Sasson (2018). At one point, for instance, it wrote:

> According to Sasson (2018), Parker's journey exemplifies the exploration of masculinity within a coming-of-age narrative, showcasing the complexities of growing up amid traditional gender expectations.

Looks to us like a sound piece of writing. The chatbot even provided a Works Cited list indicating that the essay by T. Sasson was published in the edited collection *Marvel Comics into Film: Essays on Adaptations Since the 1940s*. So all's well and good—right? The problem, however, is that, while this edited collection *does* exist—look out!—it does *not* include an essay by T. Sasson. Furthermore, T. Sasson, the supposed author, doesn't exist either! Despite its reassuringly confident tone, the bot fabricated the reference out of whole cloth.

Along similar lines, consider what happened when, prompted by this student's experience, we decided to conduct a little test by having a conversation ourselves with ChatGPT about the Spider Man movies. The conversation started out swimmingly and lasted for several days, most of it centering around an article that the bot referenced by the former *New York Times* film critic, A. O. Scott. But at the end of the exchange, when we asked the bot for a link to Scott's article so that we could read it ourselves, the bot reported matter of factly that there was no such article, that it had merely imagined what Scott "might" have written. Shocked, and a little annoyed, we typed: "But *you* were the one who told us about the article; you've been discussing it with us for hours; and, instead of using phrases like, "Scott might have said . . ." or "might have argued . . . ," you wrote, "Scott insists . . ." and "Scott appreciates . . ." or ". . . claims." GPT's response? To apologize, but simply to reiterate what it had said before: that it had been referring to "a hypothetical" article Scott could have written "based on his concerns and general outlook."

The two of us were just experimenting, of course. But a mistake like this for a student fulfilling an assignment, or someone in the world of work, journalism, or politics, say, can have serious consequences. As our sister-in-law who works for a not-for-profit company explains, while chatbots "offer increased productivity, they have their risks—like hallucinations" (Carolyn Kahn Birkenstein, The MITRE Corporation).

VERIFY, VERIFY, VERIFY

As these examples demonstrate, AI-generated writing requires critical scrutiny and investigation on your part. The lateral reading or fact-checking tips we describe in Chapter 15 can help you with this. By leaving the program momentarily and searching online, you can confirm or disconfirm the veracity of any sources—or any examples, statistics, quotations, summaries, and so forth—that a chatbot provides.

So beware. Even if a source your chatbot refers to does exist, you can't always be sure that the bot accurately represents what that source says. Most of the time, it seems to us, chatbots do a good, even brilliant, job of summarizing what others say. You just never know in advance when they will present a summary that is just plain wrong or will cite a source that doesn't exist. Chatbots often misrepresent and misquote sources, which explains why it's a serious problem when we rely on what they say about an assigned text, without bothering to read it.

Imagine, for instance, what would happen if you were to rely on the following claims made by ChatGPT about Kenneth Goldsmith's article, "Go Ahead, Waste Time on the Internet." See pp. 361–65. When asked for a summary of Goldsmith's central argument, the bot explained that Goldsmith

> posits that aimless drifting on the internet can be a creative act, drawing parallels to older forms of "wasting time" such as daydreaming or doodling, which have been recognized as sources of creativity.

Sounds plausible enough, perhaps—but not if you've actually *read* Goldsmith's article. Goldsmith does not defend "wasting time" on the internet. And he never mentions any of the examples that the bot identified like "drifting" online, or other overtly unproductive activities like "daydreaming or doodling." His title, in fact, encouraging us to "Go ahead" and "waste time on the internet" is ironic, suggesting not that we should actually waste time on the internet, but that activities often *deemed* to be wasteful—such as reading online and making social plans—are in fact edifying and productive. The only way to avoid repeating this kind of AI-generated misrepresentation is by engaging in the hard, often time-consuming work of reading every text you're writing about and double-checking everything, even tracking down material, if need be, in a library database. Your instructor will hold you responsible for your writing, so it's up to you to detect and remove any problems, which can only be done by developing a solid understanding of the sources and data you're dealing with.

Often, your understanding of these sources needs to be more than solid. It needs to be granular. For instance, when we were working with a chatbot on a project involving Gerald's essay, "Hidden Intellectualism" (see page 309), the LLM quoted Gerald as having written:

> [N]o necessary connection has ever been shown between what goes on in the street and what goes on in the school. . . .

But Gerald never wrote that sentence, which, if you think about it, makes no sense. Instead, he'd written:

> [N]o necessary connection has ever been established between any text or subject and the educational depth and weight of the discussion it can generate. (607)

We were able to spot this easily overlooked misquotation right away because Gerald is the author and we're therefore on intimate terms with his text. ChatGPT was quick once again to apologize for its mistake, but the experience made us even more vigilant than ever to double-check everything chatbots say, no matter how authoritatively they say it.

The experience also led us to rethink the claim one sometimes hears today that, were internet access to become universal, chatbots will have the capacity to democratize education by serving as a personal "tutor" or "mentor" to virtually every student.

Given how error-prone these technologies can be (and of course they may improve drastically in the near future), ceding full control to them is always a big mistake. Students themselves need to take the lead, mentoring, directing, and often even correcting the chatbots themselves, engaging with the technology in a complex collaboration in which the mentee becomes the final authority or mentor.

AI FOR ACADEMIC ARGUMENT

But problems with chatbots are only part of the story. There's also the vast potential of these technologies to help us improve as writers and thinkers. Despite having access to gigantic swaths of information (no matter how faulty that information can sometimes be), these sophisticated bots can also help you overcome that dreaded feeling of writer's block, and keep you company during a long slog of writing, breaking through the isolation of the writing process and offering stimulating feedback that can sharpen your focus—even at 2 o'clock, if it suits you, in the morning. Furthermore, as we'd now like to show, and as we suggested earlier, these technologies can also help you make what this book presents as the most important move of academic critical thinking: summarizing and responding to what "they say."

How to get chatbots to do this, however, is not immediately apparent. While there's a wealth of advice out there on how to prompt or direct such programs (a practice often referred to as "prompt engineering"), there isn't much advice on how to use them to summarize and respond to other perspectives. And part of this has to do with the nature of chatbots themselves. After all, these bots "do not," as ChatGPT tells us, "have opinions," and are instead "designed to be neutral tools." As BING explains, "I am not allowed to express subjective opinions on controversial or sensitive topics." As a result, you cannot engage with a bot in the same way you would with a noted scholar such as Michelle Alexander or a newspaper opinion writer. As they describe themselves, at least, these programs are "neutral" and, as BING puts it, "objective" tools that remain above the fray of controversies and debates (though as you may discover, because bots draw from what's readily available online, they often reproduce the biases of mainstream media).

But there are ways to prompt or guide these technologies in a dialogical, "they say / I say" direction. For one thing, despite their claims of neutrality and objectivity, chatbots do sometimes misinterpret texts, as we saw earlier, so you can argue with them within limits:

▸ **Although ChatGPT claimed that Kenneth Goldsmith argues _____, what he actually argues, on the contrary, is that _____ .**

For another thing, to the extent that chatbots don't take positions themselves, they can help you understand positions others take, your own position, and the relationship between them.

For instance, to get help understanding someone else's position—a particularly challenging reading or "they say" you've been assigned—you might write:

▸ **What does X mean when she writes, "_____"? In making this claim, is X being sincere or sarcastic?**

▸ **Author X often refers approvingly to the theory _____ . Can you explain in simple terms what that theory is?**

▸ **X often uses the term _____ . What does it mean?**

Along similar lines, to understand how an author's position fits into a larger debate or conversation, you might write something like the following:

▸ **X's argument is that _____ . Please identify another writer who names X and either critiques or builds on X's perspective.**

▸ **X's argument is that _____. Please identify another writer who doesn't name X but nevertheless offers a contrary perspective.**

And a template like the following can help with answering the "so what?" and "who cares?" questions:

▸ **A classmate who read a draft of my essay in which I argue _____ said, "Your argument is clear enough to me, but I guess I don't see why I should care one way or the other about it." Can you suggest how I might answer this comment in my essay?**

In yet other instances, you may be writing a research paper and could use some help coming up with a specific issue or debate to focus on. In such a case, you might prompt your chatbot as follows:

▸ **Please identify two or three controversies over the topic of _____.**

In still other instances, you may have a clear idea of a debate you want to address but need help seeing how two authors fit into it:

▸ **Please help me put X and Y into dialogue about _____, clarifying exactly where they agree and disagree.**

Templates like this that put authors into dialogue are extremely useful in the academic world, which values the art of synthesizing and comparing perspectives.

In prompting chatbots in this way, you may find that, despite their impressive dexterity, they do not always get things right on the first try. When we used a version of the last template above with ChatGPT, for instance, we had to prompt and re-prompt the bot multiple times before it produced a response that actually put the two authors into dialogue. In its initial responses, what the bot said about the one author seemed unrelated to what it said about the other—like two ships passing in the night. Only with persistent redirecting was the program able to pinpoint clearly and exactly where the two authors parted ways.

THE NAYSAYER ROLE

There are, of course, other ways to move chatbots in a "they say / I say" direction, but one merits special attention. It involves exploiting what these technologies seem especially good at: role playing, taking on the role of a naysayer in particular.

For example, you might ask a chatbot to play the role of a naysayer who challenges an argument you're making, as in:

▸ **I am writing a paper on the topic of X, and I would like to take the position that _____. My view, in other words, is not _____, but _____. Before I begin writing, however, I'd like you to help me refine my argument by playing the role of a skeptic. You might point out where, for instance, someone could challenge my position, from what standpoint (feminist, conservative, pro-market capitalist, and so forth) they might mount such challenges, and how they might use my evidence against me.**

Or, in revising something you've written, you might write:

▸ **When I asserted that _____ in a recent essay, my instructor wrote in the margin, "Surely, many would disagree," and I've been struggling to figure out how to respond. Can you help me identify how others might disagree with my claim?**

You can also enlist a chatbot's help in *answering* a naysayer, reversing the roles outlined above so that, instead of critiquing the position you're taking, the chatbot defends it:

▸ I just thought of a counterargument to my position. I've been making the case that _____ , but realized that a skeptic could always point out _____ . Should I radically revise my argument, or even start over, or is there some way I can rescue it?

▸ In my essay, I take the position that _____ , and at one point I address the counterargument that _____ . In my heart of hearts, I completely disagree with this counterargument. And yet, there must be some concession that I can make to it while still standing my ground. Can you help me identify such a concession by listing three or four?

Again, prompting a chatbot in ways like these isn't always a one-and-done activity, but very often a matter of prompting it again and again. You may need to remind your chatbot what you want from it, as in:

▸ Again, please remember that I'm asking you to _____ , not to _____ .

QUESTIONS OF STYLE

Chatbots can also be prompted to help you with your writing itself, as in:

▸ Please read this paragraph I've written and identify the biggest problems you see in my writing. Where, for instance, might my ideas be disconnected, my transitions weak, a quotation mishandled, or the connection unclear between the position I take and the one I'm challenging?

You can also enlist a chatbot's help with tricky questions about voice—as in:

▸ **The following sentences I've written sound a little too informal for the kind of academic essay I'm trying to write: _____. Can you please suggest how I might translate these sentences into the kind of academic professional language that scholars might appreciate?**

Conversely, chatbots can also be prompted in the opposite direction to help you include some of the non-academic language we discuss in Chapter 10, "Academic Writing Doesn't Mean Setting Aside Your Own Voice":

▸ **The following sentences I wrote contain too much jargon and sound a little stiff to me: _____." Please suggest how I could translate my point into more everyday colloquial language.**

Animating this chapter has been the question of how to use today's revolutionary AI writing technologies without over-relying on them as a shortcut that does the work for you but rather as tools that, when used responsibly, can help you make the moves that matter in academic writing. We can't put this point any better than a first-year student at Georgetown University did after reading a draft of this chapter:

> Whenever our generation talks about AI, there is a lingering notion that it's more powerful than humans, that AI overtakes what we humans can do. I believe changing the narrative to give us control over AI is exactly how we can use it to our advantage.

The ultimate goal, then, is to work collaboratively with this technology in a way in which you lead it instead of letting it lead you.

Exercises

1. Treat the privacy policy (and/or the terms and conditions) of a chatbot as a "they say" that you read and respond to.

   a. Consider the risks that users should be aware of when using this program. Which risks are stated? Are any risks left out? Does the policy say anything about data being collected on users? What about matters of copyright?

   b. Identify any passages that may be especially hard to understand. Enlist the help of the chatbot itself to parse out what such passages are saying.

   c. Use one of the "they say / I say" templates in Chapter 2 to compose a summary and response to the policy.

2. Ask a chatbot to write a few paragraphs summarizing a controversial topic that you've recently heard or written about. Does the chatbot live up to the "objectivity" and "neutrality" that most chatbots aspire to?

   a. Examine the output for signs of obvious bias or stereotypes. What do you see in the language and examples used in the argument?

   b. Does the summary leave out any important perspectives? What evidence exists beyond the internet-based dataset that the bot draws from?

   c. Describe one of these unrepresented perspectives: a personal experience, a possible interview or survey, a physical artifact. How could you revise this argument to account for this missing perspective?

3. With a partner or on your own, review a chatbot-generated text that uses sources or quotations, and, using the lateral

reading techniques discussed in Chapter 15, track down any sources or facts referenced by the bot. Do the sources actually exist? If so, are they quoted or summarized accurately? Grade the chatbot based on how well it answered the prompt and incorporated the words of others. Explain why you chose that particular grade.

4. Ask a chatbot to help you revise your writing.

   a. First, experiment with style. Ask the bot to help you make a passage more concise or revise it to include more transitional words and phrases. Were the bot's suggestions helpful?

   b. Next, ask the bot to adopt the voice of a certain perspective (a dynamic salesperson, a pompous politician, a nosy neighbor). Analyze the chatbot's answers: Did it use any language or make any moves that you could borrow to make your writing stronger?

   c. Finally, experiment with audience and different kinds of writing. Ask the chatbot to turn an argument into a slide presentation outline, a country and western song, a clickbait headline. Some of these kinds of writing may be more useful to you than others, but you may find something unexpected that helps you strengthen what you say.

READINGS

Hidden Intellectualism

GERALD GRAFF

—⊡—

EVERYONE KNOWS SOME YOUNG PERSON who is impressively "street smart" but does poorly in school. What a waste, we think, that one who is so intelligent about so many things in life seems unable to apply that intelligence to academic work. What doesn't occur to us, though, is that schools and colleges might be at fault for missing the opportunity to tap into such street smarts and channel them into good academic work.

Nor do we consider one of the major reasons why schools and colleges overlook the intellectual potential of street smarts: the fact that we associate those street smarts with anti-intellectual concerns. We associate the educated life, the life of the mind, too narrowly and exclusively with subjects and texts that we consider inherently weighty and academic. We assume that it's possible to wax intellectual about Plato, Shakespeare,

———

GERALD GRAFF, a coauthor of this book, is a professor of English and education at the University of Illinois at Chicago. He is a past president of the Modern Language Association, the world's largest professional association of university scholars and teachers. This essay is adapted from his 2003 book, *Clueless in Academe: How Schooling Obscures the Life of the Mind.*

the French Revolution, and nuclear fission, but not about cars, dating, fashion, sports, TV, or video games.

The trouble with this assumption is that no necessary connection has ever been established between any text or subject and the educational depth and weight of the discussion it can generate. Real intellectuals turn any subject, however lightweight it may seem, into grist for their mill through the thoughtful questions they bring to it, whereas a dullard will find a way to drain the interest out of the richest subject. That's why a George Orwell writing on the cultural meanings of penny postcards is infinitely more substantial than the cogitations of many professors on Shakespeare or globalization (104–16).

See pp. 62–66 for tips on disagreeing, with reasons.

Students do need to read models of intellectually challenging writing—and Orwell is a great one—if they are to become intellectuals themselves. But they would be more prone to take on intellectual identities if we encouraged them to do so at first on subjects that interest them rather than ones that interest us.

I offer my own adolescent experience as a case in point. Until I 5 entered college, I hated books and cared only for sports. The only reading I cared to do or could do was sports magazines, on which I became hooked, becoming a regular reader of *Sport* magazine in the late forties, *Sports Illustrated* when it began publishing in 1954, and the annual magazine guides to professional baseball, football, and basketball. I also loved the sports novels for boys of John R. Tunis and Clair Bee and autobiographies of sports stars like Joe DiMaggio's *Lucky to Be a Yankee* and Bob Feller's *Strikeout Story*. In short, I was your typical teenage anti-intellectual—or so I believed for a long time. I have recently come to think, however, that my preference for sports over schoolwork was not anti-intellectualism so much as intellectualism by other means.

In the Chicago neighborhood I grew up in, which had become a melting pot after World War II, our block was solidly middle class, but just a block away—doubtless concentrated there by the real estate companies—were African Americans, Native Americans, and "hillbilly" whites who had recently fled postwar joblessness in the South and Appalachia. Negotiating this class boundary was a tricky matter. On the one hand, it was necessary to maintain the boundary between "clean-cut" boys like me and working-class "hoods," as we called them, which meant that it was good to be openly smart in a bookish sort of way. On the other hand, I was desperate for the approval of the hoods, whom I encountered daily on the playing field and in the neighborhood, and for this purpose it was not at all good to be book-smart. The hoods would turn on you if they sensed you were putting on airs over them: "Who you lookin' at, smart ass?" as a leather-jacketed youth once said to me as he relieved me of my pocket change along with my self-respect.

I grew up torn, then, between the need to prove I was smart and the fear of a beating if I proved it too well; between the need not to jeopardize my respectable future and the need to impress the hoods. As I lived it, the conflict came down to a choice between being physically tough and being verbal. For a boy in my neighborhood and elementary school, only being "tough" earned you complete legitimacy. I still recall endless, complicated debates in this period with my closest pals over who was "the toughest guy in the school." If you were less than negligible as a fighter, as I was, you settled for the next best thing, which was to be inarticulate, carefully hiding telltale marks of literacy like correct grammar and pronunciation.

In one way, then, it would be hard to imagine an adolescence more thoroughly anti-intellectual than mine. Yet in retrospect, I see that it's more complicated, that I and the 1950s themselves were not simply hostile toward intellectualism, but divided and ambivalent. When Marilyn Monroe married the playwright Arthur Miller in 1956 after divorcing the retired baseball star

Joe DiMaggio, the symbolic triumph of geek over jock suggested the way the wind was blowing. Even Elvis, according to his biographer Peter Guralnick, turns out to have supported Adlai over Ike in the presidential election of 1956. "I don't dig the intellectual bit," he told reporters. "But I'm telling you, man, he knows the most" (327).

Though I too thought I did not "dig the intellectual bit," I see now that I was unwittingly in training for it. The germs had actually been planted in the seemingly philistine debates about which boys were the toughest. I see now that in the interminable analysis of sports teams, movies, and toughness that my friends and I engaged in—a type of analysis, needless to say, that the real toughs would never have stooped to—I was already betraying an allegiance to the egghead world. I was practicing being an intellectual before I knew that was what I wanted to be.

It was in these discussions with friends about toughness and sports, I think, and in my reading of sports books and magazines, that I began to learn the rudiments of the intellectual life: how to make an argument, weigh different kinds of evidence, move between particulars and generalizations, summarize the views of others, and enter a conversation about ideas. It was in reading and arguing about sports and toughness that I experienced what it felt like to propose a generalization, restate and respond to a counterargument, and perform other intellectualizing operations, including composing the kind of sentences I am writing now.

Only much later did it dawn on me that the sports world was more compelling than school because it was *more intellectual than school,* not less. Sports after all was full of challenging arguments, debates, problems for analysis, and intricate statistics that you could care about, as school conspicuously was not. I believe that street smarts beat out book smarts in our culture not because street smarts are nonintellectual, as we generally suppose, but because they satisfy an intellectual thirst more thoroughly than school culture, which seems pale and unreal.

They also satisfy the thirst for community. When you entered sports debates, you became part of a community that was not limited to your family and friends, but was national and public. Whereas schoolwork isolated you from others, the pennant race or Ted Williams's .400 batting average was something you could talk about with people you had never met. Sports introduced you not only to a culture steeped in argument, but to a public argument culture that transcended the personal. I can't blame my schools for failing to make intellectual culture resemble the Super Bowl, but I do fault them for failing to learn anything from the sports and entertainment worlds about how to organize and represent intellectual culture, how to exploit its gamelike element and turn it into arresting public spectacle that might have competed more successfully for my youthful attention.

For here is another thing that never dawned on me and is still kept hidden from students, with tragic results: that the real intellectual world, the one that existed in the big world beyond school, is organized very much like the world of team sports, with rival texts, rival interpretations and evaluations of texts, rival theories of why they should be read and taught, and elaborate team competitions in which "fans" of writers, intellectual systems, methodologies, and -isms contend against each other.

To be sure, school contained plenty of competition, which became more invidious as one moved up the ladder (and has become even more so today with the advent of high-stakes testing). In this competition, points were scored not by making arguments, but by a show of information or vast reading, by grade-grubbing, or other forms of one-upmanship. School competition, in short, reproduced the less attractive features of sports culture without those that create close bonds and community.

And in distancing themselves from anything as enjoyable 15 and absorbing as sports, my schools missed the opportunity to capitalize on an element of drama and conflict that the intellectual world shares with sports. Consequently, I failed to see the parallels between the sports and academic worlds that could have helped me cross more readily from one argument culture to the other.

Sports is only one of the domains whose potential for literacy training (and not only for males) is seriously underestimated by educators, who see sports as competing with academic development rather than a route to it. But if this argument suggests why it is a good idea to assign readings and topics that are close to students' existing interests, it also suggests the limits of this tactic. For students who get excited about the chance to write about their passion for cars will often write as poorly and unreflectively on that topic as on Shakespeare or Plato. Here is the flip side of what I pointed out before: that there's no necessary relation between the degree of interest a student shows in a text or subject and the quality of thought or expression such a student manifests in writing or talking about it. The challenge, as college professor Ned Laff has put it, "is not simply to exploit students' nonacademic interests, but to get them to see those interests through academic eyes."

To say that students need to see their interests "through academic eyes" is to say that street smarts are not enough. Making students' nonacademic interests an object of academic study is useful, then, for getting students' attention and overcoming their boredom and alienation, but this tactic won't in itself necessarily move them closer to an academically rigorous treatment of those interests. On the other hand, inviting students to write about cars, sports, or clothing fashions does not have to be a pedagogical cop-out as long as students are required to see these interests "through academic eyes," that is, to think and write about cars, sports, and fashions in a reflective, analytical way, one that sees them as microcosms of what is going on in the wider culture.

If I am right, then schools and colleges are missing an opportunity when they do not encourage students to take their nonacademic interests as objects of academic study. It is self-defeating to decline to introduce any text or subject that figures to engage students who will otherwise tune out academic work entirely. If a student cannot get interested in Mill's *On Liberty* but will read *Sports Illustrated* or *Vogue* or the hip-hop magazine *Source* with absorption, this is a strong argument for assigning the magazines over the classic. It's a good bet that if students get hooked on reading and writing by doing term papers on *Source*, they will eventually get to *On Liberty*. But even if they don't, the magazine reading will make them more literate and reflective than they would be otherwise. So it makes pedagogical sense to develop classroom units on sports, cars, fashions, rap music, and other such topics. Give me the student anytime who writes a sharply argued, sociologically acute analysis of an issue in *Source* over the student who writes a lifeless explication of *Hamlet* or Socrates' *Apology*.

WORKS CITED

Cramer, Richard Ben. *Joe DiMaggio: The Hero's Life*. Simon, 2000.

DiMaggio, Joe. *Lucky to Be a Yankee*. Bantam, 1949.

Feller, Bob. *Strikeout Story*. Bantam, 1948.

Guralnick, Peter. *Last Train to Memphis: The Rise of Elvis Presley*. Little, Brown, 1994.

Orwell, George. *A Collection of Essays*. Harcourt, 1953.

Disability in Higher Education: Building Access and Building Futures

YAEL LENGA

———

FOR ALL INTENTS AND PURPOSES, MY CHILDHOOD WAS NORMAL. I learned how to brush my teeth, tie my shoes, and change my hearing aid batteries on my own from a young age. I collected many words for myself over the years: "hearing impaired" (which would one day prickle at me), "hard-of-hearing," "disabled," and eventually, tentatively, "Deaf" with a capital D.

———

YAEL LENGA wrote this essay while enrolled at the University of Illinois Chicago. A neuroscience and sociology major with a minor in disability and human development, Lenga hopes to make mental health treatment more accessible to her Deaf and disabled communities. This essay is documented in APA style.

But as a little kid, it was easiest to say I had "bad ears," just like my mom had "bad hands."

For all that we said about my mom's hands, she had the magic touch. Her strategic mind and unwavering protective instincts made sure I had legal access to my accommodations, and every teacher from pre-K on was made aware of my deafness and what that meant in the classroom. She was the first hearing itinerant* I ever had.

I was lucky—never had to fight for my needs alone.

As I got older, I grew into the same fierce advocate my mother had been for me. Unfortunately, not every student with a disability** grows up with such a strong support system, and college rarely fills this gap. Instead, once they enter higher education, disabled students are expected to have the skills necessary to request support and navigate an overly complicated system on their own, all the while dealing with stigma and bias (Scott, 2019).

No matter how lonely it can feel, or how easily academia dismisses accessibility, there are disabled students at every

Uses personal story to establish credibility (Chapter 7).

Connects personal experience to broader public conversation (Chapter 7).

5

*__Hearing itinerant__   An advocate who provides specialized services to Deaf and hard-of-hearing students.

**__Student with a disability__   I recognize and respect that some hold tightly to their disabled identity, while others prefer to be seen as an individual first, and I therefore use identity-first and person-first language interchangeably.

school, and none of us should be left behind. Disability is a natural part of being human, after all. It can be defined in a multitude of ways, but I choose to look beyond medical terminology; instead, I focus broadly on how our bodies and minds interact with the world around us, and how this shapes our subjective experiences. Disability is fluid: anyone can become disabled at any time, and the manifestation of one's disability is also fluid. Further, disability affects everyone: Mia Mingus (2017), a queer disabled author of color, reminds us that "no matter what community you're working with, you are working with disabled people." She emphasizes that "disability is not monolithic" (2011), and indeed, disability is experienced in countless diverse ways, visibly or invisibly.

Explains why we should care (Chapter 8).

As a disabled student, I have seen the unique ways in which we interact with both the medical system and the education system to access the support we need, all while navigating our newfound adulthood. Sadly, there are still significant academic disparities among disabled students, as many of us are unprepared to handle the sheer number of barriers in higher education. Students with disabilities not only deserve but possess the legal right to access, experience, and participate in all areas of their academic life—and this right must be protected. I intend to show why educational institutions must take more responsibility in addressing ableism. Accessibility needs to be a priority and making systemic changes that not

Outlines the essay's central "they say" and previews the essay's "I say" response.

just accommodate but empower all students is ultimately an investment in the entire academic community.

To navigate higher education more easily, all students with disabilities should know their rights. The passage of Section 504 of the Rehabilitation Act and the Americans with Disabilities Act (ADA) codified the rights of disabled people in federal law. Without diving too deep into legal minutiae, I can say that this legislation applies to both public and private institutions. All campus programs, materials, and buildings *must* be made accessible to students with disabilities. While I and most of my undergraduate peers were born after the ADA's passage in 1990, we must not take for granted the significance of this legislation and the sheer volume of changes made in everyday society.

In an ideal world, the passage of the ADA and other such laws would have ushered in a utopian era of accessibility. While those outside of the disability community might naïvely assume that now everyone has unfettered access to education, disabled students ultimately fail to receive equitable treatment due to the limitations of these laws. For example, the ADA is an unfunded mandate, which means that universities are given a checklist of accessibility measures to fulfill without any federal money: it simply "establishes a minimum baseline of enforceable standards" (Axelrod & Lenga, 2020). Moreover, the decisions on how to implement these standards are left up to

Anticipates objections (Chapter 6).

schools without any guidance or supervision from the federal government. Oftentimes, academic institutions follow the *letter* instead of the *spirit* of the law, which means providing the bare minimum of accommodations to prevent a lawsuit rather than working toward equity.

Although schools may claim that they provide sufficient support, there are several instances where a lack of federal oversight lets students fall through the cracks. For instance, note-taking services are relatively common accommodations, but many students report difficulty receiving notes from peer note-takers at all (Scott, 2019). When students do receive notes, they often are incomplete or inaccessible. For example, on one memorable occasion, I saw notes submitted in illegible neon purple cursive handwriting. In other words, schools may be fully complying with the law, and yet student needs are not adequately met. Administrators can also find loopholes in the law, such as refusing to provide accommodations or dismissing the need to renovate inaccessible buildings by exaggerating the burden it will create—on the institution.

Apparently, lifting the burden on students with disabilities is not always a priority. 10

Instead, as recent data suggest, disabled students are more likely to suffer academically due to ableism. The US Census' American Community Survey found in 2019 that

> Summarizing effectively (Chapter 2).

only 18% of people 25 and older who reported having a disability had a bachelor's degree or higher—a proportion much lower than the 36% of people in the same age group who did not report a disability (PNPI, 2022). Moreover, 25% of first-time students with disabilities drop out of university by the end of their first year, and 35% drop out by the end of their second year (Shaewitz & Crandall, 2020). Unfortunately, I speak from experience when I say that there are faculty, staff, and administrators who will equate these academic disparities to individual failings rather than to a larger systemic issue. Let me be clear: these academic disparities exist because academic institutions do not properly prioritize equity and accessibility. Disabled students are just as capable of scholastic excellence as our abled peers, and we are just as worthy of accessing college as anyone else— all we need is adequate support.

Uses data to support argument (Chapter 18).

Uses metacommentary (Chapter 11).

This support does not come easily: every student with a disability must simultaneously prove that they are disabled enough to deserve accommodations while also justifying that they are worth investing in. Disabled students must advocate for their own needs to request these services, which typically requires disclosing their disability and providing the necessary documentation. For most campuses, there exists a Disability Resource Center (DRC) (or similarly named alternative) that coordinates these processes.

Anticipates
objections
(Chapter 6).

While it is true that people with disabilities know their own needs best, and must therefore be involved in the accommodations process, the existing system is filled with barriers for students attempting to self-advocate. For instance, when the National Center for College Students with Disabilities (NCCSD) conducted seven focus groups to determine how ableism manifests on different campuses, all seven named barriers in working with these centers. Once students become aware of the existence of these centers—a challenge on its own—the procedures for documenting one's disability and requesting accommodations generate a myriad of questions (Scott, 2019). Some students shared that they were unclear on which disability was eligible for support. Others weren't sure how to acquire the necessary documentation to prove their disability or were unable to pay for diagnostic testing. Even students who successfully registered with their DRCs expressed confusion with the process of acquiring their accommodations or services.

Moreover, all seven of the NCCSD focus groups mentioned that a lack of self-advocacy training was a serious concern (Scott, 2019). Without the presence of qualified advisors and case managers, disabled students are forced to take on the burden of defending themselves to faculty and staff when their accommodations are questioned. For someone living with a disability, this added stress and exhaustion can be insurmountable—and many students choose to suffer in silence instead. There is a delicate balance to strike here: students with disabilities know their needs best, and yet we cannot be expected to create solutions on our own. Besides, using the DRC can only get you so far when the school's physical infrastructure is unprepared to handle people with disabilities. Many disabled students discuss physical barriers as one of the main forms of ableism they experience, such as blocked or absent ramps, non-functioning door openers, or issues with student housing. As one student aptly puts it, "'if you can't even get to class, . . . you can't even get to the point where you have other problems'" (Scott, 2019). Ironically, when my school's DRC was constructed, it wasn't wheelchair accessible. How are students expected to self-advocate when they can't even enter their Disability Resource Center?

Introduces quotation (Chapter 3).

This has to change.

15

Ultimately, tangible improvements lie in the hands of school policymakers, but administrators often claim that there are not enough disabled students to warrant these budgetary and policy-related adjustments. First and foremost, disability is underrepresented in data since it relies on survey question phrasing, an individual's access to health care, and their comfort with self-disclosure. That being said, the National Center for Educational Statistics found that in 2015, the presence of students with reported disabilities appears to have stabilized around 11% (Scott, 2019), which is a signifi-cant percentage of students, even before the COVID-19 pandemic. It is no secret that the effects of COVID-19 have led to an increase in disabled Americans, and as we understand more about what constitutes a disability and the importance of access to health care, I only expect this percentage to increase.

Still, many administrators might insist that little time can be spent on the needs of a 'relatively small' subset of the student population. This rhetoric is frankly short-sighted: establishing a culture of inclusion benefits everyone. Renovating buildings to build ramps, improve elevator access, and install automatic door-openers helps anyone pushing wheeled carts or carrying heavy supplies. Even simpler, attendance policies that allow for multiple forms of participation are helpful to anyone experiencing a health flare, issues with commuting, or even a family emergency. It costs nothing to embed policies promoting accessibility and inclusivity on a school-wide scale. In fact, it may well be profitable! Investing in disabled students, even without apportioning any funds, can improve academic outcomes, retention, and graduation rates.

Academic institutions are capable of implementing various strategies to ensure full inclusion on campus. For instance, Dahlia Shaewitz and Jennifer Crandall's blog post on *Higher Education Today* recommends building "faculty capacity" by giving them a deeper understanding of disability bias and accessibility (2020). Further, in interviews conducted by Scott (2019), disabled students reinforced the importance of inclusive instruction and programming, as many were grateful for instructors who directed them to the appropriate services or proactively discussed accessibility one-on-one. We can conclude from this research that if disability sensitivity trainings are implemented on a school-wide basis, they will reduce the burden on disabled students to educate professors and defend their needs. When accessibility is embedded into the culture, policies, and structure of a university, all students—and all faculty—benefit.

> Explains why it matters (Chapter 8).

Our very presence challenges institutions and systems to redefine what equity looks like. Mingus (2017) writes that "we can use access as a tool to transform the broader conditions we live in, to transform the conditions that created that inaccessibility in the first place." We deserve better, and our schools are capable of doing better. Building access allows us to shape both our individual futures and the future of higher education. Disability issues must be brought out of the shadows and into the boardrooms and classrooms of universities across the world. Each and every school wants to push its students to transform the world—and disabled students have the power to do so, as long as we are given an equitable seat at the table.

As students with disabilities, we bring unique insight and perspective to our schools. As we learn, people in turn learn from us, and we can create great change. We are inheriting a rich tradition of activism: we have the Rolling Quads[*] at UC Berkeley to thank in part for the passage of Section 504 and the ADA (Abdelfatah, 2020). We must honor the perseverance of those who paved the way, both literally and metaphorically, for students with disabilities to access higher education today. As a community, we have come so far, and while there is much left to achieve, the continued work of disabled activists continues to give me hope.

Disability justice, as explained by Sins Invalid, is a framework that shifts focus away from the legal sphere and toward collective access. This movement puts forth the (somehow radical) notion that all people have inherent worth (Sins Invalid, 2015), and pushes us to redefine how we build communities. Interdependence is one of the ten principles of disability justice and exposes independence as a myth: everyone, regardless of ability, relies on others for support in one way or another. It is true that many of us need medical care from family or friends, and many others rely on a therapist or personal assistant. I myself often need an interpreter or a

[*]**Rolling Quads**   A group of physically disabled students led by Ed Roberts who fought for disability rights at UC Berkeley in the 1960s, eventually founding the Center for Independent Living (CIL) in 1972.

captioner. However, people with disabilities are not burdens for having access needs. All people have support needs of some sort, and when those needs are met, the entire community benefits. Mingus (2017) explains that practicing interdependence pushes us "towards relationships where we are all valued and have things to offer." I strongly believe that students with disabilities bring so much to academia, and deserve to be seen as contributors worth investing in.

> Introduces quotation (Chapter 3).

Tackling inaccessibility in higher education will require collaboration at every level. Administrators, faculty, and staff must work with disabled students to ensure we receive the services we are legally entitled to. By taking proactive measures to streamline procedures and implement policies that prioritize accessibility, students with disabilities are no longer made to feel like an afterthought or a burden. As such, we perform better scholastically and contribute more to the academic community. Ultimately, respecting the needs of disabled students creates a fundamental shift in campus culture: committing to students with disabilities is a commitment to making universities a more inclusive and equitable place for everyone.

> Recaps the writer's central position.

Access is a fundamental right, but it is also much more. Disability justice invites us—indeed, compels us—to reimagine access as care, as what Leah Lakshmi Piepzna-Samarasinha (2018) calls both a "collective responsibility" and a "collective joy." I firmly agree and would argue alongside Mingus (2018) that "'disability justice' is simply another term for love," and that "our work for liberation is simply a practice of love—one of the deepest and most profound there is." I write with deep and hard-won love for my ears, for my mom's hands, for the community that has taught me so much about strength and empathy. I write with love for every student defending their right to an education, and I write with hope for our futures to be filled with access and its joys.

References

Abdelfatah, R. (Host). (2020, July 30). A.D.A. now! [Audio podcast transcript]. In *Throughline*. NPR. https://www.npr.org/transcripts/895896462

Axelrod, C., & Lenga, Y. (2020, July 26). Disrupting the status quo: Accessibility as the bare minimum. *2axend*. https://www.2axend.com/disrupting-the-status-quo-accessibility-as-the-bare-minimum/

Mingus, M. (2011, February 12). Changing the framework: Disability justice. *Leaving Evidence*. https://leavingevidence.wordpress.com/2011/02/12/changing-the-framework-disability-justice/

Mingus, M. (2017, April 12). Access intimacy, interdependence and disability justice. *Leaving Evidence*. https://leavingevidence.wordpress.com/2017/04/12/access-intimacy-interdependence-and-disability-justice/

Mingus, M. (2018, November 3). "Disability justice" is simply another term for love. *Leaving Evidence.* https://leavingevidence.wordpress.com/2018/11/03/disability-justice-is-simply-another-term-for-love/

Piepzna-Samarasinha, L. L. (2018). *Care work: Dreaming disability justice.* Arsenal Pulp Press.

Postsecondary National Policy Institute. (2022, September 26). *Students with disabilities in higher education.* PNPI. https://pnpi.org/students-with-disabilities-in-higher-education/

Scott, S. (2019, April). Access and participation in higher education: Perspectives of college students with disabilities. *NCCSD Research Brief, 2*(2), 1-25. https://www.nccsdonline.org/uploads/7/6/7/7/7677280/na_focus_groups_research_brief_final_pdf.pdf

Shaewitz, D., & Crandall, J. R. (2020, October 19). Higher education's challenge: Disability inclusion on campus. *Higher Education Today.* https://www.higheredtoday.org/2020/10/19/higher-educations-challenge-disability-inclusion-campus/

Sins Invalid. (2015, September 17). *10 principles of disability Justice.* Sins Invalid. https://www.sinsinvalid.org/blog/10-principles-of-disability-justice

The New Jim Crow: Mass Incarceration in the Age of Colorblindness

MICHELLE ALEXANDER

———

JARVIOUS COTTON CANNOT VOTE. Like his father, grand-father, great-grandfather, and great-great-grandfather, he has been denied the right to participate in our electoral democracy. Cotton's family tree tells the story of several generations of black men who were born in the United States but who were denied the most basic freedom that democracy promises—the freedom to vote for those who will make the rules and laws that govern one's life. Cotton's great-great-grandfather could not vote as a slave. His great-grandfather was beaten to death by the Ku Klux Klan for attempting to vote. His grandfather

———

MICHELLE ALEXANDER is a lawyer and scholar known for her work to protect civil rights. She has taught at Stanford Law School and Ohio State University's law school, and she currently teaches at Union Theological Seminary in New York City. She is a contributing opinion writer for the *New York Times* and has written opinion pieces for many other publications. She is the author of *The New Jim Crow: Mass Incarceration in the Age of Colorblindness* (2010); this selection is from the book's introduction, and it is documented in Chicago style.

was prevented from voting by Klan intimidation. His father was barred from voting by poll taxes and literacy tests. Today, Jarvious Cotton cannot vote because he, like many black men in the United States, has been labeled a felon and is currently on parole.[1]

Cotton's story illustrates, in many respects, the old adage "The more things change, the more they remain the same." In each generation, new tactics have been used for achieving the same goals—goals shared by the Founding Fathers. Denying African Americans citizenship was deemed essential to the formation of the original union. Hundreds of years later, America is still not an egalitarian democracy. The arguments and rationalizations that have been trotted out in support of racial exclusion and discrimination in its various forms have changed and evolved, but the outcome has remained largely the same. An extraordinary percentage of black men in the United States are legally barred from voting today, just as they have been throughout most of American history. They are also subject to legalized discrimination in employment, housing, education, public benefits, and jury service, just as their parents, grandparents, and great-grandparents once were.

What has changed since the collapse of Jim Crow has less to do with the basic structure of our society than with the language we use to justify it. In the era of colorblindness, it is no longer socially permissible to use race, explicitly, as a justification for discrimination, exclusion, and social contempt. So we don't. Rather than rely on race, we use our criminal justice system to label people of color "criminals" and then engage in all the practices we supposedly left behind. Today it is perfectly legal to discriminate against criminals in nearly all the ways that it was once legal to discriminate against African Americans. Once you're labeled a felon, the old forms of discrimination—employment discrimination, housing discrimination, denial of the right to vote, denial of educational opportunity, denial of food stamps and other public benefits, and exclusion from jury service—are suddenly legal. As a criminal, you have scarcely more rights, and arguably less respect, than a black man living in Alabama at the height of Jim Crow. We have not ended racial caste in America; we have merely redesigned it.

I reached [these conclusions] reluctantly. Ten years ago, I would have argued strenuously against the central claim made here—namely, that something akin to a racial caste system currently exists in the United States. Indeed, if Barack Obama had been elected president back then, I would have argued that his election marked the nation's triumph over racial caste—the final nail in the coffin of Jim Crow. My elation would have been tempered by the distance yet to be traveled to reach the promised land of racial justice in America, but my conviction that nothing remotely similar to Jim Crow exists in this country would have been steadfast.

See Chapter 1 for tips on making what "they say" something you say.

Today my elation over Obama's election is tempered by a far more sobering awareness. As an African American woman, with three young children who will never know a world in which a black man could not be president of the United States, I was beyond thrilled on election night. Yet when I walked out of the election night party, full of hope and enthusiasm, I was immediately reminded of the harsh realities of the New Jim Crow. A black man was on his knees in the gutter, hands cuffed behind his back, as several police officers stood around him talking, joking, and ignoring his human existence. People poured out of the building; many stared for a moment at the black man cowering in the street, and then averted their gaze. What did the election of Barack Obama mean for him?

Like many civil rights lawyers, I was inspired to attend law school by the civil rights victories of the 1950s and 1960s. Even in the face of growing social and political opposition to remedial policies such as affirmative action, I clung to the notion that the evils of Jim Crow are behind us and that, while we have a long way to go to fulfill the dream of an egalitarian, multiracial democracy, we have made real progress and are now struggling to hold on to the gains of the past. I thought my job as a civil rights lawyer was to join with the allies of racial progress to resist attacks on affirmative action and to eliminate the vestiges of Jim Crow segregation, including our still separate and unequal system of education. I understood the problems plaguing poor communities of color, including problems associated with crime and rising incarceration rates, to be a function of poverty and lack of access to quality education—the continuing legacy of slavery and Jim Crow. Never did I seriously consider the possibility that a new racial caste system was operating in this country. The new system had been developed and implemented swiftly, and it was largely invisible, even to people, like me, who spent most of their waking hours fighting for justice.

I first encountered the idea of a new racial caste system more than a decade ago, when a bright orange poster caught my eye. I was rushing to catch the bus, and I noticed a sign stapled to a telephone pole that screamed in large bold print: THE DRUG WAR IS THE NEW JIM CROW. I paused for a moment and skimmed the text of the flyer. Some radical group was holding a community meeting about police brutality, the new three-strikes law in California, and the expansion of America's prison system. The meeting was being held at a small community church a few blocks away; it had seating capacity for no more than fifty people. I sighed, and muttered to myself something like, "Yeah, the criminal justice system is racist in many ways, but it really doesn't help to make such an absurd comparison. People will just think you're crazy." I then crossed the street and hopped on the bus. I was headed to my new job, director of the Racial Justice Project of the American Civil Liberties Union (ACLU) in Northern California.

When I began my work at the ACLU, I assumed that the criminal justice system had problems of racial bias, much in the same way that all major institutions in our society are plagued with problems associated with conscious and unconscious bias. As a lawyer who had litigated numerous class-action employment-discrimination cases, I understood well the many ways in which racial stereotyping can permeate subjective decision-making processes at all levels of an organization, with devastating consequences. I was familiar with the challenges associated with reforming institutions in which racial stratification is thought to be normal—the natural consequence of differences in education, culture, motivation, and, some still believe, innate ability. While at the ACLU, I shifted my focus from employment discrimination to criminal justice reform and dedicated myself to the task of working with others to identify and eliminate racial bias whenever and wherever it reared its ugly head.

By the time I left the ACLU, I had come to suspect that I was wrong about the criminal justice system. It was not just another institution infected with racial bias but rather a different beast entirely. The activists who posted the sign on the telephone pole were not crazy; nor were the smattering of lawyers and advocates around the country who were beginning to connect the dots between our current system of mass incarceration and earlier forms of social control. Quite belatedly, I came to see that mass incarceration in the United States had, in fact, emerged as a stunningly comprehensive and well-disguised system of racialized social control that functions in a manner strikingly similar to Jim Crow.

In my experience, people who have been incarcerated rarely 10
have difficulty identifying the parallels between these systems
of social control. Once they are released, they are often denied
the right to vote, excluded from juries, and relegated to a racially
segregated and subordinated existence. Through a web of laws,
regulations, and informal rules, all of which are powerfully
reinforced by social stigma, they are confined to the margins
of mainstream society and denied access to the mainstream
economy. They are legally denied the ability to obtain employment, housing, and public benefits—much as African Americans were once forced into a segregated, second-class citizenship
in the Jim Crow era.

Those of us who have viewed that world from a comfortable distance—yet sympathize with the plight of the so-called
underclass—tend to interpret the experience of those caught
up in the criminal justice system primarily through the lens of
popularized social science, attributing the staggering increase in
incarceration rates in communities of color to the predictable,
though unfortunate, consequences of poverty, racial segregation, unequal educational opportunities, and the presumed realities of the drug market, including the mistaken belief that most
drug dealers are black or brown. Occasionally, in the course of
my work, someone would make a remark suggesting that perhaps
the War on Drugs is a racist conspiracy to put blacks back in
their place. This type of remark was invariably accompanied
by nervous laughter, intended to convey the impression that
although the idea had crossed their minds, it was not an idea
a reasonable person would take seriously.

Most people assume the War on Drugs was launched in
response to the crisis caused by crack cocaine in inner-city
neighborhoods. This view holds that the racial disparities in
drug convictions and sentences, as well as the rapid explosion

of the prison population, reflect nothing more than the government's zealous—but benign—efforts to address rampant drug crime in poor, minority neighborhoods. This view, while understandable, given the sensational media coverage of crack in the 1980s and 1990s, is simply wrong.

While it is true that the publicity surrounding crack cocaine led to a dramatic increase in funding for the drug war (as well as to sentencing policies that greatly exacerbated racial disparities in incarceration rates), there is no truth to the notion that the War on Drugs was launched in response to crack cocaine. President Ronald Reagan officially announced the current drug war in 1982, before crack became an issue in the media or a crisis in poor black neighborhoods. A few years after the drug war was declared, crack began to spread rapidly in the poor black neighborhoods of Los Angeles and later emerged in cities across the country.[2] The Reagan administration hired staff to publicize the emergence of crack cocaine in 1985 as part of a strategic effort to build public and legislative support for the war. The media campaign was an extraordinary success. Almost overnight, the media was saturated with images of black "crack whores," "crack dealers," and "crack babies"—images that seemed to confirm the worst negative racial stereotypes about impoverished inner-city residents. The media bonanza surrounding the "new demon drug" helped to catapult the War on Drugs from an ambitious federal policy to an actual war.

See Chapter 6 for tips on making concessions while still standing your ground.

The timing of the crack crisis helped to fuel conspiracy theories and general speculation in poor black communities that the War on Drugs was part of a genocidal plan by the government to destroy black people in the United States. From the outset, stories circulated on the street that crack and other drugs were being brought into black neighborhoods by the CIA. Eventually, even the Urban League came to take the claims of genocide seriously. In its 1990 report "The State of Black America," it stated: "There is at least one concept that must be recognized if one is to see the pervasive and insidious nature of the drug problem for the African American community. Though difficult to accept, that is the concept of genocide."[3] While the conspiracy theories were initially dismissed as far-fetched, if not downright loony, the word on the street turned out to be right, at least to a point. The CIA admitted in 1998 that guerrilla armies it actively supported in Nicaragua were smuggling illegal drugs into the United States—drugs that were making their way onto the streets of inner-city black neighborhoods in the form of crack cocaine. The CIA also admitted that, in the midst of the War on Drugs, it blocked law enforcement efforts to investigate illegal drug networks that were helping to fund its covert war in Nicaragua.[4]*

It bears emphasis that the CIA never admitted (nor has any evidence been revealed to support the claim) that it intentionally sought the destruction of the black community by allowing illegal drugs to be smuggled into the United States. Nonetheless, conspiracy theorists surely must be forgiven for their bold accusation of genocide, in light of the devastation wrought by crack cocaine and the drug war, and the odd coincidence that an illegal drug crisis suddenly appeared in the black community after—not before—a drug war had been declared. In fact, the War on Drugs began at a time when illegal drug use was on the decline.[5] During this same time period, however, a war was declared, causing arrests and convictions for drug offenses to skyrocket, especially among people of color.

*Covert war in Nicaragua In December 1981, the then president Ronald Reagan authorized the CIA to support the Contras, an opposition group that fought the Sandinistas, a revolutionary socialist group that the United States opposed in its fight against communism during the Cold War.

The impact of the drug war has been astounding. In less than thirty years, the US penal population exploded from around 300,000 to more than 2 million, with drug convictions accounting for the majority of the increase.[6] The United States now has the highest rate of incarceration in the world, dwarfing the rates of nearly every developed country, even surpassing those in highly repressive regimes like Russia, China, and Iran. In Germany, 93 people are in prison for every 100,000 adults and children. In the United States, the rate is roughly eight times that, or 750 per 100,000.[7]

The racial dimension of mass incarceration is its most striking feature. No other country in the world imprisons so many of its racial or ethnic minorities. The United States imprisons a larger percentage of its black population than South Africa did at the height of apartheid. In Washington, DC, our nation's capital, it is estimated that three out of four young black men (and nearly all those in the poorest neighborhoods) can expect to serve time in prison.[8] Similar rates of incarceration can be found in black communities across America.

These stark racial disparities cannot be explained by rates of drug crime. Studies show that people of all colors *use and sell* illegal drugs at remarkably similar rates.[9] If there are significant differences in the surveys to be found, they frequently suggest that whites, particularly white youth, are more likely to engage in drug crime than people of color.[10] That is not what one would guess, however, when entering our nation's prisons and jails, which are overflowing with black and brown drug offenders. In some states, black men have been admitted to prison on drug charges at rates twenty to fifty times greater than those of white men.[11] And in major cities wracked by the drug war, as many as 80 percent of young African American men now have criminal records and are thus subject to legalized discrimination for the rest of their lives.[12]

These young men are part of a growing undercaste, permanently locked up and locked out of mainstream society.

. . .

The language of caste may well seem foreign or unfamiliar to some. Public discussions about racial caste in America are relatively rare. We avoid talking about caste in our society because we are ashamed of our racial history. We also avoid talking about race. We even avoid talking about class. Conversations about class are resisted in part because there is a tendency to imagine that one's class reflects upon one's character. What is key to America's understanding of class is the persistent belief— despite all evidence to the contrary—that anyone, with the proper discipline and drive, can move from a lower class to a higher class. We recognize that mobility may be difficult, but the key to our collective self-image is the assumption that mobility is always possible, so failure to move up reflects on one's character. By extension, the failure of a race or ethnic group to move up reflects very poorly on the group as a whole.

What is completely missed in the rare public debates today 20 about the plight of African Americans is that a huge percentage of them are not free to move up at all. It is not just that they lack opportunity, attend poor schools, or are plagued by poverty. They are barred by law from doing so. And the major institutions with which they come into contact are designed to prevent their mobility. To put the matter starkly: the current system of control permanently locks a huge percentage of the African American community out of the mainstream society and economy. The system operates through our criminal justice institutions, but it functions more like a caste system than a system of crime control. Viewed from this perspective, the so-called underclass is better understood as an *undercaste*—a lower caste of individuals who are permanently barred by law and custom from mainstream society. Although this new system of racialized social control purports to be colorblind, it creates and maintains racial hierarchy much as earlier systems of control did. Like Jim Crow (and slavery), mass incarceration operates as a tightly networked system of laws, policies, customs, and institutions that operate collectively to ensure the subordinate status of a group defined largely by race.

. . .

Skepticism about the claims made here is warranted. There are important differences, to be sure, among mass incarceration, Jim Crow, and slavery—the three major racialized systems of control adopted in the United States to date. Failure to acknowledge the relevant differences, as well as their implications, would be a disservice to racial justice discourse. Many of the differences are not as dramatic as they initially appear, however; others serve to illustrate the ways in which systems of racialized social control have managed to morph, evolve, and adapt to changes in the political, social, and legal context over time. Ultimately, I believe that the similarities between these systems of control overwhelm the differences and that mass incarceration, like its predecessors, has been largely immunized from legal challenge. If this claim is substantially correct, the implications for racial justice advocacy are profound.

See Chapter 8 for tips on establishing why your claim matters.

With the benefit of hindsight, surely we can see that piecemeal policy reform or litigation alone would have been a futile approach to dismantling Jim Crow segregation. While those strategies certainly had their place, the Civil Rights Act of 1964 and the concomitant cultural shift would never have occurred without the cultivation of a critical political consciousness in the African American community and the widespread, strategic activism that flowed from it. Likewise, the notion that the *New Jim Crow* can ever be dismantled through traditional litigation and policy-reform strategies that are wholly disconnected from a major social movement seems fundamentally misguided.

Such a movement is impossible, though, if those most committed to abolishing racial hierarchy continue to talk and behave as if a state-sponsored racial caste system no longer exists. If we continue to tell ourselves the popular myths about racial progress or, worse yet, if we say to ourselves that the problem of mass incarceration is just too big, too daunting for us to do anything about and that we should instead direct our energies to battles that might be more easily won, history will judge us harshly. A human rights nightmare is occurring on our watch.

A new social consensus must be forged about race and the role of race in defining the basic structure of our society, if we hope ever to abolish the New Jim Crow. This new consensus must begin with dialogue, a conversation that fosters a critical consciousness, a key prerequisite to effective social action. My writing is an attempt to ensure that the conversation does not end with nervous laughter.

NOTES

1. Jarvious Cotton was a plaintiff in *Cotton v. Fordice*, 157 F.3d 388 (5th Cir. 1998), which held that Mississippi's felon disenfranchisement provision had lost its racially discriminatory taint. The information regarding Cotton's family tree was obtained by Emily Bolton on March 29, 1999, when she interviewed Cotton at Mississippi State Prison. Jarvious Cotton was released on parole in Mississippi, a state that denies voting rights to parolees.

2. The *New York Times* made the national media's first specific reference to crack in a story published in late 1985. Crack became known in a few impoverished neighborhoods in Los Angeles, New York, and Miami in early 1986. See Craig Reinarman and Harry Levine, "The Crack Attack: America's

Latest Drug Scare, 1986–1992," in *Images of Issues: Typifying Contemporary Social Problems* (New York: Aldine De Gruyter, 1995), 152.

3. Clarence Page, "'The Plan': A Paranoid View of Black Problems," *Dover Herald* (Delaware), Feb. 23, 1990. See also Manning Marable, *Race, Reform, and Rebellions: The Second Reconstruction in Black America, 1945–1990* (Jackson: University Press of Mississippi, 1991), 212–13.

4. See Alexander Cockburn and Jeffrey St. Clair, *Whiteout: The CIA, Drugs, and the Press* (New York: Verso, 1999). See also Nick Shou, "The Truth in 'Dark Alliance,'" *Los Angeles Times*, Aug. 18, 2006; Peter Kornbluh, "CIA's Challenge in South Central," *Los Angeles Times* (Washington edition), Nov. 15, 1996; and Alexander Cockburn, "Why They Hated Gary Webb," *The Nation*, Dec. 16, 2004.

5. Katherine Beckett and Theodore Sasson, *The Politics of Injustice: Crime and Punishment in America* (Thousand Oaks, CA: Sage Publications, 2004), 163.

6. Marc Mauer, *Race to Incarcerate*, rev. ed. (New York: The New Press, 2006), 33.

7. PEW Center on the States, *One in 100: Behind Bars in America 2008* (Washington, DC: PEW Charitable Trusts, 2008), 5.

8. Donald Braman, *Doing Time on the Outside: Incarceration and Family Life in Urban America* (Ann Arbor: University of Michigan Press, 2004), 3, citing D.C. Department of Corrections data for 2000.

9. See, e.g., U.S. Department of Health and Human Services, Substance Abuse and Mental Health Services Administration, *Summary of Findings from the 2000 National Household Survey on Drug Abuse*, NHSDA series H-13, DHHS pub. no. SMA 01-3549 (Rockville, MD: 2001), reporting that 6.4 percent of whites, 6.4 percent of blacks, and 5.3 percent of Hispanics were current users of illegal drugs in 2000; *Results from the 2002 National Survey on Drug Use and Health: National Findings*, NHSDA series H-22, DHHS pub. no. SMA 03-3836 (2003), revealing nearly identical rates of illegal drug use among whites and blacks, only a single percentage point between them; and *Results from the 2007 National Survey on Drug Use and Health: National Findings*, NSDUH series H-34, DHHS pub. no. SMA 08-4343 (2007), showing essentially the same finding. See also Marc Mauer and Ryan S. King, *A 25-Year Quagmire: The "War on Drugs" and Its Impact on American Society* (Washington, DC: Sentencing Project, 2007), 19, citing a study suggesting that African Americans have slightly higher rates of illegal drug use than whites.

10. See, e.g., Howard N. Snyder and Melissa Sickmund, *Juvenile Offenders and Victims: 2006 National Report*, U.S. Department of Justice, Office of Justice Programs, Office of Juvenile Justice and Delinquency Prevention (Washington, DC: U.S. Department of Justice, 2006), reporting that white youth are more likely than black youth to engage in illegal drug sales. See also Lloyd D. Johnson, Patrick M. O'Malley, Jerald G. Bachman, and John E. Schulenberg, *Monitoring the Future, National Survey Results on Drug Use,*

1975–2006, vol. 1, *Secondary School Students*, U.S. Department of Health and Human Services, National Institute on Drug Abuse, NIH pub. no. 07-6205 (Bethesda, MD: 2007), 32, "African American 12th graders have consistently shown lower usage rates than White 12th graders for most drugs, both licit and illicit"; and Lloyd D. Johnston, Patrick M. O'Malley, and Jerald G. Bachman, *Monitoring the Future: National Results on Adolescent Drug Use: Overview of Key Findings 2002*, U.S. Department of Health and Human Services, National Institute on Drug Abuse, NIH pub. no. 03-5374 (Bethesda, MD: 2003), presenting data showing that African American adolescents have slightly lower rates of illicit drug use than their white counterparts.

11. Human Rights Watch, *Punishment and Prejudice: Racial Disparities in the War on Drugs*, HRW Reports, vol. 12, no. 2 (New York, 2000).

12. See, e.g., Paul Street, *The Vicious Circle: Race, Prison, Jobs, and Community in Chicago, Illinois, and the Nation* (Chicago: Chicago Urban League, Department of Research and Planning, 2002).

All Words Matter: The Manipulation behind "All Lives Matter"

KELLY CORYELL

I'VE NEVER UNDERSTOOD THE POPULAR SAYING "Sticks and stones may break my bones, but words will never hurt me." I grew up as a tomboy; I've had more than my fair share of scrapes, bruises, and stitches. But I've found that words inflict the most painful injuries. On sleepless nights when I toss and turn, I'm not replaying the time I broke my foot over and over in my head—I'm thinking about some embarrassing thing I said that still makes me physically cringe or

---

KELLY CORYELL wrote this essay in her first-year writing course at Diablo Valley College in Pleasant Hill, CA. An English major, Coryell works as a tutor in the college's learning center and serves as a supplemental instruction leader for multilingual students. She plans to become an English professor. This essay, which is documented in MLA Style, was nominated for the Norton Writer's Prize.

a time someone said something hurtful to me. Broken bones heal—words stay with us.

This is because words have power. A skilled wordsmith can influence us by using evocative words that elicit an emotional response. The meanings of these "loaded" words aren't located in a dictionary. There is a context surrounding them that implies a meaning beyond the basic information they convey. Loaded words and phrases appeal to our emotions, not our logic—they enter our hearts, not our minds. They can manipulate, so sometimes people use loaded language to distract us from a flawed argument.

Such is the case when people use the phrase "all lives matter" to oppose the phrase "Black lives matter." In 2012, neighborhood watch coordinator George Zimmerman shot and killed Trayvon Martin, an unarmed African American teenager returning home from a late-night snack run. In 2013, Zimmerman was acquitted of all charges. This sparked the birth of the Black Lives Matter (BLM) movement, when activists Alicia Garza, Opal Tometi, and Patrisse Cullors, frustrated with the systemic inequality and oppression exemplified by Zimmerman's trial, started using the hashtag #BlackLivesMatter on *Twitter*. As more and more Black people died during police confrontations or in police custody—Eric Garner, Michael Brown, Tamir Rice, Walter Scott, Freddie Gray—the movement, chanting the phrase

> Summarizes effectively (Chapter 2).

"Black lives matter," gained momentum and media coverage, eventually becoming a major talking point in the 2016 presidential election. And in the spring of 2020, the deaths of Ahmaud Arbery, Breonna Taylor, George Floyd, Rayshard Brooks, Dominique "Rem'mie" Fells, and Riah Milton reignited the BLM movement, leading to an overdue reckoning with racism in this country.

As a direct response, Americans who either disagreed with the BLM movement as a whole or who supported the movement but were uncomfortable with its slogan, began to chant their own phrase: "all lives matter." It should be acknowledged that some of those who have used the phrase "all lives matter" did so naïvely aiming to unify people in a time of division, thinking of the words as a positive affirmation to which no one could object. However, saying "all lives matter" as a response to "Black lives matter" is, in reality, sending a dangerous message: it steals attention from the systematic oppression of Black Americans and actively distorts the message behind the BLM movement, manipulating the American people into maintaining the oppressive status quo.

The phrase "all lives matter" belies the current racial 5 inequality in America by implying that all lives are at equal risk. The racism and prejudice endured by African Americans didn't end when slavery was abolished in 1865, it didn't

Entertains counterargument (Chapter 6).

end when Congress passed the Civil Rights Act of 1964, and it didn't end when a Black man was elected president of the United States in 2008. Racial inequality in America persists to this day, ingrained and interwoven so deeply in American society that our prison systems and manufacturing industries depend on it. It's so expertly hidden under layers of celebrity gossip in our media and blatant and bold lies from our politicians, and so "normalized" in our culture, that the privileged may not even be aware of the plight of Black Americans.

But the statistics speak for themselves. According to the NAACP, African Americans are incarcerated at six times the rate of white Americans for drug crimes ("Criminal Justice"). The Center for American Progress reported that in 2016, the median wealth of Black families was *only 10 percent* of the median wealth of white families (Hanks, Solomon, and Weller). Police shoot and kill Black Americans at *two and a half times* the rate of white Americans, according to a 2016 report by *The Washington Post* (Lowery). All these statistics point to the fact that Black lives are valued less than white lives in America. The BLM movement aims to change this depressing reality by insisting that "Black lives matter."

Responding to "Black lives matter" with "all lives matter" ignores the unique prejudices and discrimination Black

> Uses data (Chapter 18) and explains why we should care (Chapter 8).

Introduces
quotation
(Chapter 3).
people experience in America. Chimamanda Ngozi Adichie
makes a parallel argument in her essay "I Decided to Call
Myself a Happy Feminist." Adichie explains why she calls herself a feminist instead of a human-rights activist. She writes:

> Feminism is, of course, part of human rights in general—
> but to choose to use the vague expression *human rights* is
> to deny the specific and particular problem of gender. . . .
> For centuries, the world divided human beings into two
> groups and then proceeded to exclude and oppress one
> group. It is only fair that the solution to the problem
> should acknowledge that.

Explains
quotation
(Chapter 3).
Adichie's point is that not every human being suffers the
oppression that women suffer. Therefore, campaigning for all
humans, while noble, is irrelevant. It would ignore the specific plights of women, as well as the historical fact that those
behind the oppression of women were other human beings—
men. In the same way, emphasizing *all* lives takes much-needed
focus away from the oppression specifically felt only by Black
Americans—which is a direct result of the centuries of oppression at the hands of white Americans.

Later in her essay, Adichie recalls a conversation she
once had about gender: "A man said to me, 'Why does it
have to be you as a woman? Why not you as a human being?'
This type of question is a way of silencing a person's specific

experiences. Of course I am a human being, but there are particular things that happen to me in the world because I am a woman." Shifting attention away from the female gender to the entirety of humankind silences the hardships women face *simply because they are women*. Talking over them by questioning their commitment to the whole, and not allowing them to share their experiences, smothers their voices. The same is true when shifting focus from "Black lives" to "all lives." Saying "all lives matter" ignores the unique discrimination only Black Americans face, *simply because they are Black*. Dismissing the importance and relevance of their struggles because everyone has struggles misses the point entirely.

"All lives matter" implies that all lives endure an equal amount of hardship; therefore, the struggles of Black Americans deserve no more attention than the struggles of white Americans—which is demonstrably false statistically. Daniel Victor illustrates the harmful way the phrase "all lives matter" removes focus from the hardships of Black Americans in his article "Why 'All Lives Matter' Is Such a Perilous Phrase" for *The New York Times*. He writes:

> Those in the Black Lives Matter movement say black people are in immediate danger and need immediate attention. . . .

Saying "All Lives Matter" in response would suggest to them that all people are in equal danger, invalidating the specific concerns of black people.

"You're watering the house that's not burning, but you're choosing to leave the house that's burning unattended," said Allen Kwabena Frimpong, an organizer for the New York chapter of Black Lives Matter. "It's irresponsible."

To put it simply, focusing too much on the whole can divert much needed attention from crises affecting a specific group.

As one *Twitter* user notes, "#AllLivesMatter is like I 10 go to the Dr for a broken arm and he says 'All Bones Matter' ok but right now let's take care of this broken one" (@djsoap92). In this analogy, only one bone needs immediate attention—ignoring it because all bones are important to a person's health isn't an appropriate response to the situation. Nor would be putting the injured person in a full-body cast—though that would be treating every bone equally. "All lives matter" doesn't acknowledge that the lives of Black Americans are in greater danger due to the hundreds of years of systematic racism designed to devalue them. The point of saying "Black lives matter" is to bring attention to the fact that Black lives do not matter in our society. The BLM movement is not simply saying "Black people are shot and killed by the police," it's saying "Black people are shot and killed by the police *at two and a half times the rate of white people*." Replying with "all races are shot and killed by the police" can be an acceptable response to the first statement, *but not the second.* Yet that is exactly what saying "all lives matter" does—it ignores the second statement, ignores the voices of BLM activists.

> Uses metacommentary to differentiate views (Chapter 11).

Using "all lives matter" as a response to "Black lives matter" perpetuates the misconception that BLM activists do not believe both sentiments. The core of the BLM movement is the belief that *all* lives matter—*including* Black lives, which are treated differently than white lives, not just by law enforcement but America as a whole. As J. Clara Chan explains in her article, "What Is 'All Lives Matter'? A Short Explainer," for *The Wrap*,

> BLM supporters stress that the movement isn't about believing no other races matter. Instead, the movement seeks to highlight and change how racism disproportionately affects the black community, in terms of police brutality, job security, socioeconomic status, educational opportunities, and more.

The BLM movement's focus on particular inequities doesn't mean other races don't matter, but the phrase "all lives matter" is loaded language that implies they don't. Dave Bry explains this manipulation in his article titled "'All Lives Matter' Is and Always Was Racist—and This Weekend's Trump Rally Proved It" for the UK paper *The Guardian*. He writes:

> Often people who say "all lives matter" say it pointedly, correctively under the veneer of the idea that "all men are created equal." It is meant to refute the idea that "only" black lives matter.
>
> But understanding "black lives matter" to mean "only" black lives matter has been a misinterpretation from the beginning, one made in ignorance of the intent of the statement and the statistical facts that led to it.

Connects
the parts
(Chapter 9).

That is to say, "all lives matter" misinterprets the point the BLM movement is making—that all lives do matter; therefore, Black lives need to matter as much as white lives in American society. It isn't "*only* Black lives matter"; it's "Black lives matter, *too*."

"All lives matter" manipulates people into believing those who say "Black lives matter" are against other lives. Jason Stanley explains the many ways language can be used as a tool for suppression in his *New York Times* opinion piece, "The Ways of Silencing." Stanley writes, "Words are misappropriated and meanings twisted. I believe that these tactics are not really about making substantive claims, but rather play the role of silencing. They are, if you will, linguistic strategies for stealing the voices of others." In other words, a group can be silenced if the language vital to their ability to express themselves and their beliefs is co-opted by another group. Supporters of "all lives matter" co-opted the language of the BLM movement, forcing a separation between the two phrases. As a result, BLM activists cannot say "all lives matter" without sounding like they oppose the views of the BLM movement, since "all lives matter" is no longer just a phrase but a rebuttal—a counterargument.

Saying "all lives matter" is premature, since it presupposes that equality has already been achieved. If Black lives really did matter as much as white lives in American society, then saying so would be as uncontroversial as stating any other fact. In fact, America is not a postracial society: poverty, education, health, incarceration rates—all are unequal between different races in America. We must acknowledge this ugly truth if we are ever going to change it. "All lives matter" invokes a naïve reality in which all races are holding hands in a great big circle, singing "This Land Is Your Land" as the sun smiles down on the world. "All lives matter," like the statement "I don't see race, I just see people," may, at first,

Represents
objections
fairly
(Chapter 6).

seem like a beautiful sentiment. Those who say such things may truly do so with the intent of creating a world where everyone is treated equally—regardless of race, gender, creed, orientation, and so on.

But upon close examination, these phrases—however well- meaning—are harmful because, aside from robbing people of their racial identities, they ignore race-based discrimination. How can one notice racism when one does not "see race"? How can one point out discrimination against African Americans if the only response one gets is "everyone matters"? If one insists that a goal has already been met when it hasn't, why would anyone put in more effort toward reaching that goal? This is why "all lives matter" is so manipulative and damaging. It's an attempt to convince us we don't have to keep reaching for equality and justice, even though every fact around us tells us this is far from the case. Only by consciously acknowledging racial inequality will we ever be able to put an end to it.

The root of "all lives matter" boils down to one thing: 15 privilege, and the reluctance to give it up in the name of equality. As Chris Boeskool put it in a *Huffington Post* opinion piece: "Equality can *feel* like oppression. But it's not. What you're feeling is just the discomfort of losing a little bit of your privilege." Evening the playing field can feel like a bad thing to the person benefiting from the imbalance.

In the 1960s, a white bus rider may have felt oppressed when she started having to compete with Black bus riders for the front seat—she lost the privilege of getting a guaranteed front seat because of her race. In the 1970s, a man might have complained that he could no longer "compliment" his female coworkers without them accusing him of sexual harassment—he lost the privilege of being able to say offensive things because of his gender. If American society starts to accept that Black lives matter as much as white lives, white Americans will lose some of the privileges afforded to them as a result of the oppression of Black Americans. Therefore, people who either do not realize they have this privilege, or people who simply don't want to give it up, chant "all lives matter" in an effort to hold on to that privilege. If the BLM movement is silenced, the status quo of racial inequality will be maintained. The privileged must resist this unethical temptation and not mistake oppression as equality.

Works Cited

Adichie, Chimamanda Ngozi. "I Decided to Call Myself a Happy Feminist." *The Guardian*, 17 Oct. 2014, www.theguardian .com/books/2014/oct/17/chimamanda-ngozi-adichie-extract -we-should-all-be-feminists. Accessed 16 Mar. 2019.

Boeskool, Chris. "When You're Accustomed to Privilege, Equality Feels Like Oppression." *Huffington Post*, 14 Mar. 2016, www.huffpost.com/entry/when-youre-accustomed-to -privilege_b_9460662. Accessed 26 Feb. 2019.

Bry, Dave. "'All Lives Matter' Is and Always Was Racist—and This Weekend's Trump Rally Proved It." *The Guardian*, 23 Nov. 2015, www.theguardian.com/commentisfree/2015 /nov/23/all-lives-matter-racist-trump-weekend-campaign -rally-proved-it. Accessed 3 Mar. 2019.

Chan, J. Clara. "What Is 'All Lives Matter'? A Short Explainer." *The Wrap*, 13 July 2016, www.thewrap.com/what-is-all-lives -matter-a-short-explainer/. Accessed 4 Mar. 2019.

"Criminal Justice Fact Sheet." *NAACP*, 2018, www.naacp.org /criminal-justice-fact-sheet. Accessed 12 Mar. 2019.

@djsoap92. "#AllLivesMatter is like I go to the Dr for a broken arm and he says 'All Bones Matter' ok but right now let's take care of this broken one." *Twitter*, 5 July 2016, twitter .com/djsoap92/status/750563460921057280. Accessed 6 Mar. 2019.

Hanks, Angela, et al. "Systematic Inequality: How America's Structural Racism Helped Create the Black-White Wealth Gap." *Center for American Progress*, 21 Feb. 2018, www .americanprogress.org/issues/race/reports/2018/02/21/447051 /systematic-inequality. Accessed 26 Feb. 2019.

Lowery, Wesley. "Aren't More White People than Black People Killed by Police? Yes, but No." *The Washington Post*, 11 July 2016, www.washingtonpost.com/amphtml/news/post-nation /wp/2016/07/11/arent-more-white-people-than-black-people -killed-by-police-yes-but-no. Accessed 19 Feb. 2019.

Stanley, Jason. "The Ways of Silencing." *Opinionator*, New
York Times, 25 June 2011, opinionator.blogs.nytimes
.com/2011/06/25/the-ways-of-silencing. Accessed 25 Feb.
2019.

Victor, Daniel. "Why 'All Lives Matter' Is Such a Perilous
Phrase." *The New York Times*, 15 July 2016, www.nytimes
.com/2016/07/16/us/all-lives-matter-black-lives-matter.html.
Accessed 5 Mar. 2019.

Left Behind: Internet Access for People Behind Bars

JOE GARCIA

—◻—

CALIFORNIA RECENTLY PROMISED to provide free computer tablets to all state prisoners by the end of 2021, allowing prisoners like me to email our loved ones through a highly restricted prison messaging service and download content like movies and books. It's a great first step, but without more open and frequent internet access, there's no way we'll ever truly keep pace with the changing world outside our prison walls.

I've been locked up since 2003. Back then Apple had barely launched iTunes, and I was still in awe of the so-called high-speed connection I'd paid Time Warner to install in my apartment. In all the years since then, I haven't logged a single second of internet activity. My frames of reference for what it means to be online now come from network television and print media.

———

JOE GARCIA is a journalist at San Quentin State Prison and is a lead writer and editor for the prisoner-run newspaper *San Quentin News*. His writing has also been published in the *Washington Post*, the *Sacramento Bee*, and the *Prison Journalism Project*. Garcia is originally from San Francisco. This essay was published in the *MIT Technology Review* in 2021.

When my first parole opportunity arrives, in 2023, I'll be 53 years old. As a convicted murderer, I will need to convince the parole board not only that I have been rehabilitated, but also that I am able to be a productive and employable citizen. It can be hard to keep up with changes in technology even when you're experiencing them firsthand. When you're locked away, it's virtually impossible.

I'm hoping to pursue a career path in journalism when I get out of prison, and I worry every day about reentering a global economy with my grossly outdated tech skill set. I know the job market will expect internet fluency more than ever in the post-pandemic world, since much of America's media workforce has gone remote.

Roughly 2.3 million people are incarcerated in the US. Even though the internet is a given in the rest of society, access in prison is so restricted it's almost nonexistent. Prisoners are only allowed to use a tiny number of programs that might offer Zoom classes with outside teachers, or to browse an extremely limited set of whitelisted sites through intranets that are carefully cordoned off from the public internet.

At San Quentin State Prison, where I reside, the computers that prisoners can access feature preloaded interactive programs that offer the same basic experience as reading from a textbook. My only experience using a search engine has been through LexisNexis, which the prison library licenses to allow us to study case law.

In San Quentin's vaunted coding program, Code 7370, offered through the prison education organization The Last Mile, hand-selected prisoners build and sell actual websites for commercial use. But even they do not have internet access.

As a working journalist in prison, I know I have First Amendment rights, but I'm deprived of a key technology that the United Nations identified a decade ago as a means of exercising one's freedom of expression.

I understand why government officials, prison administrators, and the public might fear that giving convicted felons real-time internet access would open a Pandora's box of suspicious activity. Yet if elementary school kids can surf the web safely with parental locks and controls, how hard would it be for someone to design a system that provides incarcerated people with more meaningful access?

In Belgium, for example, an innovative platform called 10 PrisonCloud has offered limited and controlled internet access to prisoners for years. In Finland and Denmark, open prisons, which have minimal security and some of the lowest recidivism rates, also allow limited internet access.

Almost all incarcerated people in US prisons today will be released back into their communities in the future. That includes many of my peers who have been incarcerated since before the advent of the internet.

President Joe Biden has said that the majority of incarcerated Americans deserve a bona fide second chance at life—but we need some form of internet access in order to have a genuine chance of successfully reentering today's tech-driven society.

Go Ahead:
Waste Time on the Internet

KENNETH GOLDSMITH

—◳—

Is THE INTERNET A WASTE OF TIME? It's not so easy to say. When I click around news sites, am I wasting time because I should be working instead? What if I've spent hours working, and I need a break? Am I wasting time if I watch cat videos, but not if I read a magazine story about the Iran nuclear deal? Am I wasting time if I look up the latest presidential polling numbers, but not if I'm communicating with an old friend on Facebook?

The notion that the Internet is bad for you seems premised on the idea that the Internet is one thing—a monolith. In reality it's a befuddling mix of the stupid and the sublime, a shattered, contradictory, and fragmented medium. Internet

———

KENNETH GOLDSMITH is a poet and author of ten books, including *Seven American Deaths and Disasters* (2013) and *Uncreative Writing: Managing Language in the Digital Age* (2013). He is the founding editor of *UbuWeb*, an online archive, and senior editor of *PennSound*, a website for digital poetry recordings based at the University of Pennsylvania, where he teaches writing. This essay, first published on August 12, 2016, for the *Los Angeles Times*, is from his book *Wasting Time on the Internet* (2016).

detractors seem to miss this simple fact, which is why so many of their criticisms disintegrate under observation.

The way Internet pundits tell it, you'd think we stare for three hours at clickbait—those articles with hypersensational headlines—the way we once sat down and watched three hours of cartoons on Saturday morning TV. But most of us don't do any one thing on the Internet. Instead, we do many things, some of it frivolous, some of it heavy. Our time spent in front of the computer is a mixed time, a time that reflects our desires— as opposed to the time spent sitting in front of the television where we were fed shows we didn't necessarily enjoy. TV gave us few choices. Many of us truly did feel like we wasted our time—as our parents so often chided us—"rotting away" in front of the TV.

I keep reading—on screens—that in the age of screens we've lost our ability to concentrate, that we've become distracted. But when I look around me and see people riveted to their devices, I notice a great wealth of concentration, focus, and engagement.

And I keep reading—on the Internet—that the Internet 5 has made us antisocial, that we've lost the ability to have a conversation. But when I see people with their devices, what I see is people communicating with one another: texting, chatting, IM'ing. And I have to wonder, in what way is this not social? A conversation broken up into short bursts and quick emoticons is still a conversation. Watch someone's face while they're in the midst of a rapid-fire text message exchange: it's full of emotion—anticipation, laughter, affect.

The Internet has been accused of making us shallow. We're skimming, not reading. We lack the ability to engage deeply with a subject anymore. That's both true and not true: we skim and browse certain types of content, and read others carefully.

We're not all using our devices the same way. Looking over the shoulders of people absorbed in their devices on the subway, I see many people reading newspapers and books and many others playing Candy Crush. Sometimes someone will be glancing at a newspaper one moment and playing a game the next.

The other night, I walked into the living room and my wife was glued to her iPad, reading *Narrative of the Life of Frederick Douglass*. Hours later, when I headed to bed, she hadn't moved an inch, still transfixed by this 171-year-old narrative on her 21st-century device. When I said good night, she didn't even look up.

Internet critics tell us time and again that our brains are being rewired; I'm not so sure that's a bad thing. Every new media requires new ways of thinking. Wouldn't it be strange if in the midst of this digital revolution we were still expected to use our brains in the same way we read books or watched TV?

See pp. 25–27 for ways to introduce an ongoing debate.

The resistance to the Internet shouldn't surprise us: Cultural reactionaries defending the status quo have been around as long as media has. Marshall McLuhan tells us that television was written off by people invested in literature as merely "mass entertainment" just as the printed book was met with the same skepticism in the 16th century by scholastic philosophers. McLuhan says that "the vested interests of acquired knowledge and conventional wisdom have always been by-passed and engulfed by new media . . . The student of media soon comes to expect the new media of any period whatever to be classed as pseudo by those who have acquired the patterns of earlier media, whatever they may happen to be."

I'm told that our children are most at risk, that the excessive use of computers has led our kids to view the real world as fake. But I'm not so sure that even I can distinguish "real" from "fake." How is my life on Facebook any less "real" than what happens in my day-to-day life? In fact, much of what does happen in my day-to-day life comes through Facebook—work opportunities, invitations to dinner parties, and even the topics I discuss at those dinner parties.

After reading one of those hysterical "devices are ruining your child" articles, my sister-in-law decided to take action. She imposed a system whereby, after dinner, the children were to "turn in" their devices—computers, smartphones, and tablets. They could "check them out" over the course of the evening, but only if they could prove they needed them for "educational purposes." Upon confiscating my nephew's cell phone one Friday night, she asked him on Saturday morning, "What plans do you have with your friends today?" "None," he responded. "You took away my phone."

On a vacation, after a full day of outdoor activities that included seeing the Grand Canyon and hiking, my friend and her family settled into the hotel for the evening. Her 12-year-old daughter is a fan of preteen goth girl crafting videos on YouTube, where she learns how to bedazzle black skull T-shirts and make perfectly ripped punk leggings. That evening, the girl selected some of her favorite videos to share with her mother. After agreeing to watch a few, her mother grew impatient. "This is nice, but I don't want to spend the whole night clicking around." The daughter responded indignantly that she wasn't just "clicking around." She was connecting with a community of girls her own age who shared similar interests.

Her mother was forced to reconsider her premise that her daughter was just wasting time on the Internet; instead, she was fully engaged, fostering an aesthetic, feeding her imagination, indulging in her creative proclivities, and hanging out with her friends, all from the comfort of a remote hotel room perched on the edge of the Grand Canyon.

Many Internet critics yearn for a return to solitude and introspection, quiet places far removed from the noises of our devices. But those places, away from the rabble, are starting to remind me of gated communities.

"Rise of the Machines"
Is Not a Likely Future

MICHAEL LITTMAN

—▭—

EVERY NEW TECHNOLOGY BRINGS its own nightmare scenarios. Artificial intelligence (AI) and robotics are no exceptions. Indeed, the word "robot" was coined for a 1920 play that dramatized just such a doomsday for humanity (Čapek).

Recently, an open letter about the future of AI, signed by a number of high-profile scientists and entrepreneurs, spurred a new round of harrowing headlines like "Top Scientists Have an Ominous Warning about Artificial Intelligence" (Sparkes), and "Artificial Intelligence Experts Sign Open Letter to Protect Mankind from Machines" (Statt). The implication is that the machines will one day displace humanity.

Let's get one thing straight: a world in which humans are enslaved or destroyed by superintelligent machines of our

---

MICHAEL LITTMAN is Royce Family Professor of Teaching Excellence in Computer Science at Brown University. With Dave Ackley, he is the host of the podcast *Computing Up*. This piece was originally published in *Live Science* on January 28, 2015, and it is documented in MLA style.

own creation is purely science fiction. Like every other technology, AI has risks and benefits, but we cannot let fear dominate the conversation or guide AI research. Nevertheless, the idea of dramatically changing the AI research agenda to focus on AI "safety" is the primary message of a group calling itself the Future of Life Institute (FLI). FLI includes a handful of deep thinkers and public figures such as Elon Musk and Stephen Hawking and worries about the day in which humanity is steamrolled by powerful programs run amuck.

As eloquently described in the book *Superintelligence: Paths, Dangers, Strategies* by FLI advisory board member and Oxford-based philosopher Nick Bostrom, the plot unfolds in three parts. In the first part—roughly where we are now—computational power and intelligent software develops at an increasing pace through the toil of scientists and engineers. Next, a breakthrough is made: programs are created that possess intelligence on par with humans. These programs, running on increasingly fast computers, improve themselves extremely rapidly, resulting in a runaway "intelligence explosion." In the third and final act, a singular super-intelligence takes hold—outsmarting, outmaneuvering, and ultimately outcompeting the entirety of humanity and perhaps life itself. End scene.

Let's take a closer look at this apocalyptic storyline. Of the three parts, the first is indeed happening now and Bostrom provides cogent and illuminating glimpses into current and near-future technology. The third part is a philosophical romp exploring the consequences of supersmart machines. It's that second part—the intelligence explosion—that demonstrably violates what we know of computer science and natural intelligence.

Runaway Intelligence?

The notion of the intelligence explosion arises from Moore's law, the observation that the speed of computers has been increasing exponentially since the 1950s. Project this trend forward and we'll see computers with the computational power of the entire human race within the next few decades. It's a leap to go from this idea to unchecked growth of machine intelligence, however.

See Chapter 18 for tips on presenting the prevailing theories.

First, ingenuity is not the sole bottleneck to developing faster computers. The machines need to actually be built, which requires real-world resources. Indeed, Moore's law comes with exponentially increasing production costs as well—mass production of precision electronics does not come cheap. Further, there are fundamental physical laws—quantum limits—that bound how quickly a transistor can do its work. Non-silicon technologies may overcome those limits, but such devices remain highly speculative.

In addition to physical laws, we know a lot about the fundamental nature of computation and its limits. For example, some computational puzzles, like figuring out how to factor a number and thereby crack online cryptography schemes, are generally believed to be unsolvable by any fast program. They are part of a class of mathematically defined problems that are "NP-complete," meaning that they are exactly as hard as any problem that can be solved non-deterministically (N) in polynomial time (P), and they have resisted any attempt at scalable solution. As it turns out, most computational problems that we associate with human intelligence are known to be in this class.

See Chapter 6 for tips on anticipating objections.

Wait a second, you might say. How does the human mind manage to solve mathematical problems that computer scientists believe can't be solved? We don't.

By and large, we cheat. We build a cartoonish mental model of the elements of the world that we're interested in and then probe the behavior of this invented miniworld. There's a trade-off between completeness and tractability in these imagined microcosms. Our ability to propose and ponder and project credible futures comes at the cost of accuracy. Even allowing for the possibility of the existence of considerably faster computers than we have today, it is a logical impossibility that these computers would be able to accurately simulate reality faster than reality itself.

Countering the Anti-AI Cause

In the face of general skepticism in the AI and computer science 10 communities about the possibility of an intelligence explosion, FLI still wants to win support for its cause. The group's letter calls for increased attention to maximizing the societal benefits of developing AI. Many of my esteemed colleagues signed the letter to show their support for the importance of avoiding potential pitfalls of the technology. But a few key phrases in the letter such as "our AI systems must do what we want them to do" (Tegmark et al.) are taken by the press as an admission that AI researchers believe they might be creating something that cannot be controlled. It also implies that AI researchers are asleep at the wheel, oblivious to the ominous possibilities, which is simply untrue.

To be clear, there are indeed concerns about the near-term future of AI—algorithmic traders crashing the economy, or sensitive power grids overreacting to fluctuations and shutting down electricity for large swaths of the population. There's also a concern that systemic biases within academia and industry prevent underrepresented minorities from participating and helping to steer the growth of information technology. These worries should play a central role in the development and deployment of new ideas. But dread predictions of computers suddenly waking up and turning on us are simply not realistic.

I welcome an open discussion about how AI can be made robust and beneficial, and how we can engineer intelligent machines and systems that make society better. But, let's please keep the discussion firmly within the realm of reason and leave the robot uprisings to Hollywood screenwriters.

Works Cited

Bostrom, Nick. *Superintelligence: Paths, Dangers, Strategies*. Oxford UP, 2014.

Čapek, Karel. *R. U. R.* Translated by David Wyllie, The University of Adelaide, 2014. eBooks@Adelaide, https://ebooks.adelaide.edu.au/c /capek/karel/rur/index.html. Accessed 9 June 2017.

Sparkes, Matthew. "Top Scientists Have an Ominous Warning about Artificial Intelligence." *Business Insider*, 13 Jan. 2015, http://www. businessinsider.com/top-scientists-have-an-ominous-warning-about -artificial-intelligence-2015-1. Accessed 9 June 2017.

Statt, Nick. "Artificial intelligence experts sign open letter to protect mankind from machines." *CNET*, 11 Jan. 2015, https://www.cnet.com /news/artificial-intelligence-experts-sign-open-letter-to-protect-mankind -from-machines/. Accessed 9 June 2017.

Tegmark, Max, et al. "An Open Letter: Research Priorities for Robust and Beneficial Artificial Intelligence." *Future of Life Institute*, 2015, https://futureoflife.org/ai-open-letter. Accessed 9 June 2017.

CREDITS

TEXT

Michelle Alexander: Excerpt from *The New Jim Crow: Mass Incarceration in the Age of Colorblindness*–Copyright © 2010, 2012 & 2020 by Michelle Alexander. Reprinted by permission of The New Press. www.thenewpress.com

Editorial Staff of *The Eagle Eye*: Excerpt from "Our Manifesto to Fix America's Gun Laws." *The Guardian*, 23 Mar. 2018. Copyright Guardian News & Media Ltd 2023. Used with permission.

Christopher J. Ferguson and Patrick Markey: Excerpt from "Video Games Aren't Addictive." *The New York Times*, 2 Apr. 2017. From The New York Times. © 2017 The New York Times Company. All rights reserved. Used under license.

Joe Garcia: Used with permission of MIT Technology Review, from "Left Behind." *MIT Technology Review*, 30 Jun. 2021, p. 18; permission conveyed through Copyright Clearance Center, Inc.

Kenneth Goldsmith: "Go Ahead: Waste Time on the Internet." *Los Angeles Times*, 12 Aug. 2016. Reprinted courtesy of Kenneth Goldsmith.

Gerald Graff: Adapted from Graff, Gerald. "Hidden Intellectualism." *Clueless in Academe: How Schooling Obscures the Life of the Mind*, Yale University Press, 2003, pp. 211–231. Copyright © 2003 Yale University. Reprinted by permission of Yale University Press.

Michael Littman: "'Rise of the Machines' Is Not a Likely Future." *LiveScience.com*, 28 Jan. 2015. Reprinted by permission of Future Publishing Ltd.

Chris Nowinski: Excerpt from "Youth Tackle Football Will Be Considered Unthinkable 50 Years from Now." *Vox.com*, 3 Apr. 2019. https://www.vox.com/2019/3/27/18174368/football-concussion-brain-injury-cte-youth-football. Republished by permission of Vox Media, LLC.

CREDITS

ACKNOWLEDGMENTS

THIS BOOK WOULD NEVER HAVE seen print if it weren't for Marilyn Moller, our superb editor at Norton, and the extraordinary job she has done of inspiring, commenting on, and rewriting (and then rewriting and rewriting again) our many drafts. Our friendship with Marilyn is one of the most cherished things to have developed from this project.

We are also particularly thankful to our current Norton editor Sarah Touborg, whose exemplary counsel, criticism, and hands-on intervention shaped the changes we have made to this edition. We are grateful for Sarah's unflagging patience with a couple of sometimes-recalcitrant authors. Editorial assistant Caroline Fairey Meese skillfully and cheerfully coordinated the many details involved in preparing our manuscript.

Our thanks go as well to Mike Wright and Roby Harrington for their encouragement and astute suggestions (and great dinners) on their annual visits to Chicago. We extend our gratitude to Melissa Atkin and Brenda Manzanedo for their superb work managing the editing and production of this edition; and to Joy Cranshaw and Juliet Godwin for their energetic work creating the many digital resources that accompany the book. We appreciate Patricia Wong's excellent work as permissions editor and Ted Szczepanski's management of the photos for both versions of the book.

Thanks to John Darger, our Norton representative, who offered early encouragement to write this book; to Debra Morton Hoyt and Mike Wood for their excellent work on the cover. Special thanks to Michele Dobbins, Lib Triplett, and the incomparable Norton travelers for the superb work they've done on behalf of our book.

We extend our deep thanks to Laura J. Panning Davies for her many contributions to this book. Laura has done excellent work on the new e-version of this book, on the new chapter on AI, and on **theysayiblog.com**. And if that weren't enough, she has also updated the instructor's guide for *"They Say / I Say"* and expertly taken on the challenging task of editing *"They Say / I Say"* with Readings.

Many thanks to Professor Steve Benton of East Central University, who helped us not only with the first edition of this book, but with this new sixth edition. It was Steve's suggestion that we include the new chapter on writing about personal experiences. We only wish we'd thought of this ourselves! We also extend our thanks to those who provided in-depth reviews of the new chapter on drawing on your own experience: Lorelei Blackburn (Michigan State University), Velvet Pearson (Long Beach City College), Douglas Swartz (Indiana University, Northwest), Nicole Wendt (University of Minnesota), Cameron Wilson (William Jessup University), and Lacey Wootton (American University).

We would also like to thank Katharine Nicholson Ings (Manchester University) for her work on the Appendix ("Citing What They Say") as well as her superb copyediting.

A very special thanks goes to those who provided in-depth reviews of the new chapter on generative AI: Erin Ackerman (The College of New Jersey), Virginia Crisco (California State University at Fresno), Melissa Ganz (Marquette University),

Terra Joseph (Rider University), Katherine Osborne (Davis & Elkins College), Tanya Rodrigues (Salem State University), and Trish Serviss (University of California at Davis).

We're grateful to David Lipscomb, Director of the Georgetown University Writing Center, both for his clarifying suggestions on an early version of our new AI chapter and for soliciting feedback on a subsequent draft from the students in his writing courses. Thanks also to the students themselves for their invaluable responses to that draft, and finally to Georgetown student Sarah Sverdlov, to whom we give the last word of the chapter. Thanks also to our sister-in-law Carolyn Kahn Birkenstein and her colleagues at The MITRE Corporation for alllowing us to quote them on the business aspects of AI.

We are grateful to all of the instructors whose feedback was invaluable in shaping this sixth edition: Michelle Allen-Smith (Grand Rapids Community College), Valerie Ambrose (Shasta College), Stephanie Andre (Central Oregon Community College), Melissa Coss Aquino (Bronx Community College), Kim Armstrong (Metropolitan Community College), Beth Arnette Wade (Houston Community College), Gail Arnoff (John Carroll University), Sarah Baer (Moravian College), Peter Balaam (Carleton College), Molly Ball (University of Minnesota), Fredric Ball (Southwestern College), Joshua Barnes (Harrisburg Area Community College), Joshua Beall (Georgia Gwinnett College), Darlene Beaman (Lone Star College, Kingwood), Erin Beaver (Colorado Mountain College), John Bell (American River College), DeMisty Bellinger-Delfeld (Fitchburg State University), Monica Berlin (Knox College), Jessica Best (SUNY Adirondack), Brittany Biesiada (Monmouth University), Karen Birt (Grace College), Lorelei Blackburn (Michigan State University), Linda Black-Ochsenein (SUNY Oswego), Jill Bonds (West Hills Community College, Coalinga), Jesup Bonnstetter

(Des Moines Area Community College), Marci Bowden (Kirkwood Community College), Paula Boyd (Parkland College), Amber Braden (Ivy Tech Community College), Margaret Brockland-Nease (Georgia Southern University), Carellin Brooks (University of British Columbia), Bridgette Brown (University of Ottawa), Jacob Burg (Boston University), Jimmy Butts (Louisiana State University), Connor Byrne (University of British Columbia), Mary Callahan (Rhode Island College), Stacy Cameron (Oakton Community College), Rebecca Cash (SUNY Adirondack), Tom Cerasulo (Elms College), Wes Chapman (Illinois Wesleyan University), Rebecca Charry (Rochester Institute of Technology, Croatia), Song Chen (Bucknell University), Cheryl Christian (Virginia State University), Christopher Chrobak (California State University, Bakersfield), Fabrizio Ciccone (Brown University), Sara Cipriano (Bakersfield College), Erin Mae Clark (Saint Mary's University of Minnesota), Aaron Clark (Dallas College Brookhaven Campus), Patrick Clauss (University of Notre Dame), Tara Coleman (LaGuardia Community College), Sarah Collins (University of Illinois, Springfield), Glenn Collins (California State University, Northridge), Chris Corning (Pierce College), Linda Cowling (North Central Missouri College), Steve Criniti (West Liberty University), Marian Crotty (Loyola University Maryland), Sharon Dansereau (Hawaii Community College), Kevin Degnan (El Camino College), Sari Delagneau (Mission Hills High School), Robert Dixon-Kolar (College of DuPage), Ashley Dycus (University of West Georgia), Susan Erdmann (University of Agder), Greg Farber (Bentley University), Kelly Fenwick (Virginia State University), Erik Fetler (Monterey Peninsula College), Ted Fitts (Boston University), Kevin Flanagan (George Mason University), Dorritta Fong (Douglas College), Lindsay Foran (University of Ottawa), Ryan Fowler (Franklin &

Marshall College), Nicholas Frangipane (Suffolk University), Meaghan Fritz (Northwestern University), Porscha de la Fuente (Kapi'olani Community College), Erin Fujinami (Fresno City College), Anna Garcia (Middlesex Community College), Johnny Gilbert (University of Arkansas, Little Rock), Esther Godfrey (University of South Carolina, Upstate), Oscar Goff (St. Paul's Episcopal School), Nancy Gold (Northern Michigan University), Teah Goldberg (Loyola Marymount University), Sarah Gottschall (Prince George's Community College), Maura Grady (Ashland University), William Green (Douglas College), Jeremy Greenway (Huron University College at Western University), Eric Gregory (Saddleback College), Heather Greise (Allegany College of Maryland), Janet Gross (University of Maryland, Baltimore County), Edythe Hampson (University of Maine), Brooke Harrison (Central Michigan University), Natalie Hewitt (Hope International University), Meagan Hoff (Collin College), Max Hohner (Eastern Washington University), Seth Holler (Evangelical Christian School), Jessica Hoover (Baker College), Salisa Hortenstine Olmsted (Lake Land College), William Howell (George Mason University), Becky Hsu (University of California, Berkeley), Jaimie Humbert (Henderson Community College), Kirsten Iden (University of South Carolina, Salkehatchie), Scott Jackshaw (Brown University), LaToya Jefferson-James (Mississippi Valley State University), Ryan Jones (Harrisburg Area Community College, York), Christine Jones (Dallas Baptist University), Geneffa Jonker (Cabrillo College), Jamie Joseph (De Anza College), Wyatt Keener (Cumberland University), Daphne Keller (Monmouth University), Sharon Kelly (Shippensburg University), Michael Kent (Riverside Community College), Swan Kim (Bronx Community College), Heather King (Ivy Tech Community College), Timothy Klitz (Washington & Jefferson College), Jan Knispel (Mid Plains

Community College, Valentine), Carla Kungl (Shippensburg University), Scott Lankford (Foothill College), Victoria Large (Berklee College of Music), Haley Larson (Dakota State University), Aaron Lelito (SUNY Erie Community College), John Levine (University of California, Berkeley), Sarah Lincoln (Portland State University), Sara Lindey (Saint Vincent College), Susan Lipscomb (Houghton College), Catherine Loomis (Rochester Institute of Technology), Louise Lord (Bronx Community College), Karen Lowe (Solano Community College), Andrea Maciel (California State University, Bakersfield), Jennifer MacKenzie (Lehman College, CUNY), Janice Mann (Bucknell University), Rebekah Maples (California Polytechnic State University, San Luis Obispo), Meredith Marchioni (Alaska Pacific University), Selina Marcille (Southern New Hampshire University), Farah Marklevits (Augustana College), Megan Marshall (Marshall University), Liz Mayo (Jackson State Community College), Kate McCahill (Santa Fe Community College), Tim McCormack (John Jay College), Willis McCumber (University at Buffalo), Cynthia McKeag (Oakton Community College), Ildiko Melis (Bay Mills Community College), Mitchell Melter (New York University), Tiffany Messerschmidt (Polk State College), Jeremy Meyer (Arizona State University), Monica Miller (Middle George State University), Cara Minardi-Power (Florida Southwestern State), Evelina Miscin (Rochester Institute of Technology, Croatia), Kimberly Moekle (Loyola Marymount University), Stephen Molloy (Moravian Academy), Sharleen Mondal (Ashland University), John Nardone (Lehigh Carbon Community College), Emma Newcombe (Boston University), David Newman (University of British Columbia), Melody Niesen (Northland Pioneer College), Heidi Nobles (University of Virginia), Matt Norman (Vincennes University),

Acknowledgments

Oluwatosin Ogunnika (Virginia State University), David Onofrychuk (Alaska Pacific University), Michael Opolicky (Dallas College), Amanda O'Sullivan (Community College of Denver), Dennis Pahl (LIU Post), Shelley Palmer (Wake Technical Community College), Velvet Pearson (Long Beach City College), Carolina Pelaez-Morales (Columbus State Univerisity), Jennifer Penkethman (De Anza College), Alesya Petty (San José State University), Laura Phelan (St. John Fisher College), Nicola Philpott (Champlain College Saint-Lambert), Robert Pickford (San Diego Mesa College), Meenakshi Ponnuswami (Bucknell University), Katherine Preston (Brown University), Tiffany Probasco (University of Delaware), Sarah Quirk (Waubonsee Community College), John Quirk (Brown University), Ben Railton (Fitchburg State University), Alexis Ramsey (Eckerd College), Patty Rasmussen (Big Bend Community College), Katie Rasmussen (Adrian College), Angela Rehbein (West Liberty University), Yelizaveta Renfro (Saint Mary's College), Rachel Rinehart (Marshall University), Aaron Ritzenberg (Columbia University), Erin Rodriguez (California State University, Bakersfield), Linda Rogers (California State University, Chico), Kathy Rose (Dixie State University), Howard Rosenberg (Rowan College of South Jersey), Alison Rukavina (Langara College), Katie Sagal (Cornell College), Renee Schaller (Hunter College, CUNY), Cassandra Scherr (University at Buffalo), Mary Seel (SUNY Broome), Neil Segars (Freed-Hardeman University), Nicole Servino (Community College of Denver), Kayleigh Sevi (Orange Coast College), Siri Shankar (California State University, Fresno), Shantavia Shelton (Harding University), Michelle Shin (Kapi'olani Community College), John Silvestro (Slippery Rock University), Catherine Sims (Cascia Hall), Kristin Skager (De Anza College), Lisa Smith (University of Nebraska, Omaha), Amanda Smothers (Harper College), Jennie Snow (Rutgers University), Susan St John (Windward Community College), Daniel Stanford (Pitt Community College), Elizabeth Starr (Ivy Tech Community College, Bloomington), Matthew Stenson (Texas Tech University), Brian Stepanic (Newark High School), Michelle Sterling (Berklee College of Music), Carolyn Stoermer (Wright State University), Kristyn Stout (Ocean County College), Sarah Strong (University of Hartford), Trisha Stubblefield (Cottey College), Kate Sullivan (Lane Community College), Doug Swartz (Indiana University Northwest), Nanette Tamer (Stevenson University), Jayanti Tamm (Ocean County College), Marie Taylor (Arcadia University), Anne-Marie Thomas (Austin Community College, Highland), Tiffaney Tiffin (Hope International University), Travis Timmons (Butler County Community College), Melissa Toomey (Temple University), Deborah Uman (St. John Fisher College), Peter Vahle (University of California, Berkelely), Dagmar Van Engen (Arizona State University), Mark Wagenaar (Valparaiso University), Garry Walton (Meredith College), Jayne Waterman (Ashland University), Cathy Webb (Augustana College), Karen Woods Weierman (Worcester State University), Nicole Wendt (Ubah Medical Academy), Suzanne Wielgos (College of DuPage), Katrina Wilkins (Brigham Young University), Todd Williams (Kutztown University of PA), Stephanie Williams (University of Arkansas, Little Rock), Cameron Wilson (William Jessup University), Terri Woebel (Willowbrook High School), Lacey Wootton (American University), Timothy Wutrich (Case Western Reserve University), Joanne Yantz (Colorado Mountain College), Liam Young (Vancouver Island University), Jennifer Young (Cape Fear Community College), Kelly Zepp (Community

College of Denver), and Jason Ziebart (Central Carolina Community College). We owe a special debt of gratitude to Erin Ackerman for her expert contributions to the new chapter on research and for her chapter on writing in the social sciences. We also thank Chris Gillen for his chapter on writing in the sciences. Working with Erin and Chris proved to be an exhilarating experience; we learned a great deal by seeing how they applied our ideas to their disciplines.

A very special thanks goes to those who provided in-depth reviews of the chapters on research and revising: Steven Bailey (Central Michigan University), Ana Cooke (Penn State University), Courtney Danforth (College of Southern Nevada), Africa Fine (Palm Beach State College), and Traci Klass (Palm Beach State College); and to those who provided detailed evaluations of the fourth edition: Joe Bizup (Boston University), Laura J. Panning Davies (SUNY Cortland), Karen Gocsik (University of California at San Diego), and Kelly Ritter (University of Illinois at Urbana–Champaign).

We owe a special thanks to our colleagues in the English department at the University of Illinois at Chicago: Mark Canuel, our former department head, for supporting our earlier efforts overseeing the university's Writing in the Disciplines requirement; Walter Benn Michaels, another former department head; and Ann Feldman, former director of university writing programs, for encouraging us to teach first-year composition courses at UIC in which we could try out ideas and drafts of our manuscript; Tom Moss, Diane Chin, Vainis Aleksa, and Matt Pavesich, who have also been very supportive of our efforts; and Matt Oakes, our former research assistant. We are also grateful to Ann Feldman, Diane Chin, and Mark Bennett for bringing us into their graduate course on the teaching of writing; and to Lisa Freeman, John Huntington, Walter Benn Michaels, and Ralph Cintron for inviting us to present our ideas in the keynote lecture at UIC's 2013 Composition Matters conference.

We are also especially grateful not only to Steve Benton, whom we mentioned earlier, but to Nadya Pittendrigh, who together with Steve taught a section of composition with us using an early draft of this book. We are grateful to Andy Young, a lecturer at UIC who has tested our book in his courses and who continues to give us extremely helpful feedback. And we thank Vershawn A. Young, whose work on code-meshing influenced our argument in Chapter 9, and Hillel Crandus, who inspired the chapter on "Entering Classroom Discussions."

We are grateful to the many colleagues and friends who've let us talk our ideas out with them and given extremely helpful responses. UIC's former dean, Stanley Fish, has been central in this respect, both in personal conversations and in his incisive articles calling for greater focus on form in the teaching of writing. Our conversations with Jane Tompkins have also been integral to this book, as was the composition course that Jane cotaught with Gerald, titled "Can We Talk?" Lenny Davis, too, offered both intellectual insight and emotional support, as did Heather Arnet, Jennifer Ashton, Janet Atwill, Kyra Auslander, Noel Barker, Mark Bauerlein, Jim Benton, Jack Brereton, Jim Burke, Tim Cantrick, Marsha Cassidy, David Chinitz, Lisa Chinitz, Pat Chu, Harry J. Cook, Duane Davis, Bridget O'Rourke Flisk, Steve Flisk, Judy Gardiner, Howard Gardner, Rich Gelb, Gwynne Gertz, Jeff Gore, Bill Haddad, Ben Hale, Scott Hammerl, Patricia Harkin, Andy Hoberek, John Huntington, Carol Jago, Joe Janangelo, Paul Jay, David Jolliffe, Nancy Kohn, Don Lazere, Sarah Levine, Jo Liebermann, Les Lynn, Steven Mailloux, Deirdre McCloskey, Maurice J. Meilleur, Alan Meyers,

Greg Meyerson, Anna Minkov, Chris Newfield, Randy Olson, Jim Phelan, Paul Psilos, Bruce Robbins, Charles Ross, Eileen Seifert, Evan Seymour, David Shumway, Herb Simons, Jim Sosnoski, Kyle Stedman, David Steiner, Harold Aram Veeser, Chuck Venegoni, Marla Weeg, Jerry Wexler, Joyce Wexler, Virginia Wexman, Jeffrey Williams, Lynn Woodbury, Art Young, Vershawn Young, and the late Wayne Booth, whose friendship we dearly miss.

We are grateful for having had the opportunity to present our ideas to a number of colleges and high schools: University of Arkansas at Little Rock, Augustana College, Brandeis University, Brigham Young University, Bryn Mawr College, California State University at Bakersfield, California State University at Northridge, University of California at Riverside, Case Western University, Central Michigan University, Clemson University, Columbia University, Community College of Philadelphia, Daemen College, Davidson College, University of Delaware, DePauw University, Drew University, Duke University, Duquesne University, Elmhurst College, Emory University, Fairfield University, Fontbonne University, Furman University, Gettysburg College, Harper College, Harvard University, Haverford College, Hawaii Office of Secondary School Curriculum Instruction, Hunter College, University of Illinois College of Medicine, Illinois State University, Illinois Wesleyan University, John Carroll University, Kansas State University, Lawrence University, the Lawrenceville School, University of Louisiana at Lafayette, MacEwan University, University of Maryland at College Park, Massachusetts Institute of Technology, University of Memphis, Miami University, Mills College, University of Missouri at Columbia, New Trier High School, North Carolina A&T University, University of North Florida, Northern Michigan University, Northwestern University

Division of Continuing Studies, Norwalk Community College, University of Notre Dame, Ohio State University, Ohio Wesleyan University, Oregon State University, University of Portland, Purdue University at Calumet, University of Rochester, Rockford University, St. Ambrose University, St. Andrew's School, St. Charles High School, St. Francis University at Joliet, State University of New York at Geneseo, State University of New York at Stony Brook, Seattle University, South Elgin High School, University of South Florida, Southern Connecticut State University, University of Southern Mississippi, Stanford University, Swarthmore College, Teachers College, University of Tennessee at Knoxville, University of Texas at Arlington, Tulane University, Union College, Ursinus College, Wabash College, Washington College, University of Washington, University of West Virginia at Morgantown, Western Michigan University, Westinghouse/Kenwood High Schools, Wheaton North High School, Wheaton Warrenville English Chairs, Winona State University, and the University of Wisconsin at Whitewater.

We particularly thank those who helped arrange these visits and discussed writing issues with us: Jeff Abernathy, Herman Asarnow, John Austin, Greg Barnheisel, John Bean, Crystal Benedicks, Joe Bizup, Sheridan Blau, Dagne Bloland, Chris Breu, Elizabeth Brockman, Mark Brouwer, Lizabeth Bryant, Joan Johnson Bube, John Caldwell, Gregory Clark, Irene Clark, Dean Philip Cohen, Cathy D'Agostino, Tom Deans, Gaurav Desai, Lisa Dresdner, Kathleen Dudden-Rowlands, Lisa Ede, Alexia Ellett, Emory Elliott, Anthony Ellis, Kim Flachmann, Ronald Fortune, Rosanna Fukuda, George Haggerty, Donald Hall, Joe Harris, Gary Hatch, Elizabeth Hatmaker, Donna Heiland, Harry Hellenbrand, Nicole Henderson, Doug Hesse, Van Hillard, Andrew Hoberek, Michael Hustedde, Sara Jameson, T. R.

Johnson, David Jones, Ann Kaplan, Don Kartiganer, Linda Kinnahan, Dean Georg Kleine, Albert Labriola, Craig Lawrence, Lori Lopez, Tom Liam Lynch, Hiram Maxim, Michael Mays, Elizabeth McDermott, Thomas McFadden, Sean Meehan, Connie Mick, Robert Morace, Joseph Musser, Margaret Oakes, John O'Connor, Gary Olson, Tom Pace, Amy Pearson, Les Perelman, Jim Phelan, Emily Poe, Dominick Randolph, Clancy Ratliff, Monica Rico, Kelly Ritter, Jack Robinson, Warren Rosenberg, Laura Rosenthal, Dean Howard Ross, Deborah Rossen-Knill, Paul Schacht, Petra Schatz, Evan Seymour, Rose Shapiro, Mike Shea, Cecilia M. Shore, Erec Smith, Kelly Smith, Nancy Sommers, Stephen Spector, Timothy Spurgin, Ron Strickland, Marcy Taylor, Michael Theune, Trig Thoreson, Josh Toth, Judy Trost, Aiman Tulamait, Charles Tung, John Webster, Robert Weisbuch, Sandi Weisenberg, Karin Westman, Martha Woodmansee, and Lynn Worsham.

We also wish to extend particular thanks to two Chicago-area educators who have worked closely with us: Eileen Murphy of CERCA and Les Lynn, formerly of the Chicago Debate League and now director of our joint organization, Argument-Centered Education. Lastly, we wish to thank two high school teachers for their excellent and inventive adaptations of our work: Mark Gozonsky in his *YouTube* video clip "Building Blocks," and Dave Stuart Jr. in his blogs, *Teaching the Core* and *Let's Make Teaching Better*.

We would also like to express our gratitude to several people who have published interviews with us about *"They Say / I Say"*: Dave Stuart Jr., "A Conversation with Gerald Graff and Cathy Birkenstein" at **www.davestuartjr.com**; Erica Meltzer, "The Critical Reader Conversation with Gerald Graff and Cathy Birkenstein" at **www.thecriticalreader.com**; Park Howell, "How the Teaching of Argument Can Save American Education" at www.businessofstory.com; and Harold Aram Veeser, ed., in *The Rebirth of American Literary Theory and Criticism: Scholars Discuss Intellectual Origins and Turning Points* (2020).

For inviting us to present our ideas at their conferences, we are grateful to John Brereton and Richard Wendorf at the Boston Athenaeum; Wendy Katkin of the Reinvention Center of State University of New York at Stony Brook; Luchen Li of the Michigan English Association; Lisa Lee and Barbara Ransby of the Public Square in Chicago; Don Lazere of the University of Tennessee at Knoxville; Dennis Baron of the University of Illinois at Urbana–Champaign; Alfie Guy of Yale University; Irene Clark of the California State University of Northridge; George Crandell and Steve Hubbard, codirectors of the ACETA conference at Auburn University; Mary Beth Rose of the Humanities Institute at the University of Illinois at Chicago; Diana Smith of St. Anne's Belfield School and the University of Virginia; Jim Maddox and Victor Luftig of the Bread Loaf School of English; Jan Fitzsimmons and Jerry Berberet of the Associated Colleges of Illinois; Rosemary Feal, executive director of the Modern Language Association; Les Perelman of the Massachusetts Institute of Technology; and Bruce Herzberg of Bentley College and Chris Gallagher of Northeastern University.

Finally, a special thank you to David Bartholomae for suggesting the phrase that became the subtitle of this book.

APPENDIX

---□---

CITING WHAT THEY SAY

This book argues that the most important move for entering academic conversations involves referring to, and, often, <u>documenting</u> what others say (what "They Say"). And yet, documenting or citing what others say can be daunting. As even the most veteran academics will tell you, documentation is filled with seemingly countless esoteric rules for how different sources should be cited. Although this appendix does not pretend to offer an exhaustive guide to these rules (as several more comprehensive guides do), it does try to clarify several of the most basic of these rules in order to make the practice of crediting the "They Says" you're in dialogue with a little easier.

For starters, it can be helpful to note that, in the academic world, citing a "They Say" is done in two parts: within the body of what you're writing (what's called "in-text documentation") and in a list of your sources at the end of what you've written (your "Works Cited" or "References"). Depending on the documentation style you are using and the kind of source you are citing, you may need to provide parenthetical information at the end of any sentences that include material you quote, summarize, or paraphrase. This appendix offers some of the most commonly used formats or "templates" for the two most prominent academic styles, the Modern Language Association of America (MLA) and the Psychological Association of America (APA).

MLA is often used in the humanities fields (English, art, music, etc.) and APA in social sciences (psychology, sociology, political science, etc.), although there are exceptions to this rule. Always check with your instructor about which documentation style to use. If you're writing a history paper, your instructor may want you to use Chicago style, an example of which can be found in the reading by Michelle Alexander on pages 331–34 of this book.

MLA STYLE

If you were quoting this book in MLA style and using the print copy, you might write:

> As Gerald Graff and Cathy Birkenstein put it, "To write a really good summary, you must be able to suspend your own beliefs for a time and put yourself in the shoes of someone else" (33).

Or, if you didn't want to identify the authors right away by name, you could write:

> Writing a good summary means being able to "suspend your own beliefs for a time and put yourself in the shoes of someone else" (Graff and Birkenstein 33).

If you're quoting from an online source with no page numbers, such as the ebook version of this text, then no number is needed in your parenthetical reference. But if the source has chapters, as the ebook does, you would use the abbreviation "ch." in your parenthetical reference: (Graff and Birkenstein, ch. 1).

At the end of your essay, your works-cited list would give readers publication details about the book, formatted in this way:

> Graff, Gerald, and Cathy Birkenstein. *"They Say / I Say": The Moves That Matter in Academic Writing.* W. W. Norton, 2024.

To see an example of MLA style that uses a variety of sources, see student writer Kelly Coryell's essay "All Words Matter: The Manipulation behind 'All Lives Matter,'" found on pages 00–00.

APA STYLE

When you're writing using APA style, you may do more summarizing or paraphrasing of your sources than quoting them directly. But if you were quoting this book's authors in APA style, you would use their last names as well as the date in the signal phrase:

> Graff and Birkenstein (2024) assert, "To write a really good summary, you must be able to suspend your own beliefs for a time and put yourself in the shoes of someone else" (p. 33).

Or, if you didn't want to identify the authors right away by name, you could cite them this way, using an ampersand (&) instead of "and" between their names:

> Writing a good summary means being able to "suspend your own beliefs for a time and put yourself in the shoes of someone else" (Graff & Birkenstein, 2024, p. 33).

And your reference list would give readers publication details about the book, formatted in this way:

> Graff, G., & Birkenstein, C. (2024). *"They say / I say": The moves that matter in academic writing.* W. W. Norton.

To see an example of APA style that uses a variety of sources, see student writer Yael Lenga's essay "Disability in Higher Education: Building Access and Building Futures" on pages 00–00.

And to get more help with both styles, watch the videos on Using Signal Phrases and Understanding In-Text Documentation at digital.wwnorton.com/theysay6.

WHEN YOUR "THEY SAY" ISN'T HUMAN

If you are quoting from or incorporating any text or data that you've created through a generative artificial intelligence tool, like *ChatGPT*, you will need to document it. Tools such as *ChatGPT* generate a response to being asked a question, such as "How do I write a summary of a text?" And because generative AI tools generate a different response each time, even when being asked the same question, each instance must be documented.

MLA STYLE

To quote part of a large language model's response to your question in MLA style, you would include an abbreviated form of the question you asked after the quotation, and formatted as follows:

> When asked how to summarize a text, *ChatGPT* provided an eight-point response, including "Read the text carefully and identify the main ideas and key points" ("How do I write a summary?").

If you wanted to quote a description or paraphrase of *ChatGPT*'s response, you would also include an abbreviated form of the question you asked after the description or paraphrase. The format should look as follows:

> When asked how to summarize a text, *ChatGPT* provided an eight-point response ("How do I write a summary?").

Your works-cited list would give readers details about the question you asked, starting with the full phrasing, followed by the title of the AI tool, the version, the publisher, the date you asked the question, and the URL, formatted as follows:

"How do I write a summary of a text?" *ChatGPT*, 3 May version, OpenAI, 8 May 2023, chat.openai.com/chat.

APA STYLE

If you were citing a quotation from *ChatGPT*'s response to your question in APA style, and incorporating the author into your prose, you would, in the signal phrase, include OpenAI as the author followed by the year of the version you used, formatted as follows:

When prompted by "How do I write a summary of a text?" OpenAI (2023) provided an eight-point response, including "Read the text carefully and identify the main ideas and key points."

If you do not mention the author in your passage, you would follow the quotation, description, or paraphrase with a reference to OpenAI as the author and the year of the version of it you used, formatted as follows:

When prompted with "How do I write a summary of a text?" the ChatGPT-generated text provided an eight-point response (OpenAI, 2023).

And your reference list would begin with the author, followed by the year of the version you used, the name of the model, the version, any additional description in brackets, and the URL, formatted as follows:

OpenAI. (2023). *ChatGPT* (May 3 version) [Large language model]. https://chatopenai.com/chat

APPENDIX

LINKING TO WHAT "THEY SAY"

What if all your sources are online? An easy way of giving your readers instant access to what "they say" is to use hyperlinks. Anything with a URL can be linked to—blog posts, articles, social media posts, and so forth. Readers can click on the words to which you've attached links and be taken directly to those pages, as we can see in the following example:

> In the U.S., participating in youth sports is expensive and time-consuming. As writer Jill Filipovic explains, kids from wealthier families can join costly club travel teams, but because of a lack of funding in poorer communities, there are fewer options for low-cost recreational leagues and school-sponsored sports. In this essay, she makes a case that this growing divide in youth sports compounds other systemic inequities in U.S. society.

By including a link to Filipovic's website and to the article being summarized, the writer gives her readers direct access to the relevant sources she used. But in most academic writing, linking doesn't relieve writers of the need to introduce and frame what others say, so here are a few templates for framing a link:

- As X mentions in this article, "_____."

- In making this comment, X warns that _____.

- Economists often assume that _____; however, new research by X suggests _____.

Linking does create some efficiencies and allow us to connect texts and ideas in ways we couldn't before. But whatever your format, and however limited your space, in academic and professional writing too, if you want others to listen to what you say, you need to provide them with access in some form to your sources—i.e., to what others you're in dialogue with say.

INDEX OF TEMPLATES

LISTEN BEFORE YOU LEAP
(p. 10)

▶ While I understand the impulse to _____, my own view is _____.

▶ While I agree with X that _____, I cannot accept her over-all conclusion that _____.

▶ While X argues _____, and I argue _____, in a way we're both right.

THE TEMPLATE OF TEMPLATES
(p. 11)

▶ In recent discussions of _____, a controversial issue has been whether _____. On the one hand, some argue that _____. From this perspective, _____. On the other hand, however, others argue that _____. In the words of _____, one of this view's main proponents, "_____." According to this view, _____. In sum, then, the issue is whether _____ or _____.

My own view is that _____. Though I concede that _____, I still maintain that _____. For example, _____. Although some might object that _____, I would reply that _____. The issue is important because _____.

INTRODUCING WHAT "THEY SAY"
(p. 23)

▸ A number of _____ have recently suggested that _____.

▸ It has become common today to dismiss _____.

▸ In their recent work, Y and Z have offered harsh critiques of _____ for _____.

INTRODUCING "STANDARD VIEWS"
(p. 24)

▸ Americans have always believed that _____.

▸ Conventional wisdom has it that _____.

▸ Common sense seems to dictate that _____.

▸ The standard way of thinking about topic X has it that _____.

▸ It is often said that _____.

▸ My whole life I have heard it said that _____.

▸ You would think that _____.

▸ Many people assume that _____.

MAKING WHAT "THEY SAY" SOMETHING *YOU* SAY
(pp. 24–25)

▸ I've always believed that _____.

▸ When I was a child, I used to think that _____.

▸ Although I should know better by now, I cannot help thinking that _____.

▸ At the same time that I believe _____, I also believe _____.

INTRODUCING SOMETHING IMPLIED OR ASSUMED
(p. 25)

▸ Although none of them have ever said so directly, my teachers have often given me the impression that _____.

▸ One implication of X's treatment of _____ is that _____.

▸ Although X does not say so directly, she apparently assumes that _____.

▸ While they rarely admit as much, _____ often take for granted that _____.

INTRODUCING AN ONGOING DEBATE
(pp. 26–28)

▸ In discussions of X, one controversial issue has been _____. On the one hand, _____ argues _____. On the other hand, _____ contends _____. Others even maintain _____. My own view is _____.

▸ When it comes to the topic of _____, most of us will readily agree that _____. Where this agreement usually ends, however, is on the question of _____. Whereas some are convinced that _____, others maintain that _____.

▸ In conclusion, then, as I suggested earlier, defenders of _____ can't have it both ways. Their assertion that _____ is contradicted by their claim that _____.

CAPTURING AUTHORIAL ACTION
(pp. 43–44)

▸ X acknowledges that _____.

▸ X agrees that _____.

▸ X argues that _____.

▸ X believes that _____.

▸ X celebrates the fact that _____.

▸ X claims that _____.

▸ X complains that _____.

▸ X concedes that _____.

▸ X demonstrates that _____.

▸ X denies/does not deny that _____.

▸ X deplores the tendency to _____.

▸ X emphasizes that _____.

- ► X insists that _____.

- ► X observes that _____.

- ► X questions whether _____.

- ► X refutes the claim that _____.

- ► X reminds us that _____.

- ► X reports that _____.

- ► X suggests that _____.

- ► X urges us to _____.

INTRODUCING QUOTATIONS
(p. 51)

- ► X states, "_____."

- ► As the prominent philosopher X puts it, "_____."

- ► According to X, "_____."

- ► X himself writes, "_____."

- ► In her book, _____, X maintains that "_____."

- ► Writing in the journal _____, X complains that "_____."

- ► In X's view, "_____."

- ► X agrees when she writes, "_____."

- ► X disagrees when he writes, "_____."

- ► X complicates matters further when he writes, "_____."

EXPLAINING QUOTATIONS
(p. 52)

▸ Basically, X is warning _____.

▸ In other words, X believes _____.

▸ In making this comment, X urges us to _____.

▸ X is corroborating the age-old adage that _____.

▸ X's point is that _____.

▸ The essence of X's argument is that _____.

DISAGREEING, WITH REASONS
(p. 64)

▸ X is mistaken because she overlooks _____.

▸ X's claim that _____ rests upon the questionable assumption that _____.

▸ I disagree with X's view that _____ because, as recent research has shown, _____.

▸ X contradicts herself / can't have it both ways. On the one hand, she argues _____. On the other hand, she also says _____.

▸ By focusing on _____, X overlooks the deeper problem of _____.

AGREEING
(pp. 66–68)

▸ I agree that _____ because my experience _____ confirms it.

▸ X surely is right about _____ because, as she may not be aware, recent studies have shown that _____.

▸ X's theory of _____ is extremely useful because it sheds insight on the difficult problem of _____.

▸ Those unfamiliar with this school of thought may be interested to know that it basically boils down to _____.

▸ I agree that _____, a point that needs emphasizing since so many people believe _____.

▸ If group X is right that _____, as I think they are, then we need to reassess the popular assumption that _____.

AGREEING AND DISAGREEING SIMULTANEOUSLY
(pp. 70–71)

▸ Yes, it's true that _____. But _____.

▸ I'm of two minds about X's claim that _____. On the one hand, X seems right that _____. On the other hand, X seems wrong to suggest _____.

▸ Although I [must] question some of X's assumptions, I fully endorse the most important part of their argument: their conclusion that _____.

▸ Although I have no problem with X's claim that _____, I strongly disagree with their main conclusion that _____.

SIGNALING WHO IS SAYING WHAT
(pp. 78–79)

▸ Although X makes the best possible case for _____,
_____.

▸ My view, however, contrary to what X has argued, is that
_____.

▸ Adding to X's argument, I would point out that _____.

▸ According to both X and Y, _____.

▸ Politicians, X argues, should _____.

▸ Most athletes will tell you that _____.

▸ X is right that _____.

▸ The evidence shows that _____.

▸ X's assertion that _____ does not fit the facts.

▸ Anyone familiar with _____ should agree that _____.

▸ Yet _____ are real, and are arguably the most significant
factor in _____.

EMBEDDING VOICE MARKERS
(p. 81)

▸ X overlooks what I consider an important point about
_____.

▸ My own view is that what X insists is a _____ is in fact
a _____.

▸ I wholeheartedly endorse what X calls _____.

▸ These conclusions, which X discusses in _____, add weight to the argument that _____.

ENTERTAINING OBJECTIONS
(p. 88)

▸ As I write this, I can hear the reaction of some skeptics to many of the proposals in this essay: It's all fine and well for _____. But what about _____?

▸ Yet some may challenge my view on the grounds that _____.

▸ Yet some readers may challenge my view by insisting that _____.

▸ Of course, many will probably disagree on the grounds that _____.

NAMING YOUR NAYSAYERS
(pp. 89–90)

▸ Here many _____ would probably object that _____.

▸ But _____ would certainly take issue with the argument that _____.

▸ _____, of course, may want to question whether _____.

▸ Nevertheless, both followers and critics of _____ will probably suggest otherwise and argue that _____.

▸ Although not all _____ think alike, some of them will probably dispute my claim that _____ .

▸ _____ are so diverse in their views that it's hard to generalize about them, but some are likely to object on the grounds that _____ .

INTRODUCING OBJECTIONS INFORMALLY
(pp. 90–91)

▸ But is my proposal realistic? What are the chances of its actually being adopted?

▸ Yet is it necessarily true that _____? Is it always the case, as I have been suggesting, that _____?

▸ However, does the evidence I've cited prove conclusively that _____?

▸ "Impossible," some will say. "You must be reading the research selectively."

MAKING CONCESSIONS WHILE STILL
STANDING YOUR GROUND (p. 94)

▸ Although I grant that _____, I still maintain that _____.

▸ Proponents of X are right to argue that _____. But they exaggerate when they claim that _____.

▸ While it is true that _____, it does not necessarily follow that _____.

▸ On the one hand, I agree with X that _____. But on the other hand, I still insist that _____.

USING STORIES TO DRAMATIZE YOUR "THEY SAY" AND "I SAY" (pp. 102–109)

▸ Many often worry that _____. But the other night I _____.

▸ I knew there was a problem the instant I _____. When I suggested _____, I was met with _____. When I proposed _____, X told me _____. It may be true, I grant, that _____. But I still hold to my belief that _____.

▸ There was once a time when I was passionately committed to the idea that _____. I remember encountering a _____ one day and thinking _____. Now, however, having _____, I have come to realize _____.

▸ I tell this story because it shows _____.

▸ Lest anyone read this story as evidence that _____, I would point out that _____.

▸ A central lesson of my English course last semester was that _____. But author X, whom we are reading in this history course, suggests _____. My own opinion is that _____ has the better argument, largely because _____.

INDICATING WHO CARES
(pp. 115–116)

▸ _____ used to think _____. But recently [or within the past few decades] _____ suggests that _____.

▸ These findings challenge the work of earlier researchers, who tended to assume that _____.

▸ Recent studies like these shed new light on _____, which previous studies had not addressed.

▸ Researchers have long assumed that _____. For instance, one eminent scholar of cell biology, _____, assumed in _____, her seminal work on cell structures and functions, that fat cells _____. As _____ herself put it, "_____" (2012). Another leading scientist, _____, argued that fat cells "_____" (2011). Ultimately, when it came to the nature of fat, the basic assumption was that _____.

But a new body of research shows that fat cells are far more complex and that _____.

▸ If sports enthusiasts stopped to think about it, many of them might simply assume that the most successful athletes _____. However, new research shows _____.

▸ These findings challenge neoliberals' common assumptions that _____.

▸ At first glance, teenagers appear to _____. But on closer inspection _____.

ESTABLISHING WHY YOUR CLAIMS MATTER
(pp. 118–119)

▸ X matters / is important because _____.

▸ Although X may seem trivial, it is in fact crucial in terms of today's concern over _____.

▸ Ultimately, what is at stake here is _____ .

▸ These findings have important consequences for the broader domain of _____ .

▸ If we are right about _____ , then major consequences follow for _____ .

▸ These conclusions / This discovery will have significant applications in _____ as well as in _____ .

▸ Although X may seem of concern to only a small group of _____ , it should in fact concern anyone who cares about _____ .

COMMONLY USED TRANSITIONS

(pp. 127–128)

ADDITION

also	in fact
and	indeed
besides	moreover
furthermore	so too
in addition	

ELABORATION

actually	to put it another way
by extension	to put it bluntly
in other words	to put it succinctly
in short	ultimately
that is	

EXAMPLE

after all	for instance
as an illustration	specifically
consider	to take a case in point
for example	

CAUSE AND EFFECT

accordingly	so
as a result	then
consequently	therefore
hence	thus
since	

COMPARISON

along the same lines	likewise
in the same way	similarly

CONTRAST

although	nevertheless
but	nonetheless
by contrast	on the contrary
conversely	on the other hand
despite	regardless
even though	whereas
however	while
in contrast	yet

CONCESSION

admittedly

although it is true that

granted

of course

naturally

to be sure

CONCLUSION

as a result

consequently

hence

in conclusion

in short

in sum

therefore

thus

to sum up

to summarize

TRANSLATION RECIPES
(pp. 143)

▸ Scholar X argues, "_____." In other words, _____.

▸ Essentially, X argues _____.

▸ X's point, succinctly put, is that _____.

▸ Plainly put, _____.

ADDING METACOMMENTARY
(pp. 157–162)

▸ In other words, _____.

▸ What _____ really means by this is _____.

▸ My point is not _____, but _____.

▸ Ultimately, my goal is to demonstrate that _____.

- In other words, _____.

- To put it another way, _____.

- What X is saying here is that _____.

- Chapter 2 explores _____, while Chapter 3 examines _____.

- Having just argued that _____, let us now turn our attention to _____.

- For example, _____.

- _____, for instance, demonstrates _____.

- Consider _____, for example.

- To take a case in point, _____.

- Even more important, _____.

- But above all, _____.

- Incidentally, as we will briefly note, _____.

- Just as important, _____.

- Equally, _____.

- Finally, _____.

- Although some readers may object that _____, I would answer that _____.

- In sum, then, _____.

- My conclusion, then, is that _____.

- In short, _____.

DEVELOPING GOOD RESEARCH QUESTIONS
(pp. 208)

▸ Why did X happen? Was it, as _____ argues, because of _____ or, as _____ contends, because of _____?

▸ What should we do about X? Should we _____, as _____ urges, or _____, as _____ argues?

▸ Is X as harmful as _____ insists, or does it have benefits, as _____ claims?

▸ Is it true, as some assert, that _____?

▸ What is the relationship between _____ and _____? Is it X, as most assume, or could it be Y, as one source suggests?

▸ Throughout the many years that I have taken an interest in _____, I, probably like most people, have assumed that _____. When I researched the topic for this essay, however, I was surprised to discover that _____.

▸ X argues _____. In my experience, however, _____.

LET ONE GOOD SOURCE LEAD TO ANOTHER
(p. 211)

▸ X is far too pessimistic in her prediction that _____.

▸ Authors X and Y focus on the wrong issue. The issue is not _____ but _____.

▸ I agree with X in her critique of the view that _____, but _____.

STARTING WITH WHAT OTHERS SAY
ABOUT A LITERARY WORK
(pp. 236)

▸ Critic X complains that author Y's story is compromised by his
_____. While there's some truth to this critique, I argue
that critic X overlooks _____.

▸ According to critic A, novel X suggests _____. I agree, but
would add that _____.

▸ Several members of our class have suggested that the final
message of play X is _____. I agree up to a point, but I
still think that _____.

▸ On first reading play Z, I thought it was an uncritical celebration
of _____. After rereading the play and discussing it in
class, however, I see that it is more critical of _____ than
I originally thought.

▸ It might be said that poem Y is chiefly about _____. But
the problem with this reading, in my view, is _____.

▸ Though religious readers might be tempted to analyze poem X
as a parable about _____, a closer examination suggests
that the poem is in fact about _____.

RESPONDING TO OTHER INTERPRETATIONS
OF A LITERARY WORK
(p. 241)

▸ It might be argued that in the clash between character X and
Y in play Z, the author wants us to favor character Y, since

she is presented as the play's heroine. I contend, however, that
_____.

▶ Several critics seem to assume that poem X endorses the values
of _____ represented by the image of _____ over
those of _____ represented by the image of _____.
I agree, but with the following caveat: _____.

SHOWING EVIDENCE WHEN WRITING
ABOUT A LITERARY WORK
(p. 246)

▶ Although some might read the metaphor of _____ in this
poem as evidence that, for author X, _____, I see it as
_____.

▶ Some might claim that evidence X suggests _____, but I
argue that, on the contrary, it suggests _____.

▶ I agree with my classmate _____ that the image of
_____ in novel Y is evidence of _____. Unlike
_____, however, I think _____.

EXPLAIN WHAT THE DATA MEAN
(p. 261)

▶ Our data *support / confirm / verify* the work of X by showing that
_____.

▶ By demonstrating _____, X's work *extends* the findings
of Y.

▶ The results of X *contradict / refute* Y's conclusion that
_____.

▸ X's findings *call into question* the widely accepted theory that
_____.

▸ Our data *are consistent with* X's hypothesis that _____.

EXPLAINING AN EXPERIMENTAL RESULT
(p. 264)

▸ One explanation for X's finding of _____ is that
_____. An alternative explanation is _____.

▸ The difference between _____ and _____ is probably due to _____.

INTRODUCING GAPS IN THE EXISTING RESEARCH
(p. 279)

▸ Studies of X have indicated _____. It is not clear, however,
that this conclusion applies to _____.

▸ _____ often take for granted that _____. Few have
investigated this assumption, however.

▸ X's work tells us a great deal about _____. Can this work
be generalized to _____?

▸ Our understanding of _____ remains incomplete because
previous work has not examined _____.

Index of Templates

HELP ME UNDERSTAND

(p. 290–302)

▸ I am writing an essay in which I want to argue _____ and could use some help thinking through my argument. Can you help me identify who says or might say otherwise—what views my own argument might be seen as a response to?

▸ When asked why _____ , ChatGPT responded, "_____."

▸ What does X mean when she writes, "_____?" In making this claim, is X being sincere or sarcastic?

▸ X often uses the term _____. What does it mean?

▸ X's argument is that _____. Please identify another writer who names X and either critiques or builds on X's perspective.

▸ When I asserted that _____ in a recent essay, my instructor wrote in the margin, "Surely, many would disagree," and I've been struggling to figure out how to respond. Can you help me identify how others might disagree with my claim?

GERALD GRAFF, Emeritus Professor of English and Education at the University of Illinois at Chicago and the 2008 President of the Modern Language Association of America, has had a major impact on teachers through such books as *Professing Literature: An Institutional History*, *Beyond the Culture Wars: How Teaching the Conflicts Can Revitalize American Education*, and *Clueless in Academe: How Schooling Obscures the Life of the Mind*. The Common Core State Standards for K–12 cite his work on the importance of argument literacy for college and career readiness. **CATHY BIRKENSTEIN**, a lecturer at the University of Illinois at Chicago, has published essays on writing, most recently in *College English*, and, with Gerald, in *The Chronicle of Higher Education*, *Academe*, and *College Composition and Communication*. She and Gerald have given over a hundred lectures and workshops at colleges, conferences, and high schools—and are at present working on a book contending that our currently confusing school and college curriculum needs to be clarified by making the practice of argument the common thread across all disciplines.